Incorporating much information generally unavailable to the non-specialist and the reader
unfamiliar with Russian, this volume illuminates
the history, problems, and present circumstances
of the Soviet medical establishment. It is written
in clear, non-technical language and thoroughly
describes the background, basic principles, organization, and financial provisions of medical
services and research in the Soviet Union. Employing a systematic sociological approach, the
book examines Soviet socialized medicine in re-
lation to ideology and the Soviet political and
economic systems.

This comprehensive study maintains that the
"health" of a population is a basic natural resource, and that a health system contributes to
the strength of a society by preserving that resource. Soviet socialized medicine constitutes a
relevant model for today's developing nations; its
study contains valuable lessons for all societies
as an exercise in the application (rather than
generation) of medical knowledge.

For the general reader interested in Medicare
and for a wide audience of social scientists,
students of Soviet affairs, and medical specialists
and practitioners, this volume provides the basic
material needed to compare the Soviet health
service with those of our own and other nations.

ology and the *Review of Soviet Medical Sciences*
and has visited the Soviet Union in connection
with work on Soviet medicine in 1956, 1961,
1963, and 1964.

Soviet
Socialized Medicine

Soviet
Socialized Medicine

An Introduction

★

MARK G. FIELD

THE FREE PRESS, *New York*

COLLIER-MACMILLAN LIMITED, *London*

THIS BOOK IS DEDICATED TO
Anne Murray
AND TO
Alexander James
Michael Bayard
Andrew Murray
AND
Elizabeth Imbert
in the hope it will provide some compensation for the many hours
spent away from them, writing it.

Preface

AT A TIME when so much interest and concern attach to all things Soviet and when the expression the "Soviet challenge" has passed into the everyday language, it seems puzzling that so little attention has been devoted to what is generally called Soviet "socialized medicine," or what might be better termed the Soviet health service or system. There have been studies about practically every aspect of Soviet society except this one. In Chapter 1 I shall discuss some of the reasons behind this neglect and why this oversight handicaps us in obtaining a well-rounded picture of the nature of Soviet society, its strengths, and its weaknesses. Suffice it for me to state here my conviction that the health of a nation's population and the medical system that strives to maintain that health are no less strategic resources than, for example, the production of steel, the supply of food, or the capacity to launch *sputniks*, *luniks*, and other space hardware. Soviet socialized medicine must, in my estimation, be considered an important and integral component of that challenge to which I already have referred. This challenge, furthermore, is certainly not limited to the political, economic, or even military spheres; it is also part and parcel of Soviet propaganda and of its claim of having, among other things, pioneered and developed an advanced form of "socialized" health service unique in many of its features and possible only under Soviet conditions. The Soviet regime thus seeks to evoke, among its own people, an attitude of gratitude toward itself as the fountainhead of progress and the organizer of medical care; and, by inference perhaps more than by direct statements, the regime tells the people of other countries (particularly the former colonial nations) that only the adoption of a Soviet or "socialistic" form of government will make it possible for them to provide for their health needs. Until they do so, adequate care in case of illness or injury will be reserved for the rich and the powerful. Socialized medicine has, thus, an important political and ideological appeal, and becomes a part of the struggle for the minds and loyalties of men the world over. For the existence, or lack, of medical services has an intense emotional significance to all people: their life, their health, their well-being, and the welfare of those who are most dear to them. As we shall see in the next chapter, this is a question that simultaneously and intimately affects the individual and the societal; it embraces at one sweep the mother anxiously awaiting the outcome of her child's illness and the number of men declared mentally and physically fit to defend their country.

The main purpose of this book is to introduce the reader to the Soviet health service. It is intended primarily for the layman interested in learning about Soviet socialized medicine, the principles upon which it is based, and the manner in which it operates. It utilizes the best and the most recent information available, given the general and usual restrictions on this type of data imposed by the Soviet regime. It provides a fair amount of statistical material culled from Soviet sources not only to illustrate, with figures, the points made but also to provide, in English, the kinds of data usually available only with difficulty to readers without access to a specialized library and who do not read Russian. I also would like to add, in this respect, that while Soviet statistical materials on health (and other) matters are still woefully inadequate and often incomplete (we still know very little about the structure of illness, for example), what we have today is infinitely better than what was available during Stalin's days. I have tried to write the book in simple language and to avoid technical terms or to explain them if they must be used. When I use "system," and particularly "health system," I am using a shorthand name for the totality of efforts and activities (broadly conceived) a society devotes to, or invests in, the health of its people. Health is conceived here as a basic resource of society or even a source of energy. No society or social organization can, therefore, afford to be totally indifferent to the state of that resource, regardless of its political system, stage of economic development, or ideological orientation. Soviet socialized medicine may thus be defined, in its aggregate, as that specific instrumentality devised and designed by Soviet society to cope with the threats to or impairments of this resource. Like any other human enterprise or undertaking, it can be said to consist of three basic elements: a body of knowledge and techniques that must be developed and transmitted from generation to generation and serves as the base for most activities in that area; a contingent of trained and specialized personnel whose ranks must continually be replenished and whose main activities center around the maintenance of the health "resource"; and a fund of facilities—that is, the instrumentalities or resources, material or financial, necessary to carry out health-protecting and -preserving activities, whether they be the national budget for socialized medicine, a hospital, a hypodermic needle, or an aspirin. I shall attempt in this book to examine these elements and the manner in which they are combined and fit in the Soviet Union to form its health service.

I have alluded to the relative neglect of this area in the West. There are indeed very few systematic studies on the subject and even fewer that are satisfactory. W. Horsley Gantt, an American physician who had gone to Russia after the First World War to help in relief work and had then become a student of Pavlov wrote, in 1928, a series of articles for the *British Medical Journal*. These, published later in a small book entitled *A Medical Review of Russia*, present some historical interest. In 1933, Sir Arthur Newsholme and John Adams Kingsbury published *Red Medicine: Socialized Health in Soviet Russia*, a cautious but on the whole sympathetic survey of Soviet medicine. In 1937, Henry E. Sigerist wrote his *Socialized Medicine in the Soviet Union;* in 1947, the book was reissued, in a revised version, as *Medicine and Health in the Soviet Union*.

Sigerist's books, and his other writings on that topic, were well-intentioned, sympathetic, but rather uncritical (if not somewhat ax-grinding and Pollyanic) views of Soviet medical organization and public health. These views were influenced, no doubt, by Sigerist's enthusiasm for the *principle* of socialized medicine which, as a historian of medicine, he felt was *the* medicine of the future, and by his politically naïve conceptions of Soviet society, even during the worst years of Stalin's totalitarianism and terror. Sigerist shared these conceptions with many liberal writers who at that time saw or professed they saw in the Soviet Union a vision of the future that embodied the solution to the many problems that plagued (and still often plague) Western industrial societies: economic crises, unemployment, inequality, racial or ethnic discrimination, and, of course, the lack of an adequate network of welfare services, including medical care for the disadvantaged members of society. Confusing Soviet plans, programs, propaganda, and declarations with reality, these writers often saw only what they wanted to see. In the name of their ideals or beliefs they too often (and sometimes with the best of intentions) accentuated the positive and ignored or overlooked that which did not fit their preconceptions, that which would shake their faith or the faith of those they tried to convince, or that which they felt would offend the sensibilities of their Soviet hosts, who had been, in the best Russian tradition, lavish with their hospitality and their time. These writers often rendered a disservice to the West because the picture they painted of Soviet reality was distorted, incomplete, and often inaccurate. By the same token, the reverse process—that is, the emphasis on the negative—provides an equally lopsided picture of Soviet society and its institutions. An example of the latter approach in the field of Soviet health and medical organization, is Dr. Irène Lazarévitch's book, *La médecine en U.R.S.S.*, published in Paris in 1953, shortly after Stalin's death, and based primarily on official Soviet sources of the postwar period. In essence, Lazarévitch's book presents a mirror image of the Sigerist one: The worst aspects of the Soviet medical scene are piled one on top of another to illustrate the wickedness of Stalin's regime and the shoddiness of the health services available to the population. Unlike Sigerist's well-organized and well-written book, Lazarévitch's opus is a disorganized exposé, more in the form of a polemic than a serious study. The same could be said of *Medicine in the United States and the Soviet Union* (1962), which was written by George A. Tabakov, a former Bulgarian pediatrician; it is such a confused mishmash and is so stridently anti-Soviet that it can hardly be taken seriously.

My previous book, *Doctor and Patient in Soviet Russia* (published ten years ago) had a somewhat different focus. It examined, in a sociological framework, the doctor-patient relationship under Soviet conditions and how it was affected by the nature of the regime's drive for rapid modernization. The health service (called in the book "The Setting") was examined insofar as it provided the stage for the medical relationship. The present study, centered on the health service itself, is thus a continuation and amplification of my work on Soviet medicine. As such it must unavoidably make use of some materials presented earlier (particularly historical) and brings up to date many of them.

In addition to the previously mentioned books, there are available monographs on certain specific and technical aspects of Soviet medicine, translations of Soviet medical materials into English, travelers' impressions, and the official reports of delegations that visited the Soviet Union. One could, in this context, profitably mention first the series of monographs published by the Medical Section of the Osteuropa Institut, itself a part of the Free University of Berlin; especially noteworthy are the works of Professor Max Brandt and Dr. Heinz Müller-Dietz, Chief of the Section. There are, in addition, the impressive studies published under the aegis of Professor Hans Harmsen, head of the Akademie für Staatsmedizin in Hamburg; these are important contributions to our understanding of medicine, medical organization, and public health not only in the Soviet Union but also in the countries of the Eastern Bloc, including particularly (and understandably) East Germany. There is also the work done in Münich, primarily by Dr. Heinrich Schulz, a former Soviet physician and now Director of the Münich Institute for the Study of the USSR. For some years, Dr. Schulz edited the *Review of Eastern Medical Sciences,* which recently was reactivated and renamed the *Review of Soviet Medical Sciences.* In the United States there are the *Medical Reports* and occasional monographs published by the Institute of Contemporary Russian Studies at Fordham University. In addition, the Department of Health, Education and Welfare has, over the past few years, through the Public Health Service, the National Institutes of Health and the National Library of Medicine, sponsored a program of translations (including books, monographs, and journals). Through their translations from the Soviet medical literature organizations such as the Consultants' Bureau and the Pergamon Press, to name the best known ones, have played an important role in acquainting the West with Soviet practices. The Public Health Service has also published the reports of the several official medical missions from the United States that have visited the Soviet Union recently. Of particular interest are *United States-U.S.S.R. Medical Exchange Missions* (1956), *The Report of the United States Public Health Mission to the Union of Soviet Socialist Republics* (1957), *The Report of the Medical Exchange Mission to the USSR on Pharmacology and Physiology of the Nervous System* (1958), *The Report on the Medical Exchange Mission to the USSR on Maternal and Child Care* (1960), and *Medical Education in the Soviet Union* (1964). The World Health Organization has sponsored study tours or traveling seminars that have visited the Soviet Union and has published, thus far, the following reports: *Health Services in the USSR* (Geneva, 1960); *Public Health Administration in the USSR* (Copenhagen, 1961); *Maternal and Child Health in the USSR* (Geneva, 1962); *Occupational Health in Four Countries: Yugoslavia, the USSR, Finland, Sweden* (Geneva, 1963); *Health Education in the USSR* (Geneva, 1963); and the *Report of the Inter-Regional Travelling Seminar on Public Health Administration in USSR* (Geneva, 1963). In addition, physicians, specialists, and general practitioners who have visited the Soviet Union have sometimes published, in their specialty journals, their impressions and conclusions, usually gained from a whirlwind tour of a few facilities and interviews with officials of the Health Ministry, or have written informal reports for their colleagues.

In spite of the availability of these materials, no systematic effort has been made to pull them together, and the basic question remains largely unanswered: What is Soviet medicine and public health like in contemporary Soviet Russia? How efficient is it? Is it a good blueprint for other countries to emulate, particularly the economically underdeveloped ones? Is it a portent for the future in the highly industrialized countries?

The size and the format of this book preclude detailed answers to these questions; the book, however, makes a serious attempt to provide some generalized answers, and it is for this reason that it is called an *Introduction*. I welcome the opportunity provided by the publisher to place before the general public an examination, analysis, and partial evaluation of the Soviet approach to medicine and public health. Since the maintenance and the protection of health, the prevention of illness, the diagnosis and treatment of diseases and injuries, and the rehabilitation of former patients are problems that are inherent components of the human condition, it is important for us to examine the ways in which different societies have faced and attempted to meet these problems.

It may be said that in midcentury America the problem of health care—its provision to the population on an equitable basis and the financing of medical activities—are burning social and political issues, similar perhaps to those surrounding, a century and a half ago, the question of free and universal schooling. The whole issue of Medicare is symptomatic of this kind of ferment. In certain respects, and in the final analysis, the delivery of health services to the population of a nation, of any nation, is a "distributive" problem that involves, to a large degree, social policy. Illness is not the insoluble mystery it was in centuries past, and the knowledge is now available to deal with it to a very effective degree. And yet, quite often, the distribution of health services follows paths of wealth, influence, and social class rather than being uniformly available to all those who need them. While a whole American nation awaits breathlessly the new car models each year and ponders the next episode in the evolution of automotive tail fins, how many Americans have a yearly comprehensive medical examination? If the so-called Affluent Society has sometimes tended to be the Indifferent Society, it may be because the issue is more complicated than simply the application of available knowledge to the problems at hand, and because medicine and the role of health personnel are affected by a host of cultural, sociological, political, economic, and ideological factors.

It will be one of the tasks of this book to examine these questions in the perspective of Soviet society and to provide some data on the "distribution" of medical services there. The assumption is that, while such an examination is justified in that it helps us to round our picture of Soviet life, it may also be of some relevance to our society. I grant that there are many aspects that we do not share with the Soviet Union—its ideology and political philosophy, for example. On the other hand, there are many elements we do share, such as the fact that we are both large nation-states, with populations of approximately equal size, and beset with the many problems associated with industrialization, mechanization, and urbanization. We can thus, critically and cautiously, learn from each other's experience.

This volume, as indicated previously, is only an Introduction. I plan to publish, in the near future, a longer, more detailed, and more comprehensive work that will present the Soviet theory and organization of health services in most of its complexities and ramifications. That work will be intended primarily for scholars in the field of medical organization and administrators of medical programs as well as those specialists interested in Soviet affairs; its audience will thus be far more limited than that of the present volume, which is intended for the student of Soviet society interested in rounding out his knowledge, and for others who are curious about the nature of the Soviet health service.

THE USE OF SOVIET SOURCES

ONE OF THE BASIC methodological problems to be faced in any study of Soviet reality is that of the availability, reliability, and

validity of the Soviet sources or documents one uses. This is
not the place to enter into a lengthy discussion of this subject,
except to note that considerable experience has been accumulated, particularly since the late forties, on research in the Soviet field, and given general knowledge of the nature of Soviet
publications, there is a great deal of valid and reliable information that can be obtained from them. These sources, of course,
always pose certain problems of interpretation, since the regime
tightly controls all the means of mass communications. And
yet, beyond political and ideological considerations which are
not to be discussed in the Soviet Union except by the highest
authorities, there is in the literature, particularly in the one that
is relevant for this study, a great quantity of solid information
that can be used by the Western scholar. If there is any distortion, it may well be introduced by the omission of certain types
of information rather than the deliberate supply of misleading
ones. Furthermore, if we recognize that the Soviet sources
available to us in the West (and often in amazing quantities)
are precisely the same ones the Soviet readers themselves use
(and are not specially fashioned for foreign export), then we
can assume that these sources of information are legitimate. In
this study I have relied to a great extent on *Meditsinskaia Gazeta* (formerly *Meditsinskii Rabotnik*), the semiweekly organ
of the Health Ministry for the USSR (and formerly of the
RSFSR) and of the Central Committee of the Professional
Union of Medical Workers. Equally valuable has been the second edition of the *Bol'shaia Meditsinskaia Entsiklopedia* (*The
Large Medical Encyclopedia*), published in a series of 35 vol-
umes between 1956 and 1965. There are also many books,
pamphlets, and monographs in Russian which, in addition to
several journals on health organization, provided the bulk of
the information for the present work. Trips to the Soviet Union
have been useful in that they provided what I like to call a
"capstone of reality" on knowledge that, until then, had remained "historical." During these trips I was able to see the
settings of medical practice, to visit with health officials and
clinicians, and to "humanize" my acquaintance with Soviet society. In combination with other sources of information, these
visits provided a better perspective on the entire problem, and

helped in understanding the social and cultural context of health services. They would, however, have added very little without a great deal of groundwork in the library.

ORGANIZATION OF THE BOOK

CHAPTER 1 provides a general and primarily sociological orientation to the subject of Soviet society and the position occupied by the health service in that society. Chapter 2 delineates the major phases of the development of medical institutions in Russia from about the tenth century to the Bolshevik Revolution in 1917. Chapter 3 examines the interrelationship between Marxist ideology and medicine and medical institutions. Chapter 4 takes up history again, this time the development of medicine from the time of the Revolution to the present. Chapter 5 examines the organization and administration of the health service, while Chapter 6 provides information on health personnel of all categories. Chapter 7 describes the clinical facilities and services available to the population. Chapter 8 deals with preventive services, and Chapter 9 with medical research. Chapter 10 explains the financing of the health service.

ACKNOWLEDGMENTS

AS I LOOK back over the many years I have been engaged in the study of the Soviet medical system, I find it difficult to single out those individuals and institutions that have been most instrumental in channeling my interests in this direction, and in supporting and encouraging my work. I would like, however, to mention Professor Talcott Parsons who first stimulated my interest in sociological analysis and in the many problematics in the medical profession; Professor Alex Inkeles, whose personal friendship and encouragement and whose knowledge of the Soviet system influenced me in pursuing a study of the medical profession under the conditions of Soviet society; the late Professor Clyde Kluckhohn, formerly director of the Russian Research Center at Harvard, who provided the setting in which to carry out this work; my many colleagues and friends at the Center whose interest, stimulation, and criticism helped me over many a rough spot; Dr. Paul D. White who asked me to join his delegation to the Soviet Union in 1956; Drs. Heinrich Schulz in Münich and Heinz Müller-Dietz in Berlin, who have shared with me their interest in Soviet medicine; Professor Michael T. Florinsky (who has by now retired from Columbia), who originally approached me as the editor of the Russian Civilization Series of Collier Books, who suggested the format for this book and gave me valuable editorial advice once I had completed the first draft; and many others too numerous to name here. I owe, in addition, a particular debt of gratitude to the Public Health Service, Department of Health, Education and Welfare which provided, from 1959 on, the necessary support to continue this work under Grants RG-6318, RG-9644, and GM-10968 through the National Institutes of Health and CH-00002 through the Bureau of State Services, and without whose help I could not have undertaken this book, which is the first major fruit of that assistance. In addition the grants from the Public Health Service have permitted me to travel extensively in Western Europe, Eastern Europe, and the Soviet Union, in search of materials (in 1961 and 1963), and particularly to work at the Medical Section of the Osteuropa Institut in the late spring of 1963 and again in 1964. I was also able to attend the Eleventh Annual Sankelmark Seminar organized by Professor Harmsen in 1963. One important aspect of that seminar was a study trip to Yugoslavia, which provided fascinating comparative materials.

The cooperation of the Russian Research Center at Harvard University and particularly of Professor Abram Bergson, the present Director; Professor Merle Fainsod, the former Director; Professor Marshall D. Shulman, the former Associate Director; and Mrs. Helen W. Parsons, the Administrative Assistant, were prime factors in carrying out the initial phase of this work and in sponsoring and administering my Public Health Grant from 1959 to 1961. The Center continues to provide its staff and alumni a congenial place in which to work, meet colleagues interested in the Soviet field, and exchange ideas. The degree of loyalty to the Center expressed by its present and former members is witness to the strength of that institution.·The support of the University of Illinois and Boston University in carrying my research grants from the Public Health Service also deserve grateful mention.

I am very grateful to the Harvard University Press for permission to use materials from my book *Doctor and Patient in Soviet Russia* (published in 1957) as well as from an article "Medical Organization and the Medical Profession" which appeared in *The Transformation of Russian Society,* edited by Cyril E. Black and published in 1960 (pp. 541–552). The materials that form the backbone of Chapter 6 are scheduled to appear in the *American Journal of Public Health* under the title "Health Personnel in the Soviet Union: Achievements and Problems" in the fall of 1966, and the editor has graciously given his permission to use these materials.

Finally, I want to acknowledge here the help I have received from the many research assistants who, in the course of the last five years, in Cambridge and Urbana, have pored over Soviet materials and extracted the necessary ore from which this study has derived its sustenance. In particular I want to express my gratitude to Mrs. Susan Salser for the help rendered in practically every phase of the writing of this book, and to Miss Bärbel Pade, who diligently prepared the final draft for publication.

I would also like to add, as an afterthought, that the adage that writing a short book is always more difficult than writing a long one certainly proved to be true in this case.

M. G. F.

Contents

Soviet
Socialized Medicine

Chapter 1

Soviet Society
and Its Health Service

IT MAY BE difficult, at first glance, to perceive much of a
relationship between a physician at a patient's bedside and
factories, mines, canals, and highways. The first picture is likely
to evoke an emotional reaction, associated with the fact that
the physician's presence usually symbolizes illness or injury,
pain and suffering, and the ever-present possibility of permanent
disablement, disfigurement, or death. The second image calls
forth a different range of reactions. It tends to be associated
with industrialization, urbanization, and mechanization; it symbolizes wealth, national power, and strategic resources. And yet
the two pictures are linked in more ways than are perhaps
readily apparent, for they both represent national assets and
both contribute, in their own ways, to the strength and the
functioning of a society. Naturally, this relationship is far from
a simple one, for it involves an intricate linkage between the
individual and his society. A brief examination of this linkage,
in general, and with reference to Soviet society, in particular,
will be the main subject of this chapter.

It is perhaps a telling commentary on the West's fascination (one might almost say mesmerization) with recent Soviet achievements in science, engineering, and space hardware and feats that is has tended to ignore, or at least to gloss over, equally significant, although certainly not so spectacular, advances in other areas. For example, many Western observers, have smugly assumed a priori that a politically monolithic regime of the type Stalin established and maintained (albeit in a modified form) by Khrushchev and his successors was, in essence, congenitally incapable of measures that would increase its population's well-being, welfare, and health. Accustomed as we have been to thinking of Soviet Russia as a kind of vast concentration camp peopled by millions of Ivan Denisoviches[1] spending millions of days behind barbed wire in the Arctic Circle, we have found it difficult to think in terms of physicians, nurses, hospitals, clinics, and dispensaries. Or, if we have admitted (with some difficulty) that the Soviet regime was capable of taking measures to improve its citizens' life situation, we have tended to regard these measures as concessions wrung by the people from a government that was at long last becoming concerned about its popularity and earnestly trying to dissociate itself from the cruelties and inhumanities of the Stalin era. Indeed, some commentators on the Soviet scene have maintained that the Soviet regime had a vested interest in keeping the masses downtrodden, poor, and miserable, because once the regime began to improve the lot of its population it initiated an irreversible process of whetting appetites which in the long run could not be satisfied and would lead to a frustration of expectations that should never have been raised in the first place. The evidence does not seem to support this contention. The development of the Soviet health service, to take but the subject of this inquiry, began under Lenin and gathered momentum *during the years of Stalin's regime*. At the time of his death, there were more physicians per population than in any other country, with the possible exception of Israel, where the number of doctors had been artificially inflated by immigration. In the 25 years of the Stalin era (1928–53) the number of physicians more than quadrupled, from 63,000 to 285,000, and the ratio of doctors to population increased almost four times (from four to fifteen doctors per 10,000 persons). The absolute number of hospital beds more than doubled (from 532,000 to 1,177,620), and the number of beds per 10,000 persons went from 35 to 61. This expansion has been maintained (if not accelerated) under Stalin's successors, as we shall see in greater detail in Chapters 6 and 7.

It seems logical, as well as consistent with the facts, to assume that the improvement in the individual's lot, health, and longevity, instead of weakening the regime, tends to strengthen it. Furthermore, it also appears that the regime certainly has no vested interest in depressing the standard of living more than is necessary to insure the realization of first-priority goals such as capital accumulation, industrialization, and national self-sufficiency and power. Indeed, the avowed ultimate goal of the regime (which it does not cease to proclaim to its population and to the world) is precisely the creation of a life of abundance from which misery, want, and greed will have been banished forever. Or, if improvements in the population's life situation, including welfare and medical services, are acknowledged in the West (often reluctantly, because they do not jibe with the usual stereotype of a totalitarian regime), there is the tendency to brush this progress aside as being of far less importance and over-all significance than the availability of natural resources and raw materials, strides in industrialization, or the capacity to dispatch intercontinental ballistic missiles to any point on the globe. Such an approach, however, gives us an astigmatic view of the reality of Soviet power although it is quite easy to understand why it should be so widespread. For Soviet national power and potential, and the political threat they represent, are based on Soviet industrial resources and production, and in the balance of forces between the West and the Soviet bloc they are likely, in the last analysis, to prove decisive. Thus it is no accident, but the reflection of a genuine concern for the security of the West, that teams of experts are constantly at work analyzing the latest production figures and calculating when, under what circumstances, and in what areas the Soviet Union will catch up with or surpass (or fail to do so) the United States and other major Western powers.

It may be added, incidentally, that this power race or competition has been a major, if not the major, theme of *Soviet* domestic and foreign policy since Stalin decided to embark upon a program of forced draft industrialization, a program financed primarily from domestic resources (through forced savings or reduced consumption) rather than from capital borrowed abroad. But often ignored, or at least relegated to a position of secondary or residual significance, is the compelling fact that behind production figures and national power stands Soviet Russia's most important, most strategic and critical resource—its people. And it is the size and quality of a society's human resources that, to a large extent, determine the society's actual and potential power (in combination, of course, with morale, natural resources and technological know-how). Furthermore, while the sheer size of population is an important index of strength, it is important only at the very gross level. Indeed, in some cases the size of a population or its rapid increase may be a major liability, putting intolerable pressure on land, resources, and capital. This is often the case nowadays in economically underdeveloped countries. Beyond a critical point, just as important as size is the make-up or quality of a society's human materials. By quality is meant a variety of traits such as age composition, sex ratio, literacy and education, skills and expertise, and, of course, state and level of health. Health means, at the most general level, the population's over-all vitality which is measured by freedom from disabling diseases, infant and general mortality, life expectancy, and physical and mental resilience. For if we accept the premise that a country's population is one of its basic resources, then it follows that the state of that resource (its health) is also critical. In order to visualize its significance, it is only necessary to imagine what would happen to a country such as the United States or the Soviet Union if a substantial proportion of its working population were incapacitated by illness of one type or another: steel mills would shut down, production and transportation of food would diminish and stop altogether bringing famine and more disease (particularly, at first, for those most at risk, such as infants, older people, and invalids), laboratories and libraries would become deserted and useless. For it is one of the characteristics of the modern industrialized society, with its complex and advanced division of labor, that its people are dependent upon each other to a degree unknown in simpler societies, where the individuals in small groups can survive by their own efforts and activities.

If health, therefore, is considered a natural (and often a national) resource, second in importance only to life, then disease and injuries must be regarded as major threats to that resource. In addition to causing personal unhappiness, discomfort, pain, and grief, illness or injury also affects the capacity or ability to perform social roles: It keeps people from fulfilling their obligations and from meeting their responsibilities. Thus it stands to reason that the mechanisms—the health or medical system—devised to cope with this threat are of primary importance for society, and the more economically developed and interdependent the society, the more significant its health service.

The development of Soviet medicine therefore must be examined both from the viewpoint of the Communist party's professed interest in and concern with the population's welfare, well-being, and health and from the viewpoint of Soviet Russia as a national power. Indeed, historically, one might say that the early phase of the development of Soviet medicine preceded the launching, in 1928, of the program of industrialization that was to make Soviet Russia the world's second most powerful industrial nation. By 1928—a decade after the Revolution—there were about three times as many physicians as there had been before the Revolution, while the number of hospital beds increased from 175,700 to 246,500. And it was also during the ten years before the Five-Year Plans that the basic structure of the Soviet system of medical care and public health was established. It has remained in its main lines much the same until today.

These ten years (and particularly from 1925 until 1928) were also the years during which the Communist leadership debated the direction in which the Soviet Union should develop, since, with the exception of short-lived revolutions in Bavaria and Hungary, the expected European and world-wide proletarian revolutions had failed to materialize and the Soviet Union stood alone. While some favored a slow process of capital accumulation through expanded agricultural production, others supported a rapid process of accumulation financed primarily by a reduction of domestic consumption. Most parties to the debate, however, wanted industrialization as a means of raising the population's standard of living and laying the groundwork for the age of abundance that the Communist millenium promised. The Communist leadership, in addition, saw industrialization primarily as a means of ensuring the Soviet Union's national security. In a famous speech given in 1931, Stalin justified the extremely high rate of capital construction ordered after 1928 and heavily emphasized the need to build up Soviet Russia's national power in those terms:

> It is sometimes asked whether it is not possible to slow down the tempo a bit, to put a check on the movement. No, comrades, it is not possible. . . . This is dictated to us by our obligations to the working class of the whole world. To slacken the tempo would mean falling behind. . . . One feature of the history of old Russia was the continual beatings she suffered from falling behind. . . . She was beaten by the Polish and Lithuanian gentry. She was beaten by the British and French capitalists. She was beaten by the Japanese barons. All beat her for her backwardness, for military backwardness, for cultural backwardness, for political backwardness, for agricultural backwardness. She was beaten because to do so was profitable and could be done with impunity. . . . We are 50 or 100 years behind the advanced countries. We must make good this distance in 10 years. Either we do it, or they crush us.[2]

The massive program of industrialization under forced draft was cruelly executed at an extremely high human cost. But it accomplished, on the whole, its main objective of industrializing Soviet Russia. There is little doubt, furthermore, that an important component (though one rarely recognized as such) in this process was the system of medical and public health measures adopted by the Soviet regime. A major nation cannot industrialize with a disease-ridden, sickly, and weak population plagued by epidemics and a low life expectancy.

Before examining the Soviet health system in greater detail, it will be useful to take a rapid glance at the nature of Soviet society, because its medical institutions reflect, in certain respects, its sociopolitical arrangements, as well as the functional requirements to which we already have alluded.

Soviet society may be described as a large-scale national society in a process of rapid social and cultural change, moving from an agrarian and traditional type of order to industrialization and urbanization. It is a society, furthermore, in which all of the political and most of the economic power has been gathered into the hands of a militant, aggressive, and unique political organization, the Communist party of the Soviet Union. The party, which enlists in its ranks only a minority of the population, is a tightly organized, highly disciplined, hierarchic and centralized organization. Pyramidal in structure, it is controlled by a small group of men, and its policies are established by an even smaller group (or one or two men) at the apex of the pyramid. Since party rule is nearly absolute and extends to most if not all areas of Soviet life, the label totalitarianism often has been applied to the Soviet type of political organization.

Totalitarianism is a relatively new form of political organization. As Zbigniew Brzezinski has pointed out,[3] totalitarianism includes the coercive and authoritarian features one usually associates with dictatorial and autocratic regimes, but possesses one important additional trait: Its aim is *not* to maintain the status quo or a balance of power between the different contending social forces of society, but to institute a change or revolution that increases in scope and frequently in intensity as the regime stabilizes itself in power. The purpose of that revolution is to pulverize all existing social units in order to replace the old pluralism with a homogeneous unanimity patterned on the blueprint of the totalitarian ideology. It appeals, of course, in terms of a vision of the future, the realization of which requires all the efforts of the present social order. To implement that vision, the totalitarian society usually develops a single party, a technologically conditioned and nearly complete monopoly of all means of effective armed combat and of effective mass communications, and a system of terroristic police controls.

The totalitarian society thus must be seen as one whose operational mode is the bending of most human and material resources toward the realization of the plans and programs elaborated by the leadership. It tends, perforce, to regard its individual members more as soldiers, servants, or employees than as citizens. In essence, furthermore, the Communist party of the Soviet Union considers itself the embodiment of a body of theory or doctrine (the ideology) which presents not only an allegedly scientific analysis of the course of history (dialectical and historical materialism) but also a blueprint for future developments (communism). As Anastas I. Mikoyan declared at the Twentieth Party Congress early in 1956:

> Guided by the mighty Marxist method of understanding the laws of social development, the Central Committee clarifies the contemporary events of social development, explains them in a Marxist way, and arms the working man with conclusions that generalize and explain not only the facts and events of the period of the lives of Marx and Lenin, but also subsequent events both in capitalist and socialist countries.[4]

The party does not see its role primarily as one of reflecting the conscious wishes and aspirations of the masses, since the common people often do not know—nor do they have the education, wisdom, or vision to know—what "is good for them." Rather it leads, directs, and guides the masses toward a better future. The notion of the party's leadership role is prominent in Leninism and is based on Lenin's opinion that the masses under capitalism, left to themselves or even guided by labor union leaders, are capable only of "spontaneity"—that is, they react to or tend to be influenced by small economic gains, bribes, or scraps thrown to them by the capitalists and are thus easily deflected or detoured from their historical mission of bringing about the Communist millenium. The ability to see events and developments in their correct Marxist and historical perspective requires what Lenin called "consciousness," and he averred that the masses could not, of themselves, develop that consciousness: It had to be injected from without by those—that is, the party and its leaders—who, on the basis of profound historical studies, understood it and could guide its course. The goals set by the party today are thus an amalgam of the leaders' interpretation and reinterpretation of the body of doctrine, their assessment of the realistic possibility of implementing their programs, their distinction between short-range (tactical) maneuvers and long-range (strategic) objectives, and the problems inherent in their environment, domestic and foreign. While the interpretation of the ideology may vary from time to time, and the goals themselves may be changed or modified depending on the problems at hand and the leaders' personalities, the directionality of the system has been a characteristic feature from the earliest days of the Revolution, and remains so to this day.

It hardly need be mentioned that the ultimate vision communism holds to its followers, and which it claims to derive from the works of Marx, Engels, and Lenin (and formerly Stalin), is utopian; indeed it promises a sort of secular paradise on earth in which material abundance, equality, and the absence of strife will be realized once and for all.

But if the vision is utopian, the reality is not. This accounts for perhaps one of the great paradoxes of Soviet totalitarianism, a paradox that has alienated most liberals who originally were sympathetic to the Soviet experiment: In order to establish in this world what is surely the equivalent of the Garden of Eden, Communist leaders never have hesitated to use the most violent measures that are a negation of the vision itself—political repression, intimidation and terror, secret police, torture, exile, and concentration camps; the lack of personal freedom, the control of the means of mass communications, and the complex of phenomena associated with what Khrushchev called Stalin's "cult of personality," and which he described (in part only) in the famous Secret Speech delivered at the Twentieth Party Congress in 1956.

Since Stalin's death some of the harshness has been mitigated, particularly because industrial production has gradually made it possible to reward the population a little bit more substantially than before and to motivate it to work faithfully and well in order to obtain the few physical comforts it has desired for so long. On the whole, however, the basic structure of Soviet society has remained the same. Although there certainly have been small changes and adjustments, centralized direction by the party has remained intact.

The "directionality" to which we have referred necessitates a strict system of priorities in the investment of the limited resources at the regime's disposal, whether in manpower or matériel. This is true, of course, of every society and every cooperative venture, since resources are always limited. And yet in most pluralistic societies the system of priorities is implicit rather than explicit, often spontaneous rather than directed, the result of a multiplicity of decisions and adjustments, as in a market situation, with the role of the polity limited to the maintenance of order and the protection of the public. In Soviet society the presence of an explicit ideology and a series of goals and subgoals, coupled with quasi-absolute political and economic power and control, permits the regime to impose upon the entire society its scale of values, its order of priorities, its timetables, without having to contend with counterclaims and constitutional checks and without fear of antagonizing an electorate. Such an arrangement produces a mobilized society, a garrison state, in which an attempt is made to husband all social processes behind the regime's objectives, targets, and day-to-day decisions.

If managed social change is a basic component of the Soviet system, so is its system of controls designed to assure that the high priority tasks receive the necessary support, and that the scarce resources available are invested in a manner most conducive to the realization of plans and targets. This system of controls applies, naturally, with equal force to the activities of health personnel and facilities, so that allocations (personnel and material resources) appear to be dictated by the following considerations or criteria: the minimum allocation necessary to maintain that state of health in the population that will most facilitate the realization of the regime's objective, without at the same time jeopardizing other needs of equal or higher significance. In other words, were the regime to reduce its budgetary allocations to its health service below a certain point, the amount of unattended illness and its subsequent impact upon the population's work capacity might rise to a level the regime would not tolerate. If, on the other hand, the "costs" of health services were to rise above a certain point (say through a substantial increase of personnel salaries) then there would not be enough money to pay teachers or engineers, for example, or to invest in needed capital construction (plants, canals, and so on). The control on the flow of resources to the health system is administrative-financial, and since virtually every aspect of the health service, from hospital budgets to personnel salaries, is financed by the state, it is possible (within limits, naturally) for the regime to maintain a fairly tight rein on its medical expenses, just as it keeps a tight rein on all its other expenses.

To make this point more meaningful it would be enough to imagine how difficult it would be, under the present system, for the American government to impose the same control and priority upon American medicine, and to decide, for example, that only a specified percentage of the national income must be allocated to health maintenance and medical services. This would require the establishment of a complicated administrative and accounting system over funds going to medical facilities and personnel; it would mean, in one sense, the end of private practice and private medical institutions, since their budgets would be controlled and everyone in medicine would be placed on a governmentally determined salary, as is the case in the Soviet Union, where a determined portion of national resources is allocated to health. In addition, however, the placing of all health resources under governmental aegis makes it relatively easier for that government to utilize the health service than would be the case in a mixed system of private and public medicine such as exists in the United States. This is true, for example, of personnel who can be moved about "for the good of the service." With relative ease the regime also may increase its spending for health in certain areas considered more strategic than others or, by the same token, shift resources into other, more "essential" nonmedical areas, if need be. At the same time, the impression should not be conveyed too strongly that the regime has absolute freedom in manipulating its resources at will, because its free-wheeling is often limited by its very instrument of control, the bureaucratic structure, which is cumbersome and often ineffectual.

We are now ready to turn from the societal to the personal by reexamining some of the questions raised at the beginning of this chapter. One issue often posed in recent years by scholars interested in Soviet affairs is whether a totalitarian regime and a welfare state can coexist.[5] Is not, after all, the very concept of "welfare" inapplicable to a society that can be as ruthless with its members as Stalin's Russia was? Does not, when all is said and done, a democracy have a sort of self-appointed monopoly on the ability to maximize the personal happiness and well-being of its citizens? Just as industrialism can coexist equally well with the pluralistic as with the totalitarian society, so can the "welfare state," once the emotional connotations inherent in the word welfare are removed and replaced by a more functional interpretation. For, as was pointed out earlier, the health of its population is an asset to a society. This is particularly true of the industrial society. This society, by the very nature of its productive forces, depends more and more on highly trained personnel who must be educated and trained for many years and thus are, in the process, effectively kept out of the labor force. An extreme case, of course, if that of the medical specialist who, in the United States at least, does not begin to "repay his debt to society" until he has reached his thirties. If we then look upon the individual as a social and economic investment (gestation, support, training, education), it stands to reason that a short life expectancy (or an early death), in addition to being a personal tragedy, is also a net loss to the society and that, conversely, long life and good health permit the society to capitalize not only on the individual's protracted and costly training but also on his maturity and experience. It is precisely in this respect that high birth and death rates, a low life expectancy, and a high rate of disease represent a devastating drain on a nation's resources, as is the case in most underdeveloped countries today. The physician's role and that of the entire system of health care and public health aim precisely at preventing, reducing, neutralizing, and mitigating the impact of disease and reducing premature deaths or disability. From the beginning of its rule, the Soviet government has tried to establish a health service that would most expeditiously and economically deal with this most essential and "strategic" resource.

And yet the provision of medical services has much more than a purely functional, "strategic," or societal role to play. Let us then return to our earlier picture of the physician leaning over the patient at his bedside. Illness has an important emotional meaning for the individual and those around him, and so has the provision of medical services. It is in this respect that the Soviet regime has, in its system of socialized medicine, a powerful appeal. It presents itself to the population as the champion of the individual's welfare and depicts the Soviet system of health care as one more expression of this concern. Furthermore, it contrasts Soviet health services with those of tsarist Russia, when they were, by comparison, quite insignificant and almost inaccessible to the ordinary worker and peasant. It also proclaims that in Western countries medical care and a physician's services are so expensive that the poor cannot afford them. Thus in its issue of June 12, 1964, *Meditsinskaia Gazeta* published "Business and Health," an article typical of many others. The author, Professor A. Shabanov, contrasted the availability of free medical services in the Soviet Union with the high cost of such services in the United States where, he maintained, illness and injury are a source of constant anxiety to families because they are ruinously expensive.

From the individual's viewpoint, a program of socialized medicine that tries to provide qualified medical services for the entire population and at no direct cost can be interpreted as an expression of the regime's concern for the individual and his welfare. The Soviet medical press thus publishes, for example, letters of gratitude from former patients whose lives have been saved, whose eyesight has been restored, or whose work capacity has been recovered through the efforts of medical personnel.

The implication is that this is the result of the constant concern of the Communist party and the Soviet Government for the health and welfare of the toilers. On the other hand, complaints about medical services tend to be attributed officially to personal negligence, disinterest of medical personnel, formalism, and bureaucratism, and not to the medical system itself or the regime. Expressed in a different way, the regime says to the population: We are doing all that is necessary to ensure a system of high quality medical care for you, and we stint no expense to do so. Shortcomings are to be blamed not on us, or our blueprint for these services, but on the "intolerable" misbehavior of a few medical personnel who must be punished or reprimanded.

It is, therefore, not surprising that among the measures that the Soviet regime has introduced socialized medicine has proved very popular. Indeed, Soviet émigrés, who were presumably hostile to the regime, have indicated that socialized medicine was one of the measures they most approved (along with nationalization of heavy industry and free education).[6]

It appears, therefore, that the health service contributes both to the personal satisfaction of the Soviet population and to the functional needs of the Soviet Union as a national power. By catering to the deep-seated and universal anxieties associated with illness and disability, the health service strengthens, to some degree, the stability of Soviet society. By keeping the population reasonably healthy and capable of working, the system augments the power of that society. In the area of health, the interests of the regime and those of the population largely coincide.

Chapter 2

A Brief History
of Russian Medicine
Prior to 1917

THE PRE-PETRINE PERIOD

IF ONE WERE to search for the historical origins and antecedents of medicine and medical organization on the territory
that today constitutes the Soviet Union, one might have to trace
them to that small corner of the land called Armenia where,
according to the *Bol'shaia Meditsinskaia Entsiklopediia*,[1] two
centuries before the birth of Christ, King Vagarshak rehabili-
tated the districts of Taika and Yokha by eliminating malaria
and transforming these damp areas into fertile lands, where in
the first centuries of our era there were medical institutions
(presumably shelters for the poor, the sick, and the invalid)
maintained primarily by the churches, and where hospitals were
established in the second half of the fourth century. One might
also include in these antecedents the existence of medical schools
in Azerbaidzhan in the tenth century, or the rich culture of the
towns of Central Asia in the tenth and eleventh centuries, and

the activities of the Ibn-Sin. But, more realistically, one might trace them to Kievan Russia where, in the tenth century, physicians, largely from the East (Armenia, Byzantium, Syria), first appeared. They attended to the needs of the court and the nobility; the rest of the population, particularly the indigent sick and invalid, were dependent on the churches, primarily the monasteries, which maintained asylums and hostels. Monks, rather than physicians, gave whatever care was available. These activities were financed by a special tax for the poor, the orphans, and the sick. During the thirteenth and fourteenth centuries, when the Mongols dominated Russia, there were no significant medical developments except in areas not subject to that domination, such as Galician Russia and parts of Kievan Russia. In Lvov, in the thirteenth century, there appeared "lay" hospitals—that is, hospitals not run by the church.[2]

With the rise of Muscovy in the fifteenth century, physicians began to arrive in Russia, this time from the West. Indeed, until the middle of the eighteenth century, the practice of medicine and medical research as well remained largely in the hands of foreigners, most of whom did not speak Russian. As diplomatic and commercial contacts between Russia and the West intensified in the sixteenth and seventeenth centuries, more western European physicians (from England, Holland, Germany, and France) came to Moscow, there to serve the court and the tsar. They were well remunerated and, provided they did not dabble in politics, could expect to return home as men of considerable wealth. The demand for physicians, and particularly military surgeons, increased during the seventeenth century because of the growth of the army, warfare in southern Russia, and the drive toward the Baltic Sea. Many of the foreign regiments that served in Russia would not .fight without surgeons. These surgeons were, however, no longer the personal servants of the tsar or the court, but rather the servants of the state, hired to provide medical and surgical services to a designated group of individuals. Employment of physicians as state employees became firmly established as a result of the growing needs of the state, and particularly of the armed forces, and has remained the predominant pattern to this day. This may be contrasted with the development of medical practice in North America, where the predominant and culturally approved pattern has tended to be that of private practice.

In 1581, a private pharmacy that served the Kremlin was established by an English apothecary, James Frencham. And in 1672, a pharmacy was opened in Moscow to serve the population. Since drugs often contain poisons, the *Aptekarskii Prikaz* (Apothecary Board) was established in 1620 to supervise and regulate the work of the Kremlin pharmacy and the importation of pharmaceuticals. This office replaced the *Aptekarskaia Palata* (Apothecary Chamber), which had been established toward the end of the sixteenth century to supervise court medical activities.

The Apothecary Board, however, soon outgrew its original mandate and became the nation's central medical authority, setting thereby another important benchmark in Russian medicine: state direction, financing, administration, and centralization of medical services. The board appointed physicians and surgeons to the army and outfitted field pharmacies. Foreign physicians presented their credentials to it, and later were examined by it. In 1654, the board established a school to train *lekars*. (A lekar, or "treater," was equivalent to the barber-surgeon of the West, who treated patients but knew very little medicine; a doctor, by contrast, knew medicine but did not usually treat patients.) *Lekars* trained from four to six years and then served in the army. This school, however, existed for only a short period. Military hospitals began functioning in 1656 in Smolensk and in 1678 in Moscow. The Apothecary Board became the Apothecary Chancellery in 1707 and was moved to St. Petersburg in 1712, to be renamed the Medical Chancellery in 1725 and the Medical Collegium in 1763.

FROM PETER THE GREAT TO
THE ZEMSTVO REFORMS

PETER THE GREAT'S EFFORTS to modernize and westernize Russia bore fruit in the development of science, in general, and medical science, in particular. For example, in the military (1716) and naval (1720) rules, and in the regulations of 1721–22 there are many references to the need to maintain and strengthen the health of the men and to the provision of medical personnel for this purpose. In 1692, Peter sent R. V. Postnikov, a young Russian, to Padua and, in 1698, one Volkov and others to study medicine abroad. Peter also invited 150 foreign physicians to practice medicine in Russia. In 1701, a decree was issued, permitting the opening of "voluntary"—that is, private—pharmacies under the control of the Apothecary Board.

In 1707, a military general hospital, patterned after the Greenwich Hospital in England, was opened in Moscow. The term "general" meant that a medical school was attached to the hospital. Dr. N. Bidloo of Leiden directed the training of students in medicine and surgery. Similar hospitals (with medical schools) were established for the Navy in St. Petersburg (1710) and Kronstadt (1720) and for the Army in St. Petersburg (1733). These schools were called "hospital schools" and later "medicosurgical schools." The first attempt at a crude sort of census of vital statistics was made in 1712. Every four months priests were to report to the synod the number of male births and deaths in the area under their jurisdiction.

In 1721, a licensing system began in Russia; the state reserved to itself the right to determine who was competent to practice medicine; in addition, since in most cases the state paid the physician, it wanted to know what the physician did. With the beginnings of small-scale industrial production in the eighteenth century, some measures, of a minimal nature, were taken to provide medical services for workers. Hospitals were built at the Botkin Mining Works (1759) and at the Izhevski Iron Works (1760), financed by a 1 per cent deduction from workers' salaries as well as fines and donations.

Peter the Great laid the foundation for scientific work by importing scientists, books, and scientific collections from Europe, including many relating to medicine, and by suggesting the foundation of an Academy of Sciences. The academy, which began its work shortly after Peter's death, had a physician, Lorenz Blumentroost, as its first president, and in the years that followed many distinguished medical men were among its members. Russian medicine then became part of the mainstream of European medicine.

Another important milestone was the founding of Moscow University in 1755; a medical faculty began functioning in 1764. The first academic medical degree, however, was not bestowed until 1794. Prior to that time, the right to grant such a degree in medicine was reserved to the Medical Chancellery or Collegium. In 1798, a Medical-Surgical Academy was founded in St. Petersburg, with a branch in Moscow. New universities and medical schools (faculties) were founded in Yuryev (Dorpat, now Tartu) in 1802, Kazan (1804), Kharkov (1805), and Kiev (1834). Schools for the training of *feldshers*[3] and nurses were established in the middle of the nineteenth century.

In 1775, as part of the measures introduced to strengthen local governments, Boards of Social Assistance were established. Their jurisdiction embraced all charitable and medical institutions, and they were charged with building orphanages, hospitals, pharmacies, poorhouses, homes for incurables, and mental asylums. The position of *uyezdnii* (district) physician was also instituted, and, in 1797, medical administrations were established in all provincial towns to provide some modicum of medical assistance to the needy population.

At the beginning of the nineteenth century (in 1802), there were 1,519 physicians instead of the 150 physicians and *lekars* of a century before. Of these, 422 served in the army, 218 in the navy, and 879 in medical districts of the civilian service. There were thirty military hospitals. And the number of pharmacies increased from two at the end of the seventeenth century to fourteen at the end of the eighteenth century.

Administratively, the Medical Collegium was replaced, in 1802, by the Medical Department of the Ministry of Internal Affairs, which remained generally in charge of medical matters for the country until tsarism fell. However, certain medical functions began to be assumed by other ministries and administrations, so that by the time of the Revolution the direction of medical affairs in Russia was fragmented among different state agencies. There was no central planning and coordinating medical agency for the country as a whole, a situation the Soviet regime, almost immediately after its seizure of power, tried to remedy by establishing a single and unique medical center to coordinate and standardize all medical activities, military and civilian. Experience soon showed, however, that this was unrealistic, and at the present time there are several more or less autonomous health authorities, although (as will be seen later) the Soviets claim this does not violate the unity of Soviet medical administration.

Russian medicine truly came of age in the nineteenth century, as a result of the general flowering of cultural and scientific life and increased contact with the West that followed the Napoleonic Wars. Medical students and physicians who wanted to complete special studies or postgraduate work or to do research often went abroad, particularly to Germany, Austria, and, to a lesser degree, France.

FROM THE ZEMSTVO REFORM (1864) TO 1917

AN IMPORTANT FEATURE of the development of Russian medicine and medical organization in the nineteenth century were the zemstvos created in 1864, as part of the reforms introduced after the Emancipation Proclamation which freed the serfs. The reforms aimed at a partial decentralization of governmental operations, reduction of the power of the bureaucracy, and the development of limited local self-government in the countryside. Similar self-government units were established for the towns. Zemstvo functions were broad and diversified, embracing such local activities as road building, supervising prisons, education, public welfare, social assistance, and medical care and public health. The central government, on the other hand, retained control of such functions as policing and recruiting, and appointed provincial governors who had the right to intervene in the work of the zemstvos.

In the area of public health Russia had been lagging behind western Europe through lack of financial resources, interest, initiative, and personnel. Most physicians practiced in the large cities, treating primarily the middle and upper urban classes, leaving the worker and the peasant with very little or practically no professional attention. Whatever assistance the peasantry received came primarily from medicine men, feldshers, and midwives, who had scarcely any professional training. As S. I. Mitskevich wrote, the nobility and gentry felt that

> The peasant [*muzhik*] is not accustomed and does not need scientific medical assistance, his diseases are 'simple' and for this a feldsher is enough—a physician treats the masters, and a peasant is treated by a feldsher.[4]

Deplorable health conditions in the countryside and among the urban lower classes and the consequent high illness rates were further compounded by frequent and disastrous famines and epidemics. A first step in the development and modernization of medical assistance for the population as a whole came primarily as a result of the public health and medical functions assumed by the zemstvos.

The zemstvos inherited the medical institutions that were the responsibility of the Boards of Social Assistance (established, it will be remembered, in 1775). Most of these institutions had been neglected and poorly maintained in the years preceding their transfer.

The immensity of the tasks faced, the paucity of the resources available, and the lack of trained and experienced personnel made progress, at first, extremely slow, sporadic, and irregular; the zemstvos allotted only the most minimal resources to public health. Peasants, who often had to pay for medical assistance, saw the fees abolished only in the middle eighties. Because of the shortage of funds, zemstvos frequently hired physicians' assistants (feldshers) rather than full-fledged physicians. The few doctors who were employed by the zemstvos worked at first on a "circuit" (*razyezdnaia*) basis, going from district to district and village to village, seeing patients usually on market days. They also went to the villages upon request of the organs of justice or to carry out measures against epidemics. Those who needed continuous medical attention had to resort to the feldshers. It was only in the nineties that the circuit system was abolished and physicians were appointed to reside and practice in one locality. In 1870, there were 1,350 medical dispensaries manned by feldshers; in 1910, there were 2,620. Over the same period the number of zemstvo physicians rose from 610 to 3,100, and the number of beds per 10,000 inhabitants, which was 1.5 in 1870, more than tripled.

Yet, as noted, the development of zemstvo medicine was extremely uneven. Initiative and resources varied from one zemstvo to another. There was no over-all nation-wide, coordinated medical assistance program for Russia.

One of the achievements of the zemstvo was its pioneering the system of city and rural medical microdistricts. A microdistrict (*uchastok*), a territorial or geographical unit for the delivery of medical care, was designed to provide complete and comprehensive medical coverage for its population. The basic organizational medical nucleus was an outpatient clinic to which was added, later, a small hospital. In addition, there were to be attached public health or sanitation services and provisions for antiepidemic work and for research in the area's general health conditions. Ideally, the microdistrict was to provide both preventive and clinical services, and to afford medical coverage in different specialties. This remained, however, mostly a blueprint.

In the cities some measures to bring medical assistance to the workers were adopted. According to a decision of the Committee of Ministers passed in 1866, ten hospital beds were to be made available for every one thousand workers at the expense of the employer, but this remained largely a dead letter. It was only after the 1905 Revolution that laws permitting the creation of hospital funds (*bol'nichnie kassi*) were enacted; they were patterned loosely after the German social insurance system.

It may be said that the zemstvo system not only provided Soviet medicine with a partial organizational blueprint, but also gave rise to a distinctively new social and professional type, that of the zemstvo physician, who combined traditional medical ethics with the humanitarianism and reformism of the "Populist" movement. The Populists, or *Narodniki*, as they were known, felt they had to "go to the people" and bring them the benefits of science, education, progress, and of course, medical care. This movement best embodied the spirit of mission, dedication, and activism that was found among large segments of the Russian intelligentsia. The physician and the teacher were perhaps the most outstanding representatives of this voluntary movement to assist and educate the "dark and deaf" masses of rural Russia. Members of the intelligentsia who foresook the comforts of the "center" for the dreary life on the "land" were making, in the eyes of the city population, a substantial sacrifice. In addition to difficulties and deprivations, these intellectual missionaries also faced a frequently hostile and suspicious peasantry. Sometimes they were murdered; sometimes, driven out or turned over to the police by the peasants, the intellectuals returned to the towns discouraged and disheartened, having experienced an inability to communicate with "the people." Yet, despite these conditions, the number of zemstvo physicians increased almost tenfold between 1865 and 1910.

While zemstvo physicians certainly did not constitute a majority of the medical profession (in 1913, about 22 per cent of all physicians worked in the countryside), they played a role quite disproportionate to their numbers. They created the model of the "socially conscious" physician who devotes himself to the welfare of others without regard for his own comfort, safety, or well-being. To their credit, they went beyond the sick individual to the social and economic conditions that produced sickness. But in addition to social and economic conditions, there were political factors that to a large extent determined many, if not most, other conditions. Confronted in their daily activities, as they were, with the misery, poverty, corruption, inequalities, and sufferings of the population, the zemstvo physicians soon began to realize that even the best medical care would be of little avail unless matched by political reforms that would pave the way for improvements in sanitation, food, and living standards in general. They were truly appalled by the terrible waste, both in human lives and in economic terms, which was the direct result of the deplorable health conditions in the countryside as well as in the towns, and by the low life expectancy of the population. What contributed most to their dissatisfaction, of course, was the realization that most of these conditions *could* be remedied if only the appropriate measures were taken and the necessary funds made available. For example, at a meeting of the St. Petersburg Society of Russian Physicians held in 1885, a resolution was taken approving a report presented by Dr. Nikolai Ekk [later published in *Mezhdunarodnaia Klinika* (*International Clinic*)] on the extraordinary mortality rate in Russia and the need to take measures to improve the situation. Dr. Ekk's viewpoint was perhaps more economic than humanitarian. He argued that low life expectancy (compared to that of western Europe) was a definite economic liability, since premature death robbed the society of the productive capacities of its members. "Nor should one imagine," Dr. Ekk went on, "that Russia by refraining from improving health conditions actually does effect economies. On the contrary, since in Russia sixteen more persons out of 1000 die annually than in England, one million and a half die each year who need not. More than half of these, almost two thirds, die without having earned a living, without having repaid their debt to society." The cost of this loss was estimated at fifty million gold rubles yearly. Further, Dr. Ekk's report continued:

> Death from a majority of diseases is an artificial (violent) death and not a natural one, and results from the failure to take the appropriate preventive measures indicated by science and the usefulness of which has been demonstrated by the experience of many cities and countries; the extraordinary mortality among the Russian population lowers its working capacity and damages the national economy; an increase in the work capacity of the population, as well as its prosperity and education in our country, is impossible without a decrease of mortality, and this is why a decrease in mortality by means of an improvement of sanitation constitutes our first governmental necessity.

Dr. Ekk concluded by emphasizing, once more, that the knowledge for decreasing mortality already existed: "It only remains for us to translate into our local conditions the practical data gathered by England . . . the more spent for health, the better for the people."[5]

Under these circumstances it is not surprising that the medical profession, in general, and, of course, most of the zemstvo physicians held "liberal democratic" ideas and were part of the revolutionary ferment of the times. A change in the political structure would allow them, so they thought, to improve the population's medical care and health. While the financial and organizational support would naturally have to come from the state, the medical profession expected to retain its professional autonomy. Indeed, it would advise and suggest. In this expectation, as in many others, the profession was to be disappointed after the Revolution: It was the Soviet regime that did the advising and the medical profession that did the obeying.

Zemstvo medicine, furthermore, also contributed to the solution of the problem of providing medical care for groups that could not afford it. It raised health and preventive services to the level of a public service provided by and for the community, which financed them from tax funds and general revenues. In this respect the scheme differed somewhat from insurance plans in which specific groups of wage earners (and sometimes employers) made a definite and regular contribution to a central fund which would, in turn, pay for the services of the physician and for hospital and related care.

At the same time, it should be noted that the allocations for medical care were not generous (4.5 kopecks per capita in 1871, 20.4 in 1890, and 56 in 1904), and that, in some instances, the principle of free care was not observed, the peasant population at times being made to pay for outpatient and hospital care, prescriptions, and drugs in addition to the medical tax. As the *BME* comments: "Zemstvo physicians insisted on the principle of free medical care, but were not able to realize it in all the zemstvos. The ideals of zemstvo medicine did not correspond to the reality."[6]

Politically and socially, the medical profession in the latter part of the nineteenth century and the early part of the twentieth had achieved a considerable amount of professional autonomy and political influence. In addition, the formation of professional associations or societies gave the physicians, collectively, a platform from which they could express their social and political views. Although the Medico-Physical Society was founded in 1808, and the Moscow Society of Russian Physicians in 1861, perhaps the most influential organization was the Society of Russian Physicians in Memory of N. I. Pirogov. The society, founded in 1885 and named for one of Russia's ablest military surgeons and physicians, campaigned actively both for medical *and* economic-political reforms, stating in effect that an improvement in medical care and public health would, by itself, accomplish little unless paralleled by similar improvements in the life and working conditions of the Russian population. The Pirogov Society also tried to disseminate health information (what the Soviets call "health propaganda"). The Commission for the Dissemination of Health Knowledge, organized in 1894, was quite active. By 1905, more than two million leaflets and about 300,000 brochures had been issued. In 1919, the task of that commission was delegated to the RSFSR Health Commissariat, and health propaganda became one of the regular and constant concerns of the Soviet health authorities (see Chapter 8).[7]

As such, of course, the Pirogovists were very much within the tradition of liberalism and good works of the Russian *intelligentsia*. But perhaps the most significant aspect of the Pirogovists was their ability, even under tsarist conditions of autocracy and lack of political freedom, to band together into a corporate group and act in concert, assuming and maintaining a position with heavy political overtones. Furthermore, as physicians they cherished their ability to act independently, particularly in professional matters, because this was for them a guarantee of high ethical standards of medical practice, free from outside (nonprofessional) dictation; it was a guarantee also of high social status. This was true even in the case of the zemstvo physicians who were salaried. As we have seen, the principle of "public practice," regarded favorably by the medical profession, was upheld by some of its most respected members and spokesmen. At the same time, this principle entailed a degree of professional autonomy from nonprofessional direction and dictation quite at variance with Soviet conceptions in this area, as we shall see later.

A few figures will provide a general idea of the extent of the Russian Empire's medical resources immediately prior to the First World War. In 1913, there were 23,143 physicians for a population of 159,200,000 (on the territory corresponding to that of the USSR today) or 1.45 physicians per 10,000. In addition, there were about 54,000 semiprofessional medical personnel,[8] of these 29,000 were feldshers, 15,000 were midwives, and 10,000 were nurses (sisters of charity).[9] In 1913, there were 207,300 hospital beds (or 13 beds per 10,000 population).[10] The distribution of medical resources in Imperial Russia was, however, very uneven. According to Vinogradov, 35 per cent of all towns had no hospital whatsoever, and only 21 per cent of all hospitals had more than 20 beds (26 per cent of the hospitals had five or fewer beds).[11]

The tsarist regime was not, of course, unaware of the country's tremendous medical needs, and several commissions between 1886 and 1917 investigated these needs, produced voluminous reports, and made recommendations; but, in general, progress was slow. In addition, many proposals for the creation of a single health authority were opposed by some of the progressive physicians on the ground that another bureaucratic authority would not solve the country's basic problems: Medical reforms would not be of much avail unless matched by similar improvements in other areas.

Prior to the Bolshevik Revolution, in the period of democratic ferment that followed the February 1917 Revolution and the establishment of the Provisional Government (which was to last only six months until the Bolsheviks overthrew it), two other significant developments took place in medicine and public health. The medical profession, as a corporate body, undertook to reform and improve the medical system along the lines discussed and elaborated in the fifty years preceding the Revolution. Indeed, the Provisional Government was for the profession the opportunity to pass from talk to action. It thus sponsored the formation of a Central Medical Sanitary Council that was the embodiment of this movement and a clear indication of the principle that while medical care for the population and public health should have central governmental—and, naturally, financial—backing, this was to be in partnership with the medical profession, which would retain a strong directing and advisory role. The Pirogovists played a critical role in the formation of the council. Thus the February Revolution strengthened the hand and the power of the medical profession.

Parallel to the growth of labor unions, there also arose several medical unions based primarily on the physicians' specialties and places of employment: hospital, city, army, navy, transportation, and factory. (In 1905, an All-Russian Union of Medical Personnel had been established.) In May, 1917, these unions or associations amalgamated into the Council of the Petrograd Union of Physicians. From that city the movement rapidly spread to others, leading later to the creation of a central organization, the All-Russian Union of Professional Associations of Physicians.

Therefore, while the Medical-Sanitary Council was more of an official body with "service" functions (concerned with the organization of medical services) working closely with the government, the All-Russian Union represented the organized or the unionized medical profession attempting to define its place, role, and status vis-à-vis other occupational groups in the new democratic and liberal society that was to emerge from the February Revolution. It should be noted, furthermore, that these organizations, and the physicians as such, did not look favorably upon the Bolshevik bid for power. By virtue of their social and professional position, the medical corps tended to hold "liberal" rather than "proletarian" political views, and the Bolsheviks also tended to regard the physicians (except the few who had made common cause with them) somewhat as "bourgeois"—that is, class enemies. The October Revolution was to bring this antagonism into the open.

On the other hand, when socialized medicine was introduced in the Soviet Union, "public" practice did not emerge as an innovation imposed upon a reluctant professional body (as it might be in the United States), but as the extension of a cultural tradition that had been upheld by some of the most respected members of the pre-Revolutionary intelligentsia. And yet, in its attempts to unify medical services, centralize all the health activities, and direct medical practice in general, the Soviet regime introduced a series of changes that largely destroyed the spirit of spontaneity and voluntariness that had characterized medical practice, particularly the zemstvo physician's work, in the pre-Revolutionary years. The well-meaning, philanthropic activities of the medical profession became incompatible with a bureaucratically organized and politically controlled health system, embracing the totality of medical personnel, and subordinate to a political ideology toward which most physicians initially felt hostile. This ideology, in addition, led to a policy and directives that were contrary to the basic ethics of medical work as they had been known until then; they were resisted by the medical profession. In turn, as we shall see, the regime took steps to break down this resistance by destroying the pre-Revolutionary associational bases of the medical profession and substituting other structures more responsive to its directives.

Chapter 3

Marxism and
the Ideology of Medicine

THE CENTRAL POSITION occupied by ideology and ideological questions in Soviet society makes it imperative at this juncture, to examine certain aspects of ideology, particularly as they relate to the theory behind the organization and philosophy of the Soviet health service and medical institutions. Insofar as medical theoreticians and organizers of medical services operate, or profess to operate, in terms of ideological propositions and commitments, these are germane to an understanding of the specific forms medicine and medical organization have taken in the Soviet Union.

We must specify at the outset that we are dealing with two analytically distinct, although closely related, types of "ideologies." There is, first and foremost, the basic, official ideology upon which the regime theoretically rests. This is, of course, Marxism, today called Marxism-Leninism in order to include the modifications and additions introduced by Lenin, who is considered the founder of the Soviet Union and Marx's greatest disciple (a position shared, until a few years ago, by Stalin).

Second, and of greater relevance for this study, is the "ideology" of Soviet medicine, which might briefly be described as a set of principles derived, for the greater part, from Marxism-Leninism, but adapted and modified to serve as the ideological foundations of the Soviet health service and to justify and support that service. As we shall see, these modifications consist, in part, of selected "national" additions obtained by tracing the origins of the Soviet medical system to the historical traditions of Russian "progressive" medicine (and particularly the zemstvo system) of the second half of the nineteenth and the early twentieth centuries, as well, of course, to Marxist theory, and combining these with a praise of Soviet socialized medicine and a critique of health services of countries outside the Soviet bloc.

There is no dearth of controversy among observers and students about the nature of Marxist ideology (is it a tool of sociological analysis, a theory of history, a philosophy, a program of action?) and its relevance to Soviet society. In other words, the question often is posed: Does ideology really matter, does it make a difference? Opinions on the subject run the entire gamut from the belief that ideology today plays no significant role, that it is only the frosting of rationalization on the cake of action and that the regime is motivated only by considerations of self-interest, national power, and control over its population, to the conviction that the Soviet regime operates according to the blueprints and timetables drawn up by Marx and Lenin, so that an understanding of that society can be achieved only through a thorough knowledge of the works of these men and their followers. (This view often is justified by arguing that one might have learned of Hitler's plans and designs through a careful reading of *Mein Kampf*.)

The answer must lie somewhere between these polar viewpoints. As the history of the Soviet Union and policies of its leaders have demonstrated, ideological considerations often have gone by the board, particularly in situations when there was little choice between survival and catastrophe. And yet, in just as many situations, and particularly when there were alternative choices of action, a course consistent with the ideology was selected, often when a more expedient choice might have produced better and cheaper results. (This is true, for example, of Soviet agricultural institutions, particularly the state and collective farms, which appear inadequate to meet the consumer and industrial crop needs of the country. Reform, however, might create private, capitalistic farming which the Soviet regime has consistently rejected since collectivization.) It is, thus, our contention that theories, values, ideologies (particularly when they are supported by the entire apparatus of the regime) tend to shape human actions—that is, they are normative—and that violations of these premises are psychologically more difficult to accept and justify than compliance with them.

Even a surface acquaintance with Soviet society will disclose not only the overwhelming importance of ideology but also the fact that the Soviet regime derives its legitimacy, its *raison d'être*, from Marxism-Leninism, even though the tenets of this ideology are sometimes not observed, or observed only in the breach. Indeed, it would not be too much to assert that the Communist party of the Soviet Union, the one and unique organization that retains the ultimate power to make secular decisions in Soviet society, considers itself the embodiment of the Communist vision and the instrument by which the utopian society that this vision promises to mankind will be achieved.

THE IDEOLOGY OF SOVIET MEDICINE

IT MUST BE MADE clear to the reader that in what is to follow we will deal with ideological questions and interpretations primarily *in Soviet terms*, regardless of the objective validity of these terms. In other words, we are interested in showing how the Soviets view and describe their situation, since it is in terms of this view and description that they act.

Marxism, as such, must be viewed as a *Weltanschauung*, a world view defining the nature of reality, man, society, and the unfolding of history. Because of the integral, all-embracing quality of this world view, it is only natural that it should include a definition and interpretation of medicine and medical institutions. The "laws" for the prevention and treatment of diseases, the conservation and development of the population's work capacity, the achievement of a long life expectancy—these are all to be derived, it is claimed, from the teachings of Marx and Lenin. It is seriously maintained, at least among official medical circles, that a physician's education (or that of any specialist) is incomplete if it consists only of technical, professional knowledge and skills. Thus one can read in the semi-weekly organ of the Health Ministry USSR, *Meditsinskii Rabotnik* (*The Medical Worker*), that "In order to be a worthy representative of the physician's noble profession, it is necessary not only to have an excellent professional education, but also to be well acquainted with the principles of Marxism-Leninism."[1] (In the current medical school curriculum about 250 course hours are devoted to the study of Marxism-Leninism.)

Therefore, were one to consult exclusively Soviet sources on the subject, one might easily come to the conclusion that a correct interpretation of health and illness, the nature of the physician's work in society, and the rational organization of medical services, medical research, and public health is possible only within the framework of dialectical materialism and through the prism of Marx's and Lenin's wisdom and vision in particular.

Actually, Marx, Engels, and Lenin paid relatively little attention to these problems, except insofar as their analysis of health conditions was part and parcel of their general view of capitalism and their description of the working conditions and exploitation of its industrial proletariat. They held that the owners of capital were supremely indifferent to the health of the workers, and that in their search for profits they did not hesitate to ruin the health of the workers, including women and children, by making them toil under inhuman conditions for twelve, fourteen or even sixteen hours a day. Marx held that capital

> . . . in its unrestrainable passion, its were-wolf hunger for surplus-labour . . . oversteps not only the moral, but the merely physical maximum bounds of the working day. It usurps the time for growth, development and health maintenance of the body. It steals the time required for the consumption of fresh air and sunlight. It higgles over meal-time . . . so that food is given to

the labourer as to a mere means of production, as coal is supplied to the boiler. . . . It reduces the sound sleep needed for the restoration, reparation, refreshment of the bodily powers to just so many hours of torpor as the revival of an organism, absolutely exhausted, renders essential. . . . Capital cares nothing for the length of life of labour-power. . . . The capitalistic mode of production . . . produces thus the premature exhaustion and death of this labour-power itself.[2]

Furthermore, Marx pointed out, it would seem to be in the self-interest of the owner of capital to care for and maintain his labor-power (workers) in the same way as it is in his interest to care for and maintain, say, a horse or a piece of machinery. Presumably, the maintenance cost would prolong the useful life of the labor-power and would be cheaper than replacement. But these considerations in most instances do not apply, he contends, because there is a constant supply of very cheap labor available, and it is economically more advantageous to use labor-power intensively for a short period of life than to keep maintaining it, since in this case replacement is cheaper than repair or maintenance. As a result of such an attitude, no attention is paid to the working and living conditions of the proletariat. Hence, as Marx further wrote:

. . . Capital is reckless of the health or the length of life of the labourer, unless under compulsion from society. To the outcry as to the physical and mental degradation, the premature death, the torture of overwork, it answers: Ought these to trouble us since they increase our profits?[3]

Actually, Marx, as a determinist, was not passing a "moral" judgment on the owners of capital. Rather, he concluded, their actions did not derive from good or ill will, but from, as he put it, "free competition [which] brings out the inherent laws of capitalist production, in the shape of *external coercive laws having power over every individual capitalist.*"[4]

The juxtaposition in this picture of the bourgeoisie lining its pockets in a limitless drive for profits, on the one hand, and the broken bodies and minds, twisted existences, and shortened lives of the proletariat, on the other, is a most powerful indictment against the kind of ruthless exploitation of labor that accompanied (and often still accompanies) the initial stages of industrialization and urbanization—when the worker, so to speak, pays by decreased consumption and increased exertion for the accumulation of the capital necessary for industrialization. This indictment was perhaps best formulated by Engels who, writing before Marx and providing him with a great deal of data, had pointed out, in his *Condition of the Working Class in England,* that capitalistic production led to a progressive deterioration of the workers' health through factory-caused diseases and injuries:

> A fine list of diseases and injuries due solely to the revolting greed of the middle classes: Simply in order to fill the pockets of the bourgeoisie women are rendered unfit to bear children, children are crippled, while grown men are stunted and maimed. The health of whole generations of workers is undermined and they are racked by diseases and infirmities. . . . Stuart reports that children were dragged naked out of bed by overseers and driven with blows and kicks to the factories, their clothes over their arms. . . . We read of hundreds of children who come home from the factory every evening so tired that they cannot eat their supper from lack of sleep and lack of appetite. Their parents had found them on their knees at their bedside, where they had fallen asleep while saying their prayers. . . .[5]

Lenin, conceding that legislation had sometimes been passed by bourgeois governments under pressure from the working class in the second half of the nineteenth century to provide for some form of medical treatment, asserted that in most instances these provisions were evaded by owners of capital and remained a dead letter. The government of a bourgeois country, he insisted, was nothing more than the executive committee of the bourgeois class. No real improvement in the lot of the workers could be expected until the proletariat had seized political power and begun to operate the state to benefit the workers.

In the Draft Program of the Social Democratic Party elaborated in 1895–96, Lenin proposed, among other things, that a law be passed in Russia to make manufacturers responsible for injuries sustained by workers in production and to oblige them to maintain schools and provide medical services for their employees. And in his book *The Development of Capitalism in Russia,* Lenin made fairly extensive use of the materials (particularly statistics) gathered by the zemstvos and zemstvo physicians, and there found indications that he felt fully confirmed Engels' and Marx's conclusions that work under capitalistic conditions leads to serious diseases and injuries for workers and their children. He also described in some detail the conditions of what he called "capitalistic agriculture," tracing, for example, the consequences of the introduction of machinery into agriculture:

. . . Another consequence of the use of machinery is the growing employment of female and child labor. The existing system of capitalist agriculture has, generally speaking, given rise to a certain hierarchy of workers, very much reminiscent of the hierarchy among factory workers. . . . Often they work merely for their food and clothes. The introduction of agricultural implements "depreciates the labor of the full worker" and renders possible its replacement by the cheaper labor of women and juveniles. Statistics on immigrant labor confirm the fact of male labor being displaced by female labor. . . . The capitalistically employed machine creates here (as everywhere) a powerful stimulus to the lengthening of the working day. . . . Finally, the systematic employment of machines results in traumatism among agricultural workers; the employment of young women and children at machines naturally results in a particularly large crop of injuries. The Zemstvo hospitals and dispensaries in Kherson gubernia, for example, are filled during the agricultural season almost exclusively with traumatic patients and serve as field hospitals, as it were, for the treatment of the enormous army of agricultural workers who are constantly being disabled as a result of the ruthless destructive work of agricultural machines and implements. A special medical literature is appearing that deals with injuries caused by agricultural machines. Proposals are being made to introduce compulsory regulations governing the use of agricultural machinery. The large-scale manufacture of machinery imperatively calls in agriculture, as in industry, for public control and regulation of production. . . .[6]

A special section on the protection of the workers' health was included in the Party Program adopted by the Second Congress of the Party in 1903, and in the Project of the New Program of the Party drafted in April, 1917. Lenin included demands for the protection of the workers and of their health which he considered indispensable ". . . in the interest of protecting the working class from physical and mental debilitation, and also in the interest of the development of its capacity in the struggle for liberation."[7]

It must be understood that these programs and demands were addressed to the government of a "bourgeois" society, and aimed at the protection, insofar as seemed feasible, of the health of the workers under capitalistic conditions. It was only after the seizure of power, in October, 1917, that Lenin and the new Soviet government could turn to the problem of organizing medical and public health services under conditions of Soviet rule.

Theoretically, according to the Marxist analysis, medicine and the medical institutions of any social system must be considered part of the superstructure of that society, resting on its socioeconomic base. By "base" Marx meant the means of production of commodities and their exchange. It is the base, in this view, that determines the nature of the superstructure, and as the base changes under the impact of technological changes and the application of knowledge, so do the superstructures, whether they be political, ideological, religious, or medical institutions. The scope of the medical system, the extent of its coverage, the scheme of its organization, and the forms of public health are determined both by the level of the development of the productive forces in the society and the nature of the social relationships that obtain in that society. Just like religious, political, and legal institutions, the medical system, according to Marxist theory, also serves the interests of the ruling class, which in a capitalistic society exploits the proletariat in order to increase its own profits and well-being. In the Soviet Union, on the other hand, the official contention is that the elimination of the private ownership of the means of production has led to the elimination of antagonistic classes and the exploitation of man by man. The health system is thus said to serve the needs of the entire population.

Like other historical and ideological interpretations, Soviet evaluation of the contributions to Soviet medicine made by Marxist theory, the early Russian historical background, the traditions of progressive and zemstvo medicine, and Soviet modifications of the medical system, have varied, reflecting thereby the ideological and political vicissitudes of Soviet history. In the early twenties, it was still fashionable to emphasize, in addition to Marxism and zemstvo medicine, the contributions made to Soviet public health by the English and the Germans; later, during the heyday of Russian chauvinism under Stalin, these "foreign" contributions were gradually ignored or denied until Lenin and Stalin began to emerge as the exclusive founders of the Soviet medical system. Thus, according to M.I. Barsukov, in a book written in 1951,[8] Soviet health protection is *sui generis* a unique phenomenon in the history of mankind, completely (or almost completely) divorced from medical developments and progress in other societies and even from pre-Revolutionary Russian history. Therefore, Barsukov vehemently rejects the thesis advanced in 1926 by Skorokhodov (when such views could be advanced with impunity) that Soviet medical theory and medical organization had its antecedents in, and combined features of, English social medicine (with its mass preventive emphasis), German insurance medicine (with its class character), and Russian zemstvo medicine (with its ideal that free care should be available to all). Rather, Barsukov asserts, "only the theory of revolutionary Marxism, most developed in the works of Lenin and Stalin, permitted Soviet health protection to solve scientifically the problems of the (health) protection of the broad masses, a protection which is in practice fully realized only in our country, the country of victorious socialism." The main role in the creation and the development of the Soviet medical system is thus attributed not to physcans and public health specialists, but to the Bolshevik party, and primarily to its leaders, Lenin and Stalin, who are credited with laying down the theoretical foundations of Soviet health protection and with guiding it through all stages of its development and its struggles. This view, it will be remembered, was propounded in 1951, when the cult of personality of Stalin was at its zenith, and when even genuine Russian contributions to the sciences and other areas of human endeavor were deemphasized by comparison with the brilliant (and almost divine) personality of Stalin (and to some degree to that of his mentor, Lenin). At the present time, a somewhat more balanced evaluation is used. It stresses the progressive humanism of nineteenth-century Russian thinkers, philosophers, and socially conscious physicians and the "materialism" of Marxist philosophy.

Soviet medical care and the health service are also considered important propaganda elements, domestically and abroad. Since the government claims to follow Marxist-Leninist theory, it holds Soviet society to be a socialistic system in which medicine can *truly* serve the interests of all the people because the inequities characteristic of capitalism have been removed and the exploitation of man by man has been abolished. The critique of capitalistic medicine is therefore addressed both to pre-Revolutionary Russian medicine and to contemporary medicine in capitalist countries. We are thus told that the Bolshevik Revolution eliminated the basic antagonistic contradictions between the socioeconomic structure and the health of the people and thus did away with the basic source of illness for the workers:

> . . . It is only in the Soviet era that it becomes possible in the full sense of the term to realize that directing role of Marxist-Leninist philosophy in the development of natural science and of medicine. . . . The theoretical basis of Soviet health protection is the theory of Marxism-Leninism, based on the dialectical method of the study of nature and of society, and on the materialistic theory of consciousness . . . (it) gives the key to a correct understanding of the influence of the external environment on physiological processes of the organism of man and permits the discovery of the etiology of many morbid processes.[9]

Thus the humanism and progressiveness of pre-Revolutionary Russian medicine, as beneficial as they may have been in creating a tradition for Soviet medicine, were, under the conditions of tsarist autocracy, doomed to failure. As Professor Anichkov described it: "For the best representatives of our national medicine it was a characteristic striving to serve the masses of the people, to give free medical care to the workers, to organize social popular medicine, to imbue in the new generations of doctors a feeling of love for their great people . . . but *they were stars in a dark atmosphere.*"[10]

By the same token, Soviet medical ideologists, when confronted with measures expanding and improving health care in capitalistic countries, deny that these measures are significant, arguing that a capitalist society by definition exploits the workers and is incapable of providing for a substantial improvement of their standard or living and health care. Indeed, most Soviet pronouncements on the subject are apt to stress the increasing pauperization of the masses under capitalism and argue that medical care is largely inaccessible to them because they cannot afford the private services of rapacious physicians, costly pharmaceuticals, or exhorbitant hospitalization expenses. Taking their cue from the frequently repeated cliché that under capitalism the law of the jungle predominates and man is another man's wolf, they tend to dismiss summarily Western programs of socialized medicine or medical insurance as pure sham.

To enter the field of Soviet ideology, even as it applies to medicine and public health, is thus for the Westerner to penetrate a strange house, populated by heroes and villains, by the good socialistic society and the bad capitalistic bourgeois world; it is a house replete with fulsome praise for itself and violent invective against outsiders; it is a house whose members are convinced they have the correct viewpoint and interpretation, and that all others are wrong. In other words, the very tone of ideological pronouncements and discussions resembles that of the religious and theological arguments of centuries past.

"Bourgeois medicine" as the expression goes, is contrasted with "Soviet medicine" and is accused of playing an important role in defending capitalism, "often under the mask of humanism." Soviet readers are told, for example, that recommendations of "some bourgeois authors" to decrease fat intake in the diet in order to decrease heart disease are,

extremely advantageous for the ruling classes of the capitalist
society who, at the present time, are carrying an active campaign against the living standards of the masses of the population and the wages of the workers, and increase the prices of
foodstuffs, especially fats. . . . The situation of the large masses
of the workers in capitalist countries is . . . characterized by the
unemployment of many millions of workers in the USA and other
countries, by the especially sharp deterioration of the living
standard, . . . a considerable decrease in real wages, an increase
in the prices of food products, especially fats, the starving of
millions of people. . . . In the contemporary capitalist countries millions of people suffer not from a surplus but a lack of
fats and calories. . . . [This entirely contradicts the statements of
some foreign authors], who try, contrary to the facts, to prove
that the "increase in standard of living" in Western countries is
allegedly linked with the increased danger of coronary disease.
It is the task of Soviet medical science to unmask these false and
deceitful attempts to embellish the capitalist order.[11]

Thus, for Soviet ideologists, peaceful coexistence does not, by
any means, imply a decrease in the "ideological struggle"; on
the contrary, it requires its intensification. As two Soviet writers
recently put it: "In the conditions of a sharp ideological struggle
between the two opposing systems——capitalism and socialism
. . . the dialectical-materialistic interpretation of biological and
medical questions is one of the most important areas in the fight
against bourgeois ideology."[12] The main "sin" of bourgeois scientists is their attempt to prove that within the framework of a
capitalistic society it is possible to realize he idea of the individual's complete physical and spiritual development. At the
same time, capitalism is said to stamp the physician's professional activities, because "he sells his knowledge for money . . .
the toilers, the exploited are deprived of the possibility of af-
fording medical assistance and are, as a rule, deprived of that
assistance."[13] This also means that the physician who works under capitalistic conditions, even if he sincerely wishes to diminish illness and suffering, must inevitably come into conflict with
the conditions of his society. This society, because of the capitalist mode of production, produces unavoidable illnesses. In addition, as Professor Bakulev, former President of the Academy of

Medical Sciences, stated, the fact that some medical theories claim that the origins of disease lie only in the organism of the individual himself "arose precisely because under a bourgeois system it is impossible to change the conditions of life in order to sharply decrease illness."[14]

It is hoped that these few comments will convey some idea of the weight given ideological matters and interpretations even in an area so apparently nonideological as medicine and medical organization. We can turn our attention now to more practical matters, such as the principles that are said actually to determine the Soviet health service.

ORGANIZATIONAL PRINCIPLES

IF ONE WERE to ask a Western physician to enumerate the basic principles and operational characteristics under which medical care and public health services are made available, he might be hard put to give a definite and unequivocal answer. He might dredge up such ideas as a mixture of private, charitable, voluntary, and governmental efforts, different schemes for the financing of medical services (insurance, taxes, fee-for-service), overlapping authorities, unnecessary duplications coupled with a variety of approaches, and other similar characteristics that would suggest congeries of really uncoordinated efforts. A Soviet physician would have little difficulty in enunciating the basic principles on which health services rest in the Soviet Union. He might, indeed, contrast what he would regard as the inchoate nature of medical organization (particularly in the United States) with the regal grandeur and unambiguous schema of the Soviet health service.

In the Soviet Union the provision of medical and public health services proceeds within a clearly defined ideological-political framework and a series of well-stated principles. These principles constitute the basic charter, organizational framework, and practical guide for the entire health service and the activities of the regime in this field. It is, of course, an open question whether these principles are always observed; whether they are (and often, for many reasons, they are not or cannot be), they constitute a sort of guideline that is meaningful to those involved in the medical system, and gross violations, distortions, or departures are bound to bring about negative sanctions of a social or even a legal nature.

At the most general level, as we have seen, the Soviet health service is described as a socialist system of governmental and community or collective measures having as their principal purpose the prevention and treatment of illness, the provision of healthy working and living conditions, and the achievement of a high level of work capacity and long life expectancy for the individual (to be gained primarily through a reduction of the mortality rate). As such, this system has several well-defined operational characteristics that spell out and elaborate these basic principles. These characteristics can be regarded as the bridges between the general charter, mandate, or mission and the organization and administration of health services (which will be examined later). They are the following:

1. *Public health and medical care are a responsibility of the state and a function of the government.* The provision of health services and all related health activities are, first and foremost, a state responsibility and considered a public service. Private practice, private initiative, and independent or charitable activities are rejected in favor of placing all health work under the aegis of the state. As a public service, therefore, medical care is given in much the same way as public education is offered in most countries. True, even in the Soviet Union, with its highly socialized medical system, private medical care has not totally disappeared. It exists on a minor scale, offered primarily by professors who see patients for relatively high fees after their work hours. Private practice, however, is ideologically frowned upon as a survival of "bourgeois medicine" left over from tsarism and not only is subject to heavy taxation, but also is slated to "wither away." There are, as far as we know, no private medical clinics, hospitals, or other medical installations. The fact that the health service is governmentally operated permits, in Soviet estimates, a unity, control, and standardization of medical and other services that cannot be attained in mixed systems, where

private or independent facilities coexist with those operated as a public service. As Maistrakh has pointed out in a textbook on Soviet health protection:

> Government control of Soviet public health is responsible for the unity of purpose, tasks, forms, and operational methods of medical establishments. All of them, whether part of the Ministry of Health system or of other departments, function throughout the country in accordance with a uniform plan and uniform methods, interlinked and so designed as to achieve the same objective—a reduction in the death rate of the population, continuous betterment of health, and an increase in the average life span by ameliorating working and living conditions.
>
> In the bourgeois countries public health services are scattered among a host of state, social, private and philanthropic institutions and organizations, which are uncoordinated and lacking in uniformity of plan or method of operation.[15]

2. *The development of all public health and medical measures takes place within the framework of a single plan.* The health service is not considered a separate entity operating independently of the goals, decisions, priorities, needs, and commitments of the Communist regime and of Soviet society. Rather, it is made to fit, like all other organized activities in the Soviet Union, within the over-all plans the regime elaborates in the pursuit of its own goals. This provides a guideline for a rational use and allocation of personnel, funds, and other limited resources and for the organization of medical facilities and services with the maximum efficiency, as well as the standardization of these services for the whole country. As also pointed out by Maistrakh:

> The plan for public health is part of the over-all state economic plan. The planned nature of public health ensures an even apportionment of funds, sound distribution of medical resources, and organization of the medical network for maximum efficiency and optimum satisfaction of the people's needs. It provides for a differentiated approach to the deployment of medical services in the various regions and provinces, enabling lagging areas to be strengthened, and tends to eliminate the differences between urban and rural medical facilities.[16]

3. *The centralization of the entire health service.* As a planned governmental responsibility and a state activity, the general direction and supervision of all health activities is concentrated in a central organization whose function it is to direct, coordinate, and standardize (within limits) all medical and public health efforts in order to permit the least amount of waste and duplication. This is accomplished through the establishment of a single and supreme health authority (the Health Ministry USSR) with subordinate units in all major administrative-territorial divisions. It is true, however, that certain organizations and administrations maintain their own health network, administratively independent of the Health Ministry (armed forces, Ministry of Internal Affairs, republican ministries of social welfare, Ministry of Communications, Ministry of Transportation), but these medical networks are run (with minor modifications and alterations to fit the particular circumstances) on the basic principles and standards established by the Health Ministry. They are not, therefore, held to constitute a violation of the principle of centralization and so-called "uni-directionality." It would, at the same time, be erroneous to assume that this centralization implies lack of local initiative and maneuverability. Thus, according to a description by the World Health Organization, the "basic principles of this structure are the highly centralized planning and supervision, coupled with an almost complete executive and operational decentralization, permitting almost ninety per cent of the problems to be dealt with at local levels, without disturbing the general and basic pattern in any way."[17]

4 *Health and allied services are made available to the population at no direct cost.* Health and allied services are financed as a public service—that is, their costs are underwritten by the state through general revenues and taxation, and are parts of the all-union, republican, and other governmental budgets. The Soviet citizen who applies for medical services of any type does not, therefore, have to pay for these services directly. He pays for them, indirectly, it is true, through taxes and particularly through the relatively high turnover tax, which is a hidden sales tax from which most revenues are derived. There are some minor exceptions to this rule, such as private practice and the so-called

paying polyclinics, which are state institutions where, for a modest fee, the patient can avail himself of the services of better qualified professionals. The one major and important exception to this principle is that the patient must pay for drugs prescribed for outpatient use (but not drugs for the treatment of specified chronic conditions, such as tuberculosis and malaria). The Third Party Program adopted in October, 1961, states that in the future all payments for drugs will be abolished, but does not say when.

5. *Prevention.* In Soviet medical theory prevention is said to be the cornerstone of the medical system. According to Semashko, the first Commissar of Health, prevention "must be understood not in the narrow and administrative sense of a task of the health organs, but broadly and deeply as the concern of the Soviet state for strengthening the health of the Soviet people."[18] Soviet writers claim that it is only under their kind of system that this principle can really be implemented on a national scale. It also is assumed that in the future the activities of medical personnel will, more and more, be oriented toward prevention rather than clinical treatment. Most medical installations bear the official title of preventive-clinical institutions, although if one were to make a strict accounting of the total efforts and work of medical personnel, in the majority of cases the work would undoubtedly be of a clinical rather than a preventive nature.

6. *Unity of practice and theory.* This principle, derived from Marxist philosophy, is constantly invoked in discussions of medical care. Originally it derives from the Marxist postulate that in order to know nature one must act upon it, and that there is no knowledge only for the sake of knowledge. Concretely, this consists of stressing the application of research findings to clinical activities and of urging practicing physicians to engage in research. Most Soviet health officials working at the Health Ministry USSR insist that they either practice medicine or do research or both, in addition to their administrative responsibilities. According to Vinogradov, more than one third of the articles published in medical journals are written by practicing physicians or medical administrators.[19] The unity between theory and practice is symbolized, furthermore, by the role played by the

Academy of Medical Sciences, which serves as the most important consultative body to the Ministry and is financially supported by the Ministry. According to Maistrakh, there is not a single branch of clinical or preventive medicine that is not directed by a corresponding scientific research institute.[20]

7. *Need for "popular" support.* While Soviet principles reject private medical care or independent activities, they support, on the other hand, the idea that medical care, being for the people, should to some degree involve their participation and support. This implies, for example, that by themselves the efforts and activities of health personnel cannot ensure the success of public health and preventive measures. The health service must be, so to speak, "backstopped" and supported all the way by the people themselves, acting either as volunteers or through other, nonmedical, organizations (party, state, trade union, Red Cross, and so on). This participation often takes the form of voluntary councils whose function might be, for example, to help patients at home, give support to the local hospital, clean up streets, yards and parks, and so on. As an English commentator has expressed it,

> In a sense, the whole of Soviet society is an exercise in social medicine. This is particularly noticeable in the way in which committees of citizens deal with welfare, care, and aftercare. Stalingrad has 401 "street committees"—local committees of citizens—in streets, blocks of flats, and other units. These undertake social-welfare work under the direction of a committee of the Stalingrad council, with a prominent member as chairman. They are responsible for sanitary matters, for taking steps to see that those in need of care get it, for work in connection with problem families and marital disharmony, for following up school children (in collaboration with parents' committees) and much else. This organization was described as a most important agent in promoting community health.[21]

8. *A system of priorities in providing medical services.* Soviet medical principles also emphasize that as long as health services remain scarce those who perform more important tasks and functions must have priority over those whose work is not so

critical to the national interests and national economy. This has led to the establishment and maintenance of a system of priorities by which workers in certain occupations (mining, for example) are offered better care (such as a higher staff-to-patient ratio, periodic preventive examinations, and the like) than those in less critical jobs.

It should be made clear that the principles discussed in this chapter are the official ones enunciated by Soviet medical ideologists and specialists in medical organization. While in some instances these principles are more programmatic than descriptive of reality, they nonetheless constitute the basic model toward which the system of medical care and public health strives. As a "blueprint" they are therefore often useful in examining the realities of the Soviet health service.

Chapter 4

The Development of
the Soviet Health Service:
From 1917 to the Present

POLITICAL EVENTS, economic conditions, health conditions, and ideological considerations in the early days of the Soviet regime helped shape the health service into a characteristic mold which it retains to a considerable extent even today. The system was born, so to speak, in a period of dire stress and emergency, one of insufficient economic resources and almost insurmountable crises of all types. The basic philosophy and framework of the health service elaborated at that time, therefore, reflect to some degree at least the difficult nature of the conditions confronting Lenin and his followers after they seized power on the night of October 25–26, 1917 (old style). They also reflect, but perhaps to a lesser degree, the nature of the ideology on which the new Soviet state was founded. While health conditions and problems have, naturally, changed in the Soviet Union, and while many changes and adaptations as well as extraordinary growth and expansion have taken place in the health service, the critical period of gestation, which occurred immediately after the Revolution deserves, if only from the viewpoint of the historical record, special attention. Hence, in this chapter we shall examine the period between the Revolution and the establishment of a Health Commissariat for the Russian Socialist Federated Soviet Republic, or RSFSR, in July, 1918, at some length. We shall then follow, more briefly, the development of the health service afterward. Our aim certainly is not to trace the history of the Soviet regime. Rather it is to relate the unfolding of Soviet medicine to the development of the regime, and to show that this unfolding was not, by any means, a spontaneous process, but was closely managed by the regime in response to current problems and programs.

DEVELOPMENT OF THE HEALTH SERVICE
AFTER THE OCTOBER REVOLUTION
(1917 TO MID–1918) ·

THE INCLUSIVE or "totalitarian" nature of Bolshevik ideology meant that every aspect of society, including the organization of medical care and public health, was to be reshaped by the new regime. Almost immediately after the seizure of power, a small group of physicians who had espoused the Bolshevik cause proceeded to bring medicine into line with the other changes that were being made in Russia, and to mold the health service and the nature of the medical profession along lines best calculated to further the regime's aims and programs. In medicine this meant, among other things, that the members of the "formerly exploited classes" (workers, soldiers, peasants) were to receive medical care before members of the "formerly exploiting" classes (members of the nobility, clergy, bourgeoisie). It also meant that the typically "middle-class and bourgeois ideas" that dominated the thinking of the majority of practitioners (and particularly the Pirogovists) were to be replaced by a new proletarian medical ideology. But aside from these ideological and political considerations, the very nature and magnitude of the health problems the regime faced immediately after the Revolution were instrumental, to a large degree in shaping the new

Soviet state's medical institutions and planning and giving them a certain "stamp" or character. It is therefore difficult to examine the development of the health service without looking both to the ideological and political factors, on the one hand, and to the dictates of reality, on the other. In combination, they determined the shape of the health service and gave it its typically "Soviet" countenance.

When the Bolsheviks wrested power from the weak and confused Provisional Government, they simultaneously inherited many of the problems that had plagued that government. These problems were a legacy of the general unpreparedness with which the country had entered the war in 1914, as well as of the general disorganization, ineptitude, and corruption that had characterized the first three years of the Russian war effort, particularly the second and third. The Bolsheviks inherited a system that not only was politically corrupt, economically bankrupt, and militarily on the verge of collapse, but also was endangered by a shortage of medical personnel, supplies, and facilities. Epidemics had found fertile ground among an already ill-nourished, exhausted, and weakened population. This crisis was further compounded by the lack of soap and other disinfectants. Ruling as a precarious minority from Petrograd, the new regime could not fail to regard the people's steadily deteriorating health as a serious political threat. Statistical data we have for the period amply confirm the magnitude of the epidemics and the threat they presented to the new Soviet state. These figures are certainly incomplete, because of the general disorganization and chaos that reigned in these years; and while they purport to reflect the number of registered cases of various diseases, we must assume that they are probably underenumerations. In any case, the reader familiar with descriptions of this period (fiction such as *Dr. Zhivago*, or nonfiction) will remember that Soviet life was dominated by the ever-present lack of food and danger of epidemic diseases.

Typhus was a particularly grave threat. In 1913, there were 7.3 registered cases of typhus per 10,000 people; in 1918, the figure was 21.9; in 1919, it was 265.3; and by 1920, it rose to an all-time high of 393.9. According to conservative estimates, twenty to thirty million were ill with typhus, and 10 per cent or more, perhaps three million, died of the disease. The number of deaths from all epidemics between 1916 and 1924 was estimated at ten million. Indeed, from 1917 to 1926, the Russian population decreased each year. "This typhus," Lenin declared shortly after the Revolution, "in a population [already] weakened by hunger and sickness, without bread, soap, fuel, may become such a scourge as not to give us an opportunity to undertake socialist construction. This [must] be the first step in our struggle for culture and for [our] existence."[1]

In 1919, at the height of the epidemic, Lenin tersely faced the Seventh Congress of Soviets with the choice: "Either the lice defeat socialism or socialism defeats the lice," and on March 20, 1920, at the Second All-Russian Congress of Medical-Sanitary Workers, he said: "Perhaps, after the military front, no other task than yours has had so many victims. We must turn all (our) resolution, all the experience of the civil war to the fight against epidemics."[2] This was, undoubtedly, an emergency situation requiring emergency measures. It was not a question, at least for the time being, of worrying whether factory workers were receiving the kind of medical services and other social welfare assistance that Lenin and his colleagues had demanded in the pre-Revolutionary period. It was a question of attempting, with the limited resources available, to stem the tide of epidemics or at least to diminish their spread and impact on the population's working and fighting capacity. For as the *Journal (Gazeta) of the Workers' and Peasant's Government* had warned in December, 1921: ". . . the war, the economic ruin and the ensuing famine, as well as the weakening of the population pose for the workers' and peasants' government the problem of a struggle, at the governmental level, against disease, mortality and the unsanitary living conditions of the large masses of the population."

Prior to the Revolution (on October 12, 1917, old style) a Military Revolutionary Committee had been formed in the Petrograd Soviet of Workers' and Soldiers' Deputies to seize power from the Provisional Government. The committee assumed power during the night of October 25–26, and the Provisional Government fell almost of its own weight. A Medical-Sanitary

Committee, consisting of Bolshevik physicians to which we have already referred, was formed on October 26. This was the Soviet regime's first medical center or organization. Its mandate, at first only local and practical, was to organize medical services "for the soldiers and workers" of the Petrograd area. Soon, however, it was destined to be the nucleus of a Soviet medical organization that would operate at a national level.

Lenin perhaps felt it was premature, immediately after the Revolution, to create a Commissariat of Health—that is, a central organization responsible for medicine and public health in the country at large with "cabinet" rank. Rather—and this may have been due to his still lingering belief that under a socialist government the "masses" would undertake many social functions themselves and eventually take over all governmental functions—he wanted to have, at least in the area of health services, a sort of grassroots movement that would involve the peoples' full participation in the provision of these services. Indeed, even today Soviet medical ideologists, as we have seen in the previous chapter, maintain that medical and public health measures cannot be successful unless they have the full support and cooperation of the "collectivity"—that is, the local population. Lenin thus advised that a first step should be the establishment of sections of medicine and public health in the local Councils (Soviets) of Workers' and Peasants' Deputies. This should then be followed by intensive explanatory work among the masses (propaganda and agitation) urging the organization of a central coordinating medical administration, and later by the convening of a meeting or congress of medical workers (from these sections) that would adopt a resolution on the formation of a central Health Commissariat. And, in one sense, this is what happened.

In addition to the Medical-Sanitary Section, other Soviet medical institutions were established at the central (or national) level. Special medical boards, called *collegia*, were organized (or taken over) in the Commissariats of Internal Affairs, Transportation, and Social Welfare in November, 1917. Two months later, a decree over Lenin's signature established a Council, or Soviet, of medical collegia to unite, supervise, and coordinate their activities. This council, which was then dubbed the "highest medical organization of the Workers' and Peasants' Government," also simultaneously assumed the functions of the Medical-Sanitary Council.

The next step, the elimination of the Central Medical-Sanitary Council, was a logical one from the viewpoint of establishing Soviet control over all matters of a medical or public health nature. This council, as we have seen in Chapter 2, had been established earlier as a link between the medical profession and the Provisional Government. It was not, however, a "Soviet" organization and was not responsive to the demands of the Soviet health authorities. A decree of February, 1918, eliminated the council on the now familiar grounds that it was counter-revolutionary, although we are told that an attempt had been made by the regime to reach some kind of agreement with the council. Since the type of agreement demanded by the Bolsheviks usually required subordination in all respects to the new government, it is quite understandable that the council would not agree, particularly in view of the fact that many of the regime's ideas and programs ran counter to the medical profession's deep-seated convictions. The refusal to cooperate with the regime was interpreted as the result of the bourgeois class origins and class interests of the majority of the physicians. This left no alternative, according to Soviet sources, but to form Soviet medical institutions that "could be trusted and which would work honestly and without refusals."[3]

As Lenin had suggested should happen, the Council of Medical Collegia called a conference of local medical-sanitary sections in Moscow on June 15–18, 1918. This conference was chaired by Dr. N. A. Semashko, at one time an exile companion of Lenin, and Dr. Z. P. Soloviev. It resolved that qualified and free medical care must be part of the Soviet health program and that the time was now ripe for the establishment of a medical organization with cabinet rank—that is, a commissariat— to carry out this decision. Less than a month later, on July 11, 1918, Lenin signed a decree formally establishing a Commissariat of Health Protection (*Narodnii Kommissariat Zdravookhraneniia*).

This decree, which may be considered the basic charter of the Soviet health service, stressed that the commissariat's primary task was to take over the jurisdiction as well as the resources of the soviet of the medical collegia. Thus the reorganization and centralization of medical services was accomplished on Soviet terms and in less than one year after the Revolution. On July 29 of that same year, a decree was issued by the Council of People's Commissars of the RSFSR mobilizing medical personnel for service in the Red Army, and on August 18, a commission to deal with epidemic diseases was formed within the Commissariat of Health Protection. Its mandate included "questions related to the problem of fighting against cholera, plague and typhus, as well as other acute epidemic illnesses, if their spread will be considered by the NKZ as a threat to the state." These measures, in one sense, symbolized the major problems the new Soviet state was facing: the need for military power to ensure its existence against domestic and foreign foes, and the control of epidemic diseases that were sapping the population's strength.

Another important matter agitated medical circles during this period: the question of the relationship between the pre-Revolutionary medical profession, not committed to and often antagonistic to Bolshevik ideas, and the Soviet regime. This problem was primarily political and ideological, involving the nature of the interconnection between a society and its professional bodies. By Marxist definition the typical pre-Revolutionary physician was a "bourgeois," a member of the intelligentsia who by his political views was considered an ineffectual liberal (a political position scorned by the Bolsheviks), an individual content primarily with reforms and thus devoted to the maintenance of the old order and of capitalism. It would, therefore, be inconceivable for the Bolshevik leadership to leave medical and public health affairs in the hands of the pre-Revolutionary associations, particularly the Pirogov Society. Initially, however, the Bolsheviks made appeals to the society hoping that it would espouse the Bolshevik cause, but this effort was doomed to failure, especially since many in Russia and abroad felt that the new regime would not last. Furthermore, the Bolsheviks knew (or sensed) that

some of their ideas about the role of medical services in the new
society clashed with some of the basic medical ethics of most
physicians.

What the Bolsheviks wanted, of course, was a medical organization and group of physicians that would do as it was bid.
This bidding, derived from the belief in the importance of
classes, meant that medical care ought to be made available on
a class, but inverted class, basis. Defining the pre-Revolutionary
society as one in which only the exploiters and the well-to-do
could affort medical services (and the pre-Revolutionary physician as one who sold his knowledge and skills to those who could
pay for them), the Bolsheviks claimed they were, in a period of
revolution, inverting the social pyramid, so that now those who
had everything would become have-nots and vice versa. This
meant that medical services were to be made available exclusively, or at least on a first priority basis, to those who before
the Revolution could not (according to this theory) have obtained them: ordinary workers, peasants, and soldiers. Medicine
and the physician were now to serve the proletariat, the new
ruling class: "Toward this goal, workers and peasants must take
into their hands the protection of health in the same way as
they have seized all the political and economic power in the
republic."[4] Medical care on a "class basis" simply meant differential treatment in accord with an individual's class position,
a principle that clearly ran against the ethical universalism of
medicine. The Bolsheviks countered that this "ethical universalism" had certainly not existed before the Revolution, except as
a hypocritical maneuver masking the physician's true class
interests.

Those physicians who either refused to side with the Bolsheviks, or who allegedly refused to treat members of the new
"ruling class," were accused of "medical sabotage," an expression
that was to become all too familiar later, during the purge trials
of 1937 and 1938, when well-known professors of medicine con-
fessed to having murdered their patients, and in the now famous
"Doctors' Plot" of 1953. Barsukov gives several examples pur-
porting to demonstrate that "bourgeois" physicians deliberately

withheld their assistance from the Bolsheviks, while at the same time treating White Guardists and using medical installations to hide "counterrevolutionaries." He quotes, for example, A. Okhapin, who wrote as follows about events in one of the Moscow districts:

> . . . They brought the wounded to the secondary school on the Krimsky Ploshchad. The old gatekeeper, under a series of pretexts, did not open the door. I ordered to beat on the window panes. After the first blow a key was found, and I myself, with difficulty, found the doctor in another room; he started to beat around the bush and to bare his teeth; knowing that we were Reds, he found a pretext to refuse to operate. I called some of our own people, ordered the doctor to go into the operating room, forced him to boil his instruments, asked the attendants to look after the wounded, put someone on duty, and then brought in the rest of the wounded.[5]

Aside from the melodramatic nature of this narrative (with the villainous and teeth-baring physician), one may well wonder how many authenticated cases there were in which physicians actually refused to treat patients because of political reasons. Yet this alleged medical sabotage was one more justification for the gradual elimination of the medical profession as a corporate body, with its traditions and strong sense of social duty and professional ethics (which makes the alleged refusal to help wounded men difficult to believe).

Another point of friction between the medical profession and the regime was the general policy, in line with proletarian and egalitarian notions, of reducing the status of physicians (and other professionals) to that of "workers"—that is, medical workers. As a "worker" the physician was to be considered a social (and even a professional) equal of the other medical workers, whether they be nurses, morgue attendants, hospital receptionists, or ward sweepers. As such, his authority over other medical personnel was correspondingly decreased. Apparently, it was the lack of enthusiasm with which most physicians viewed both the "class approach" to medicine and the decline in their social position as intellectuals that led to what Soviet medical historians called "medical sabotage."

In medical circles opposition to the regime and to its medical policies centered in the Pirogov Society. The society, as such, constituted an independent locus of power and opposition which the regime was unwilling to tolerate. As a corporate association the society was thus officially dissolved along with the Central Medical-Sanitary Council in 1918.

One more organization had to be subdued. This was the All-Russian Union of Professional Associations of Physicians. Unable to capture the leadership of the association, the regime was more successful in obtaining control over the unions of junior medical personnel who, having been formerly also "exploited" by the physicians, were now in a favored ideological and political position. An All-Russian Federated Union of Medical Workers (*Medsantrud*) was founded in 1918 and began its work in 1919 without, however, the formal participation of the physicians' unions or associations (or the pharmacists and veterinarians). The few physicians who did join this union numbered less than 10 per cent of its initial 900 members. At the end of 1919, the pharmacists and veterinarians withdraw their objections, and at the beginning of 1920, they joined the union, although in special sections. Only the physicians remained outside. Then followed a familiar action. The All-Russian Union of Professional Associations of Physicians was dissolved by a decree of the All-Russian Council of Trade Unions, with which the Medical Workers Union was affiliated. In 1920, an arrangement was made whereby physicians could joint the union, but in nonpartisan sections not committed to its political aims. In 1924, the nonpartisanship clause was dropped. With the gradual emasculation of all labor unions after 1930, these unions became to an even greater degree agencies of the state for the control of workers, including the medical workers, among whom were the physicians. The medical profession as an organized, self-governing occupational group had been captured, neutralized, and now eliminated. The profession had become, in the terms of Lewis and Maude, a "body of expert officials" trained and employed by the state.

SOVIET MEDICINE FROM 1918
TO THE PRESENT

THE HISTORY of the Soviet regime can generally be divided into six periods, each associated with its own particular health problems and policies. They are (a) War Communism, 1918–21; (b) the New Economic Policy, 1921–28; (c) industrialization and collectivization, generally known as the period of the Five-Year Plans, 1928–41; (d) the Second World War, 1941–45; (e) the Stalinist postwar period, 1945–53; and (f) the Khrushchev and post-Khrushchev era, 1953 to the present (1966).

(a) *War Communism* (1918–21). From the moment Lenin seized power toward the end of 1917, and particularly from 1918 on, the Soviet regime was literally fighting for its existence against domestic and foreign enemies. This period, known as War Communism, was characterized by an almost complete disruption of the economy, military attacks from the outside and civil war inside the country, famines, and epidemics. The breathing spell obtained at Brest-Litovsk came to an end in the first half of 1918 with landings by the French, English, Americans, and Japanese, the renewal of the German offensive, particularly in the Ukraine, and the formation of White Russian forces. War Communism was marked by an attempt, perhaps naïve in view of the conditions of the times, to put into practice many of the ideological precepts of the classless society derived from Marxist ideology. For example, the decrease and near disappearance of a money economy and equalization of wages were interpreted as the first steps toward the creation of an egalitarian society. From the medical viewpoint, the period was dominated by epidemics. Most statements on the medical situation emphasize the mortal danger that these epidemics (and the conditions that gave rise to them, such as shortages of goods, medicines, disinfectants, personnel, facilities, transport, and so on) engendered.

At the Eighth Party Congress held in Moscow March 18–23, 1919, a new party program was adopted. This program emphasized, with respect to health protection, the following points: "Fundamental in its activity in the sphere of the protection of the health of the people is, first of all, the implementation of broad measures of a sanitary and health-reinforcing nature, having as their goal the prevention of disease." In addition, the program reaffirmed the party's conviction that the toilers should receive medical care free of charge and of good quality, as well as free pharmaceuticals. (A decree at the end of 1918 had already nationalized the pharmacies of the RSFSR.) The program went on to say that "The dictatorship of the proletariat has already had the opportunity of putting into practice a whole series of measures that could not be realized within the framework of the bourgeois society: the nationalization of pharmacies, of large privately owned medical installations, resorts, liability of medical personnel to a work draft, and so on." Among its immediate tasks the party saw the following:

1. A determined effort to carry out far-reaching public health measures for the benefit of the toilers, such as (a) sanitation of living quarters (protection of soil, air, water); (b) establishment of communal feeding on the basis of scientific hygiene; (c) organization of medicine to prevent the development and spread of contagious diseases; and (d) health legislation.
2. Combating social diseases (tuberculosis, venereal diseases, alcoholism, and the like).
3. Guaranteeing the availability of qualified health and medical services to all without charge.

It should be noted, furthermore, that medical services for the Red Army, which was fighting against both the White Russians and Allied troops, were organized and administered by the Commissariat of Health. There was, in a sense, little distinction between what might be called civilian and military medical services, and in territories recovered by the Red Army military physicians organized medical services and public health for the inhabitants. There existed an "indissoluble connection between military medicine and public health in general."[6] It was only later that the medical services of the armed forces were detached from the jurisdiction of the commissariat and placed under that of the armed forces.

(b) *The New Economic Policy* (1921–28). With the end of

the civil war and foreign intervention, Lenin called a halt to War Communism and proclaimed the New Economic Policy (NEP). This policy, one of minor retreat ideologically, was calculated to permit Soviet Russia to recover from the damage and trauma of seven years of wars, revolutions, epidemics, famine, and the almost complete collapse of the economy. The policy involved, among other things, the elimination of grain requisitioning from the peasantry and its replacement by a tax in kind. The "commanding heights" of the economy, however, remained firmly in the hands of the regime, particularly heavy and extractive industry, transportation, communications, and foreign trade.

In the medical area similar concessions were made, most of them of a minor nature; in some instances, for example, nationalized pharmacies were returned to their owners. Physicians were permitted to choose between public or private practice. While official policy and ideology dictated that eventually private practice, like private trade, was to disappear as a survival of capitalism and petty bourgeois ideology, the country's economic situation was not yet ripe for such a move. This was particularly true of areas where socialized medical institutions could not, because of lack of funds, give free medical care.

With the cessation of hostilities, the gradual return to a better food supply, and a general improvement in the economy, the threat posed by the mass epidemics that had ravaged Soviet Russia in the early days gradually began to recede.

Freed from the overwhelming problems caused by epidemics, Soviet health authorities began to turn their attention to different questions, and to organize the health service for Soviet society along the blueprints dictated by their ideological convictions and their reality problems. Two major groups were the objects of special concern: the workers in critical industries and the peasantry (particularly the poorer peasants) in the countryside. Maintenance and expansion of the work capacity of those employed in essential industries was crucial for economic recovery and for sustaining economic growth. Thus at the First All-Union Congress of Microdistrict (*uchastok*) physicians, held in December, 1924, Z. P. Soloviev, Deputy Health Commissar and the regime's foremost medical ideologist, demonstrated the close and meaningful interdependence of economic indices and vital statistics (birth and death rates) as well as illness rates, particularly the development of parasitic typhus.[7]

The commissariat also began to pay some attention to the hitherto largely neglected health needs of the peasants who at that time constituted the overwhelming majority of the population. Since the growth (and indeed the very existence) of towns and industry depended upon the peasants' ability to produce enough surplus food to feed the urban areas, their health and living conditions, acquired economic significance.

Because prevention and preventive services stood at the core of Soviet medical philosophy, a special effort was made to translate this commitment into reality during the years of the NEP. In 1923, the Health Commissar Semashko had written that special attention to preventive measures and a social approach to protecting the health of the population had characterized Soviet medicine from the beginning, noting, however, that

> . . . Earlier we were deprived of the opportunity to approach these tasks with the degree of organization, planning, quietude, and design with which we can do it at the present time. Emergency work at the military and epidemic fronts tore us away from this task. Now with the liquidation of these fronts, we can attack these questions in a more planned manner.[8]

At the Fifth All-Russian Congress of Health Departments, held in Moscow between June 27 and July 4, 1924, Soloviev spelled out in some detail what was meant by "preventive principles of Soviet Health protection." Soloviev's statement is interesting because it links, in an unambiguous manner, health protection, ideology, political structure, and practical matters.

1. The transfer of state power to the hands of the workers, the organization of the Soviet government and, in particular, as one of its results, the development of a single (system) of Soviet medicine, form the necessary prerequisites for putting into practice the beginnings of a preventive medicine.
2. The basic difference between Soviet medicine and the medicine

of capitalist countries is that the latter cannot, without impinging upon the very foundations of the capitalist system, embark on prevention; it [the capitalist country] limits itself to so-called "general" measures and becomes caught in the narrow circle of individual charity.

3. Social medicine in the Soviet system basically differs from the "social" medicine of the pre-Revolutionary period in that it is a part of the Soviet government and is indissolubly linked to all organs of state power by unity of purpose and unity of plan.

4. Social medicine was created, developed, and will develop in the conditions of Soviet society, [which is] founded on the extensive spontaneous activity of the worker and peasant masses and embraces all aspects of economic and cultural life [conditions] inherent solely in the Soviet system.

5. The [above] enumerated characteristics of the Soviet state form a firm organizational basis for solving the tasks of improving the lives and labor of the working people.

6. The preventive measures carried out up to now in this sphere, measures which have achieved significant and real progress, must be broadened and deepened by involving *all* medical-sanitary institutions in this work.

7. The principle of unity of purpose of sanitary and medical work, united by an understanding of the medical-preventive tasks, hitherto realized only in a limited circle of special institutions for the struggle against social diseases (tuberculosis and venereal diseases) and for maternity and child protection, must lie at the basis of the work of *all* medical institutions.

8. Medical institutions must undertake two kinds of tasks: (a) the study of the living and working conditions of the patients, and (b) organized action as to their improvement.[9]

A meeting of the health commissars of the four republics constituting the Soviet federation at that time had been held in August, 1922, under Semashko's chairmanship, to coordinate their efforts. Although the republics and commissars were in theory equal partners, the Russian Republic, of course, played the leading role and the Health Commissariat of the RSFSR directed, in effect, health affairs for the entire Soviet Union.

A thorn that remained in the side of the commissariat and of Soviet medicine was the medical profession's generally cool response, particularly those who had "Pirogov" leanings, to the measures adopted by "Soviet" medicine. In 1922, a journal expressing these leanings, *The Social Physician,* had renewed publication and severely critized many of the regime's health measures. At the Second All-Union Congress of Medical Workers held in 1922, these physicians presented and defended their viewpoint. They were later criticized in a resolution of the Congress which complained that "the majority of physicians' sections, in spite of their three-year existence within the Union, have not been penetrated by the general spirit of the proletarian professional movement."[10] The resolution went on to say that the doors of the union remained open to physicians, but that the presence in the union of "alien class elements" was inadmissible. By the end of the NEP physicians' resistance to Soviet health policies had practically disappeared.

(c) *The Five-Year Plans* (1928–41). The end of the NEP officially came in December, 1928, although the party had been debating industrialization since 1924–25. The Fifteenth Party Congress, held in December, 1928, decided to push industrialization immediately to make the Soviet Union economically and militarily self-sufficient and to move toward "socialist construction." Also the collectivization of agriculture was decreed in order to destroy the power that the regime (and particularly Stalin) feared the *kulaks,* or prosperous peasants, might acquire through their control of the food supply. With the end of the NEP came a revival of the proletarian and equalitarian spirit that had dominated War Communism and which had lain more or less dormant during the partial revival of capitalism. The decision to industrialize was to launch an economic and social revolution that by far overshadowed the seizure of political power in 1917.

Since ideological and practical considerations precluded any large-scale borrowing abroad, the capital necessary for industrialization came almost exclusively from domestic sources. It was obtained through a draconic reduction of consumption levels and coercive measures that affected the entire population, but were applied with particular severity to the peasantry, who were made, as Stalin once said, to pay a tribute to the rest of society. Large masses were moved to cities and industrial centers, leading to extreme overcrowding, because the regime had neither the resources nor the inclination to provide new housing. The speed and forcible nature of collectivization resulted in a mass slaughter by the peasantry of cattle and a decrease in food production which forced the reestablishment of rationing in the latter part of 1928.

In December, 1929, the party's central committee rebuked the Health Commissariat of the RSFSR for lagging behind the tempo set by the regime and by the needs of the workers and the peasantry. Health organs were criticized for laxity in utilizing the Soviet collectivity, failure to obtain the participation of professional unions in operating the medical system (in other words, the medical personnel had not been sufficiently indoctrinated), and poor management of local health affairs. And the Central Committee bid the health commissars to restructure their work so that it would more accurately reflect the regime's proletarian, or class, policy. Special attention was to be paid to the health needs and health conditions of the Donbas, Kuzbas, and Urals—regions critical from the viewpoint of mineral fuels and the whole industrialization program. The Central Committee's resolution also called for an improvement in the training of medical personnel and particularly for their better and more rational distribution. In addition, the commissars were urged to order the health service in general to wake up and take notice of the degree to which it also fitted into the party plans and the programs. It was urged to take any measures that would keep it from slowing down the success of the Five-Year Plan. Medical work was thus to fit within the framework of the plan. As a textbook on the subject puts it: "1929 was a pivotal year for Soviet health protection also. The historical decisions of the Central Committee of the Communist Party of December 18, 1929 forced the organs of health protection to make a decisive turn in the direction of a differentiated approach to the medical care of the leading group of industrial workers and the socialist sector of agriculture." The rest of the population, by implication, was to receive the crumbs.

Several major medical problems preoccupied the regime and the health authorities after the decision to industrialize. These problems were, of course, all connected in one way or another with the massive program of industrialization and the resulting dislocation of the population, the crowding of workers into newly established industrial areas, the lack of appropriate municipal services of all kinds, as well as the needs of the rural population on the collective farms.

The enormity of the task necessitated not only massive investments in the health service but also an increase in personnel and facilities, all rendered extremely difficult by the high priority granted industrial management for all scarce resources. And yet, in many instances, health authorities faced an impossible task that no amount of prodding or high-minded and sanctimonious resolutions of party or government could resolve. In 1930, Dr. M. S. Vladimirsky, who had replaced Semashko as Commissar of Health for the RSFSR, had pointed in a *Pravda* article to the importance of the physicians' work as an adjunct of production and of worker productivity. He noted that in Leningrad alone in 1928–29, economic losses due to illness and recovery from illness had amounted to an equivalent of one quarter of its annual production. Remarking that any significant decrease in illness (and length of illness) could add substantially to total production, he called not only for improved medical services, but also for improved living and working conditions for the workers. He stressed the fact that management must consider the physician's work a factor in the rationalization of work, and cited statistics showing that between 1928 and 1930 one half of all cases of illness and loss of time due to illness were the result of epidemic and infectious diseases, digestive and skin problems, all of which, he felt, could have been prevented.

In 1935, the sixteenth All-Russian Congress of Soviets again noted that the health service lagged behind the country's needs, particularly in agriculture and in the area of medical personnel, who were, apparently, being trained in insufficient numbers. Criticism was also addressed to the supply of equipment and pharmaceuticals and to the medical services available to outlying areas and national districts. By that time Vladimirsky had been replaced as Health Commissar by Dr. G. N. Kaminsky. Kaminsky (who was shot during the purges in 1937) pledged, among other things, significant improvements in medical services for women and children. Because of the manpower shortage more and more women were being drawn into the labor force, particularly into industry, thus necessitating special medical services for their care, as well as the care and supervision of their children. This required the organization of thousands of kindergartens and crèches, most of which were placed under the health authorities' supervision.

A major step in the administration of medical services and their formal coordination at the national level was the formation on June 20, 1936, of a Peoples' Commissariat of Health for the USSR, headed by Kaminsky. Two administrations that had been organized earlier were placed directly under the new Health Commissar. One, the Health Commissariat's research arm, was the All-Union Institute of Experimental Medicine which had been established on the base of Pavlov's research institute in Leningrad. (The institute, in turn, was the predecessor of the Academy of Medical Sciences founded in 1944.) The other administration was the All-Union State Sanitary Inspectorate, the head of which became a First Deputy Health Commissar. The necessity of subordinating preventive public health services to clinical services had become apparent in the years following 1928. The over-all preoccupation and commitment to prevention that was writ large in the Soviet conception of health services had led, understandably, to an underemphasis on clinical and medical services, with dire results for the population's health. Two types of medical institutions appeared as a result of this reemphasis on clinical medicine. One was the *Zdravpunkt*, or medical station, which was to bring medical and preventive services directly to the worker. The physician's role in the factory medical stations was not only to provide medical care and first-aid services, but also to take active measures that would reduce traumatism or injuries. Second, in agriculture there were organized medical brigades made up of doctors and junior medical personnel who were sent from the towns to the countryside, particularly at harvest time.

In addition to an increase in the number of students to be trained in medical schools and in the number of middle medical schools for junior personnel, an important change took place in 1930. University medical faculties were detached from the universities and placed under the direction of the Health Commissariat. It was felt that since the Commissariat was to use the individuals trained by these institutions it ought to have a deciding voice in determining the curriculum. Medical schools were divided into three basic faculties: general medical, pediatric, and public health, each instructing physicians in their specialty almost from the beginning of their training. In the Ukraine a fourth faculty was available—the stomatological, or dental faculty. When the Health Commissariat was created for the Soviet Union, the largest medical schools and the Institute of Postgraduate Studies of Physicians were placed under its jurisdiction, in addition to many research institutes. The Health Commissariat USSR also took over supervision of the production of pharmaceuticals and medical supplies, tasks which up to that time had been scattered under different commissariats. Furthermore, efforts were made to improve the standardization of medical services and the reporting forms and accounts kept for statistical purposes. A scientific Council was created to advise the Health Commissariat and facilitate the actual management and planning of these services.

On the ideological front the battle was also fought with great vigor, on one side by the Health Commissariat and on the other by those who were called "Menshevik idealists" and "Right Opportunists." These terms denoted those who, in one way or another, did not approve of the health authorities' policies, such as the ideas that medical care ought to depend on the recipient's economic contributions, or that industrialization should be pushed even to the detriment of the population's health, or that, in essence, there was no difference between workers' health problems under socialism or capitalism.

Thus the period from 1928 to 1941 in health care reflected the turmoil caused by industrialization and collectivization and the frenzied efforts of the Communist leadership to direct the entire Soviet system toward the goals of the Five-Year Plan. By the time the Second World War broke out, the Soviet Union had improved its medical system significantly. It had been centralized, tightened, and better coordinated. Doctrinal opposition among the members of the medical profession had practically vanished, particularly because new physicians had been trained entirely under the Soviet regime. By 1928, for example, there were three times as many physicians as in 1917, and, by 1940, the increase was sevenfold over 1920. The percentage of women in medicine increased from 10 per cent in 1917 to 60 per cent in 1940.

(d) *The Second World War* (1941–45). The German invasion and occupation of 1941 put the Soviet regime to an extremely severe test. German armies advanced rapidly, particularly during 1941–42, occupying large areas vital to Soviet agriculture and industry and inflicting enormous losses on Soviet armies and the civilian population. Defeat was averted, in part because of the immensity of the Soviet Union: manpower and industry could be evacuated to the east. And Hitler, like Napoleon, was thwarted by the Russian winter which ground the German advance to a halt and permitted Soviet forces to regroup and be reinforced by fresh troops from the area east of the Urals. No less important was the grim determination of the Soviet leadership to resist at all possible costs. The Soviet war effort was also considerably strengthened by economic assistance provided by the United States and Great Britain.

The war imposed new demands and strains on the health service—a test all the more severe because of immense losses of manpower, facilities, and equipment. From all evidence, however, Soviet medicine, which even in its civilian form had been organized on a quasi-military and easily mobilizable footing, was equal to its manifold tasks at the front and in the rear. Several measures were quickly adopted to turn all available medical resources to the war effort.

One problem—epidemics—haunted Soviet health authorities. Only twenty years before, the nation had been ravaged by epidemics. And only even fewer years before had the threat of epidemics been eliminated. Health authorities naturally devoted a great deal of their attention, energies, and resources to preventing the possibility (always present under wartime conditions) of their recurrence.

Almost immediately after the outbreak of war a State Defense Committee, under Stalin's chairmanship, was formed to direct the Soviet Union's efforts in its struggle against Germany. The committee placed Health Commissar G. A. Miterev in charge of all anti-epidemic matters. To complement this work, special commissions were formed in most local executive committees of the Soviets, with the chairman of the executive committee acting as head of the commission. An order of the Health Commissariat dated May 22, 1942—"on the antiepidemic work of the municipal polyclinics and outpatient clinics, and on the strengthening of the microdistrict territorial system of the medical care of the urban population"—placed special obligations on the urban medical institutions. They were to exercise tight control and vigilance over communicable diseases, immediately hospitalize anyone sick or suspected of being sick with an infectious disease, search for other persons with whom the patient was in contact, and supervise as well as disinfect actual and potential foci of infection. *Pravda*, on March 8, 1942, emphasized the importance of vigilance in this matter, urging the cooperation of the entire population with medical authorities and stressing that the quality of the public health work determined the contribution the rear could make to the front. Special attention was also paid to such carriers of infections as railroad and water transportation, which could easily spread disease from one part of the country to another. It is a tribute to the efforts of the Health Commissariat (as well as the medical corps of the Red, later Soviet, Army) that no major epidemics were registered or allowed to spread to the proportions experienced during War Communism. E. I. Smirnov, in 1945 head of the army medical service (later appointed Health Minister of the USSR) wrote that

All previous wars were accompanied by a significant increase of epidemic diseases. However, neither our army nor our country knew epidemics during these years. This is indeed the result of the heroic work of the communicable disease personnel of the Soviet Army and the public health workers of the rear.[11]

Next in importance to the problem posed by potential epidemics was the care and treatment of sick and wounded soldiers and officers. This treatment was placed under the joint direction of the Red Army Medical Department and the (civilian) Health Commissariat of the USSR. A system of evacuation hospitals (to which wounded and sick soldiers were directed) was organized by the Health Commissariat. A department of evacuation hospitals was established within the all-union and republican health commissariats to manage these hospitals. Soviet sources indicate that more than 70 per cent of the wounded and sick were returned to their units.

Special measures were also instituted to safeguard the health of children (many of whom were evacuated to the rear without their parents), orphans, adolescents who were employed in industry, and women, who during these years provided the bulk of the civilian labor force.

The training of medical personnel was intensified. An accelerated medical course introduced in 1941 was, however, abandoned almost immediately as inadequate. Indeed, in the course of the war it was decided to lengthen the training of physicians from five to six years; but the six-year course was not introduced until after the end of hostilities. Five new medical institutes were organized during the war years, far from German attacks. They replaced institutes that had been destroyed or were located on enemy-held territory. The shortage of physicians trained to treat casualties led to an order that sent thousands of medical specialists (obstetricians, pediatricians, gynecologists, anatomists, and others) to special retraining courses where they learned military surgery. An important milestone was the formation, in 1944, of an Academy of Medical Sciences to supervise and direct medical research.

(e) *The Stalinist Postwar Period* (1945–53). Politically and socially the Soviet Union emerged unchanged from the Second World War, although it had suffered vast destruction in human resources and in physical and industrial facilities. The population deficits directly traceable to the war and the early postwar period, in terms both of lower birth rate and of excessive mortality, probably amounted to close to 45 million, or about 16 per cent of the population expected by 1950. Capital losses were even more difficult to assess. According to Soviet estimates, they amounted to 679 billion rubles. By the end of the war the Soviet medical system had been seriously damaged, the loss being estimated, on the basis of incomplete data, at 6.6 billion rubles. Losses in medical buildings destroyed or partly destroyed alone are impressive. According to Soviet data almost 6,000 hospitals and clinics were completely destroyed, and 7,369 were partly destroyed. Of children's medical institutions and crèches, 838 were destroyed completely and 1,211 partly destroyed; 472 scientific and medical research institutes were destroyed and 758 partly destroyed. Similarly distressing figures are cited for medical schools or institutes.

And yet there were more physicians in the Soviet Union in 1946 than at the beginning of the war, and organizationally the health service remained the same after the ordeal. The majority of physicians are still trained, placed, and remunerated by the state, and medical services remain a public service dispensed by the state.

Just as in the period following War Communism, the first postwar task in medicine, as in other areas, was reconstruction and rehabilitation. Regions that had been conquered and then defended by the enemy, had a heavy legacy of illness. In addition, continued attention had to be given the problem of epidemics; the end of hostilities did not automatically put an end to that danger. Again, with top priority allocated to heavy industry, health programs could be undertaken only with difficulty and in most instances unsatisfactorily.

In addition to the organization of medical services for the urban population, the regime and the health authorities also turned their attention to the perenially neglected health problems of the rural population, particularly to the question of making specialized (as well as general) assistance available. Several measures were adopted by the Health Ministry (the Commissariat of Health had been rechristened a "Ministry" in 1946) in an effort to make more specialized medical care available to the rural population. An obstacle of major proportion was (and is) the reluctance of physicians to practice in the countryside, not only because of the backwardness of rural culture but also because of the harrowing living conditions. Physicians' efforts to get themselves reassigned to more urbanized areas have led to enormous turnover rates for rural medical personnel, rates which have made providing medical services in rural areas more difficult. Efforts were also made to improve medical services for children and women in rural districts, the aim being to have all children delivered in maternity homes.

On the ideological front, the battle was joined by two groups which Soviet ideologists defined as the "materialists"—that is, those who believed that nature operates according to the rules of dialectical materialism— and the "idealists," broadly tagged as Weismanite-Morgan reactionaries, thereby echoing in the medical field the controversy between Lysenko and those who opposed him. The new line was to derive from the theories of Pavlov, who became the ideological godhead in the medical field. Placing the entire medical system on Pavlovian rails was the result of a Joint Session of the Academy of Sciences and the Academy of Medical Sciences in 1950. This session resolved that the two academies must in the shortest time take the necessary organizational and scientific steps for the "further development of the creative bases and introduction of Pavlov's theory into medical practice, pedagogy, physical education and animal husbandry." In addition, the academies, the Ministry of Higher Education, and the Ministry of Health were to reexamine research projects in physiology and the medical disciplines (internal diseases, hygiene, psychiatry, neuropathology, and others) on the basis of Pavlovian theory. At the same time, this ideological reorientation had a strong nationalistic tinge. It aimed at demonstrating the superiority of Russian and Soviet medicine over Western, bourgeois medicine. This was in line with then current determination to "prove" the general superiority of Soviet cultural achievements in all fields, including the priority of Russian inventions and discoveries. It was only after Stalin's death, and particularly after 1956, that a less rigid and dogmatic line was permitted in medical research and practice.

(f) *The Khrushchev and Post-Khrushchev Era* (1953–

present—1966). After Stalin died, certain changes and new programs resulted from reforms introduced by the Khrushchev regime. One of these was a decentralization of the administrative apparatus designed to relieve the bureaucratic paralysis that had crept over the entire Soviet administrative apparatus under Stalin. Many executive functions hitherto performed by the Health Ministry USSR were transferred to the health ministries of the republics, which thus were accorded greater latitude in devising programs and measures best suited to the nature of their population, resources, and disease patterns. An attempt was also made, first on an experimental basis and later on a much larger scale, to simplify the administrative apparatus of health services in the countryside. As a result of the decentralization trend, the functions of the Health Ministry USSR have tended to be more and more in the direction, not of ordering and commanding, but rather of providing suggestions, necessary standardization, and advice. The Health Ministry continues, of course, to perform tasks that are of national health significance and cannot be delegated to the republican health ministries, such as standardizing, testing, and approving drugs.

Taken in its broadest context, the function of the health service in the second half of the sixties is to consolidate the gains made in the previous fifty years, increase the flexibility of its administrative structure, and improve the quality of services by increasing specialized medical care and making this care more available to the hitherto somewhat neglected rural population.

We have, in this chapter, reviewed the development of the Soviet health service in the light of the major phases in the history of the Soviet regime. In the next chapter we turn to the administrative structure of the Ministry of Health and other health organs.

Chapter 5

Organization and Administration
of the
Soviet Health Service

THE ROMANTIC days of the solo medical practitioner with his little black bag and his all-night (though often futile) vigils at the patient's bedside are about as much a thing of the past as his horse and buggy. Because of the complexity (and the cost) of contemporary medical techniques, medical services tend to be given more and more within an organizational context, uniting and coordinating the activities of many individuals at the professional, semiprofessional and nonprofessional levels, and necessitating an ever more complicated administrative structure. This is particularly true in the Soviet Union, where medical services are administered and financed by the state and where the emphasis on planning, coordination, and over-all national control necessitates a large bureaucratic structure. Thus, in the Soviet Union, perhaps more than in countries where the medical system is of a more mixed type, actual health services must be seen as the last link in a long chain of events. These events are, to a large extent, the organization, administration, and management of the health service.

We have examined (Chapter 3) the ideological premises and the basic principles that undergird that service. In this chapter we turn our attention to the machinery without which the "charter" would remain only a theoretical program, majestic and comprehensive in design and purpose, but with no real connections to the health problems faced by the regime and the population. As we have seen, this process of translation from idea to action in medicine and public health is primarily the responsibility of the state, carried out by a formally designated branch of the governmental apparatus as a public service. However, for ideological and sometimes practical reasons, certain auxiliary and supportive functions are considered the province, not of the formal health institutions and personnel, but of nongovernmental, voluntary, and community organizations which supplement the work of the service.

It is beyond the scope of this work to present a detailed description of the workings of the Soviet government, but an understanding of the administration and the organization of the health service should necessarily start with the governmental structure, because the health service is a part of that structure. While the Communist party is intimately involved in all aspects of Soviet society and retains the ultimate power of making secular decisions, formally speaking, health services are a *governmental* and not a *party* function. We shall, at the appropriate moment, pay due respect to the party's role in medical and health matters.

In formal terms, and according to the Constitution of 1936 (the present fundamental law), the Supreme Soviet is the highest organ of state power in the Soviet Union. Between sessions of the Supreme Soviet its powers are assumed by the Presidium of the Supreme Soviet. The executive and administrative powers are vested in a Council of Ministers which is accountable either to the Supreme Soviet or (when it is not in session) its Presidium. The Council of Ministers consists of a Chairman, First Deputy Chairman, Ministers (heads of ministries), committees, and officials. In all the Council has more than sixty members.[1]

The Health Minister of the USSR is a member of the Council of Ministers and, as the head of one of the ministries, is of "cabinet" rank. Actually, there are two types of ministries in the Soviet Union. One is the so-called *all-union ministry*, which directly administers its subordinate organs wherever they may be located on Soviet territory. The jurisdiction of an all-union ministry is thus strictly national and transcends other administrative-territorial divisions. The Ministry of Foreign Trade or of Defense, for example, is an all-union (or in American terms, a "federal") ministry. The second type of ministry is the *union-republican ministry*, which embodies a division of functions and jurisdictions between the all-union and the republican (or in American terms, the "state") levels. This type of ministry thus operates through counterpart ministries in the constituent republics (of which there are fifteen) and the relatively minor autonomous republics. The union-republican ministry embodies, to some extent, the principle of decentralization and the granting of a small amount of autonomy to the republics in order to increase their flexibility in dealing with local problems. The Health Ministry USSR belongs to this second category. In essence, the functions of the over-all, national direction, the planning, supervision, and financing of health matters, are the responsibility of the Health Ministry of the USSR, which is located in Moscow. The republican health ministries, on the other hand, bear direct responsibility for the over-all planning of health matters in their respective territories and for actual operations, although, of course, under the basic tutelage of the Health Ministry USSR.[2]

Structurally, the ministries in general and the Health Ministry USSR in particular are subordinate to their respective councils of ministers and carry out their general directives. Specifically, the Health Ministry USSR may be considered as the medical, public health, and health protection arm of the government of the Soviet Union, and more directly of the Council of Ministers USSR. It is entrusted, and this at the highest national level, with responsibility for the health of the Soviet nation. As such it disposes of certain powers in addition to its responsibilities. These are powers of health legislation. Health legislation issued at this "federal" level is valid throughout the Soviet Union and supersedes legislation adopted by the republics (which is valid only over the territory of the republic). The Council of Ministers of each republic, in turn, has the right to suspend the regulations, orders, decisions, and instructions of the health organization of lower territorial-administrative units —for example, those of the autonomous republics, as well as those issued by executive committees of provinces, regions, and autonomous regions—if they are inconsistent with or contradictory to those of the Soviet Union, the republic in question, or any superior health authorities. Local soviets and their executive committees manage health services according to all-union and republic legislation.[3]

We shall return later to the Health Ministry USSR and to its inner administrative structure. We now turn our attention to the health administrations below that of the Health Ministry USSR.

Essentially, the same relationship that exists between the Council of Ministers USSR and the Health Ministry USSR obtains at the republican level, with the exception, of course, that a republican council of ministers is itself subordinate to the Council of Ministers USSR, and a republican health ministry is subordinate to the Health Ministry USSR. Below the republican level (and with the exception of the autonomous republics, which have their own health ministries), the top executive governmental body is the executive committee of the soviet of the province, region, district, or city, and the top executive health organ is the health department of that soviet. (See Chart 5-1.)

Thus, with the exception of the Health Ministry USSR, every health organization is responsible to *two* agencies: its own council of ministers (or executive committee of the soviet, as the case may be) and the next higher health organization. Generally speaking, there is a division of labor between these two jurisdictional lines. The governmental organs (the councils or executive committees) provide the general "political" directives which must, of course, follow the regime's general policies goals, and plans. In addition, the governmental organs must

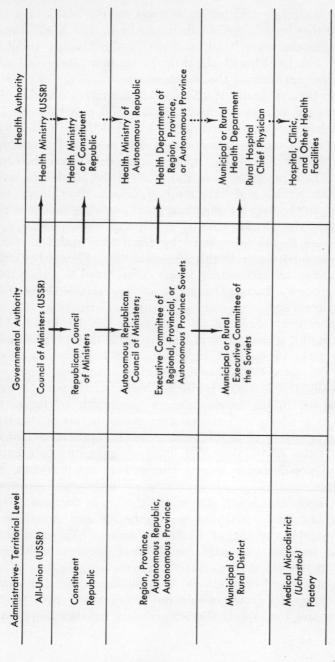

Chart 5-1—The Administration of Health Services in the USSR

Administrative- Territorial Level	Governmental Authority	Health Authority
All-Union (USSR)	Council of Ministers (USSR)	Health Ministry (USSR)
Constituent Republic	Republican Council of Ministers	Health Ministry of Constituent Republic
Region, Province, Autonomous Republic, Autonomous Province	Autonomous Republican Council of Ministers; Executive Committee of Regional, Provincial, or Autonomous Province Soviets	Health Ministry of Autonomous Republic — Health Department of Region, Province, or Autonomous Province
Municipal or Rural District	Municipal or Rural Executive Committee of the Soviets	Municipal or Rural Health Department — Rural Hospital Chief Physician
Medical Microdistrict (Uchastok) Factory		Hospital, Clinic, and Other Health Facilities

→ Administrative Authority
┄┄► Health Administration

provide budgetary and logistic support for the health organizations so they may carry out their functions. The health organizations, on the other hand, from the Health Ministry USSR on down to the local health department, are more concerned with the *modus operandi* of the health service.

Until Stalin's death, the Soviet administrative structure was characterized by extreme centralization and unwieldiness. The Khrushchev regime, to some degree loosened that structure with measures that would decentralize it and give local administrations a modest amount of autonomy and control over their own affairs. These measures have also affected the administration of the health service and have resulted, among other things, in a decrease in the over-all importance and executive functions performed by the Health Ministry USSR and, correspondingly, in an increase in the role played by republican health ministries and their subordinate health administrations. Khrushchev's successors have, to some extent, reversed this trend in certain parts of the economy, but no changes of any appreciable degree have taken place (at this writing) in health administration.

The general mandate or mission of the Health Ministry USSR in the second half of the sixties is that of performing certain tasks of national importance which cannot or should not be delegated to the health ministries of the republics. More specifically, the Ministry is charged with (1) the over-all planning of the future development of the health service of the nation as a whole, and the working out of norms or standards for the provision of health services to the population (for example, ratios of physicians of different specialties to different types of population in large urban centers, small centers, and rural communities); (2) providing methodological assistance to the republican health ministries, whether in the area of specialized medical assistance, public health and antiepidemic work, or the training of health personnel; (3) coordinating medical research and assistance to the republican health ministries in the elaboration and the practical application of the results of medical research; (4) determining the needs for medical supplies (pharmaceuticals and instruments) both for the country and for export, allocating orders for these supplies to industry, and supervising their production and distribution among the republics; and (5) maintaining international relations in the field of medicine, public health, and the protection of health (for example, dealing with foreign physicians or delegations who come to the Soviet Union).[4]

The Health Ministry USSR also manages the activities of certain institutions, organizations, and enterprises of national significance and importance placed directly under its jurisdiction and carried on its own operational budget. It is also charged with the responsibility of issuing decisions and instructions on health protection deriving from the laws passed by the Supreme Soviet USSR and the decisions of the Council of Ministers USSR, and of verifying their fulfillment.

The Health Minister is chairman of a collegium (or committee) which appears to function as an advisory as well as executive committee. Members of the collegium, in addition to the Minister are the Deputy Ministers and other important or leading persons of the Ministry, presumably those in charge of major departments and those designated by the party organization at the Ministry.

At its regular meetings the collegium examines questions pertaining to the practical management of the health service. The decisions of the collegium are implemented by orders of the Ministry. In cases of disagreement between the collegium and the Minister, the latter carries out his decision but informs the Council of Ministers of the disagreement, and the members of the collegium have the right, in turn, to appeal to the council.

As in any bureaucracy, the Ministry's inner structure or organization consists of specialized departments headed by a responsible official and his staff. In the Health Ministry these are called main administrations, administrations, and departments, in that order of decreasing importance. Over the years the number, types, and functions of these administrative divisions have changed, reflecting not only the vicissitudes of the general Soviet administrative philosophy, but also the varying and changing problems faced by Soviet society in the prevention of illness and the maintenance of health.

At the time Stalin died, and for two or three years afterward, the Health Ministry USSR was a large, somewhat unwieldy, bureaucratic organization, with a proliferation of departments and personnel, and the problems usually associated with this kind of organization, particularly in the Soviet Union: "formalism" (the ritual of adhering to the letter of regulations rather than to their spirit), slowness of action, interminable red tape, delaying of decisions, and inertia. This condition was compounded by the fact that, because of the extreme centralization of power in Moscow favored by Stalin, relatively little initiative or autonomy was left to the republican health ministries. Practically every major decision, and often many minor ones, had to be referred to the "center," a lengthy process which tended to paralyze the health service. As a result of the reforms introduced by Khrushchev, an attempt was made to slim down the Health Ministry USSR through decentralization and a simplification of its administrative structure and a reduction in staff. At the present time the Ministry has the table of organization shown on Chart 5–2, page 83.

The republican health ministries have more departments than the Health Ministry USSR, and their administrative structure is somewhat more complex (a reversal of the situation that obtained before the Khrushchev era). Chart 5–3 illustrates that structure, using as an example the Health Ministry of the Russian Soviet Federated Socialist Republic, the largest of the constituent republics, and the one that presumably serves as a model for the other republics. There are, undoubtedly, minor variations from one republican health ministry to another to account for local conditions and variations in population distribution, but the basic structure is apparently uniform from republic to republic. In addition, it must be assumed that many administrative divisions at the republican level are already more concerned with "operational" tasks than with "planning, methodological, and supervisory" duties. The republican ministries have thus assumed the management of matters that until the Khrushchev era, had been largely the province of the Health Ministry USSR.

The next administrative rung below the republican ministry is either the (relatively minor) health ministry of an auton-

Chart 5–2—The Structure of the Health Ministry USSR*

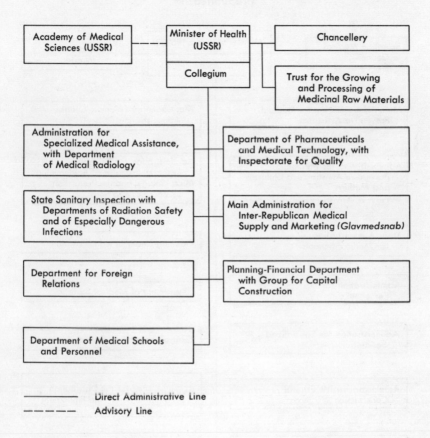

—————————	Direct Administrative Line
— — — — —	Advisory Line

* N. A. Vinogradov, *Organizatsila*, 2d ed., p. 607. Brought up to date by M.G.F.

Chart 5–3—The Structure of the Health Ministry RSFSR (Republican)*

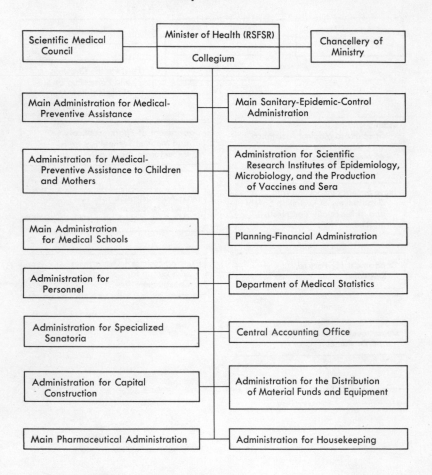

* N. A. Vinogradov, *Organizatsiia*, 2d ed., p. 608.

omous republic or the health department of a province (*krai*) or region (*oblast*). Administratively, the health ministry of an autonomous republic has about the same status in the medical hierarchy as the provincial and regional health departments. Typically, a regional health department consists of an executive, an advisory committee (medical council), a secretarial and accounting staff, four administrative and operational departments (called sectors), and a sanitary inspectorate, as seen in Chart 5–4.

Attached to the sectors are the so-called "chief specialists" (therapy, surgery, gynecology, obstetrics, pediatrics, epidemic diseases, and, in some cases, other specialties). These chief specialists are responsible for the level and the quality of services in their area of jurisdiction. For example, they establish standards of practice and staffing, supply personnel, and give them further training and specialization.[5] The regional or provincial health department has, thus, an internal structure geared to "practice" and to practical problems to a greater degree than the republican health ministry. In addition, the regional or provincial health department maintains, on its own budget, clinical facilities of regional significance (the regional hospital, for example).

The lowest administrative health organs are either the municipal or rural health departments. These departments direct and supervise, as well as finance, local medical facilities in the community; they appoint and pay health personnel; they supervise and are responsible for the health level of the population under their jurisdiction, and must carry out preventive measures. They, in turn, derive their logistic and financial support from the local soviet to which they are attached and of which they are a component part. They are also expected to maintain contact with paramedical organizations such as the Red Cross and Red Crescent Societies, and community or voluntary organizations which cooperate with health authorities. The structure of a municipal health department is quite simple, as can be seen from Chart 5–5.

While the municipal health departments have not experienced much change in the last few years, the rural ones have.

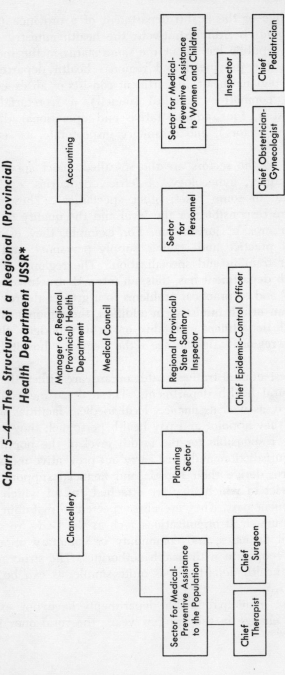

Chart 5-4—The Structure of a Regional (Provincial) Health Department USSR*

* N. A. Vinogradov, Organizatsiia, 2d ed., p. 610.

Chart 5–5—Structure of a Municipal Health Department USSR*

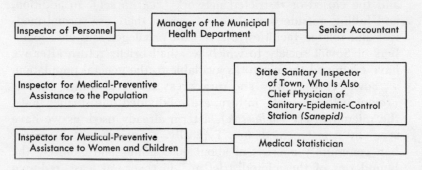

* N. A. Vinogradov, *Organizatsiia*, 2d ed., p. 610.

Beginning in the late fifties, the rural health departments gradually have been abolished and replaced by an even simpler organization: the rural district hospital. The director of that hospital became, in fact, the manager of the rural district's health services. The rural sanitary-epidemic-control station (*Sanepid*) also became a department of the hospital. The hope was that this would eliminate a great deal of useless bureaucratic red tape and duplication (parallelism), and that more operational management could be obtained from a physician actually involved in clinical services. Actually, the elimination of the health department as a separate administrative unit in the countryside was possible because rural medical facilities are relatively simple and small in numbers. A similar elimination apparently was impractical in the urban centers, because of the greater complexity and the multiplicity of their medical resources and the patent inability of the chief physician of a municipal hospital to take over these administrative functions. And yet a glance at the administrative structure of the municipal health department, coupled with the fact that most of the staff carry the title of "inspector," suggest that a conscious attempt has been made at that level to eliminate needless bureaucracy, a step quite in line with the decentralization philosophy that distinguished the Khrushchev regime.

The ultimate units for the actual delivery of medical services are the so-called general medical network (*obshchii set*) and the closed or restricted network (*zakritii set*). In addition, and falling outside these two categories, there are special medical and related facilities reserved for privileged and elite members of Soviet society to which we shall briefly return after we have examined the networks available to the general population.

Soviet cities, towns, and rural areas are divided into districts (*raiony*); the districts, in turn, are subdivided into smaller units, the microdistricts (*uchastok*), a term already used, as we have seen, by zemstvo medicine. Typically, a microdistrict in an urban community consists of about 4000 adults and children; the boundaries of the microdistrict are, in theory at least, redrawn to keep pace with changes in population and to maintain an even number of persons in each. In recent years experimental microdistricts with only 2000 persons have been established to determine whether halving the number of people would improve the medical services. Under the microdistrict system, a person is assigned to a health-territorial unit on the basis of his *residence*, and if he moves to another area, he is assigned to the corresponding microdistrict. In the countryside a microdistrict is, because of the low density of population, geographically much larger than in the cities. Some rural microdistricts have their own small hospitals to ensure inpatient services for the inhabitants, particularly when the distances are great and there are transportation difficulties (a common situation in the Russian countryside). In the urban areas, on the other hand, where there are large densities of populations, the microdistrict has no medical facilities of its own. Rather, the district (*raion*) is the first unit to have such facilities, usually a polyclinic and sometimes a hospital, although hospitals in most urban areas serve more than one district. The number of microdistricts per district is usually ten, although this may vary. Thus the model district, as conceived in Soviet planning, is one with a population of 40,000, divided into ten microdistricts of 4000 each. A graphic representation of rural and urban microdistricts is available in Chart 5-6. This constitutes the "general" or "residential" network and it is the one that services by far the greatest majority of ordinary Soviet citizens. The mainstay of this network

Chart 5-6—Overview of Local Administrative Organization in the USSR*

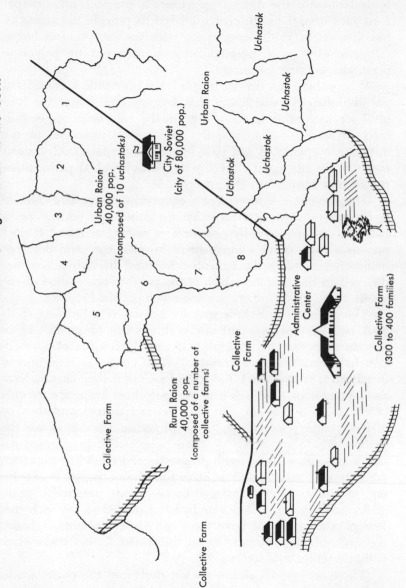

City Soviet
(city of 80,000 pop.)

Urban Raion
40,000 pop.
(composed of 10 uchastoks)

Uchastok

Uchastok

Uchastok

Uchastok

Uchastok

Urban Raion

Rural Raion
40,000 pop.
(composed of a number of
collective farms)

Collective Farm

Collective Farm

Administrative
Center

Collective Farm

Collective Farm
(300 to 400 families)

* The Report of the United States Public Health Mission to the Union of Soviet Socialist
Republics. Public Health Service Publication No. 649, Washington, D.C., 1959, p. 16.

is undoubtedly the district polyclinic, a comprehensive outpatient facility and health center, geared to provide the gamut of health services in the community with the exception of hospitalization; but even hospitalization is arranged by polyclinic personnel in most instances.

Where there is a district hospital, the polyclinic is considered an administrative division of that hospital, and where the hospital services more than one district, the polyclinics are considered divisions of that hospital. The health personnel of the district are appointed and paid by the municipal health department in the cities and either by the rural health department or the district hospital in the countryside.

The polyclinic is in essence a community outpatient medical facility; it provides services either to ambulatory patients or to patients who are seen by polyclinic personnel at home. It does not, as a rule, provide inpatient or hospital care and does not maintain hospital beds. Patients who must be hospitalized are directed to the hospital which is the parent organization of the given clinic, or to other, specialized, inpatient facilities.

The standard polyclinic may be housed in a building of its own, or it may occupy part of a building (the lower floor of an apartment house, for example). It usually consists of a reception hall where patients report either to obtain an appointment in advance, or to be directed to a physician if they already have an appointment. The office of the polyclinic keeps the records of the patients (usually classified by microdistrict and then by address) and sends these to the physician who is to see the patient. There are rooms or offices where doctors examine patients, procedure rooms with diagnostic and medical equipment, laboratories for tests, and an office for administrative, bookkeeping, and other clerical tasks. Because private practive is negligible, and because at any rate housing conditions are such that few physicians would have the room to see patients at home, the bulk of medical practice in the Soviet Union takes place within a polyclinic setting.

There are specific norms for the staffing of the polyclinic, as well as for the number of hospital beds that are reserved for each microdistrict. Thus the size of the polyclinic staff will vary with the number of microdistricts it services, as will the number of hospital beds set aside for the population of the microdistricts.

We present below the current organizational table for the microdistrict, keeping in mind, of course, that the correspondence between the table of organization and the actual situation throughout the Soviet Union may often be at considerable variance. In other words, this table represents an ideal toward which the health authorities are striving. Furthermore, it must be noted that norms for staff are stated, naturally, in terms of medical positions, implying that one physician may have more than one full-time job. The possibility, and often the necessity, both from the viewpoint of the "good of the service" and of the low pay of medical personnel, of multiple jobs, has naturally led to abuses. At the present time a physician is officially not permitted to hold more than two full-time medical positions, and he must obtain official permission from the republican health ministry to hold more than one and one half staff positions. Multiple jobs are made possible because the official workday of professional medical personnel is six and one-half hours.

Table 5–1—Specialized Medical Personnel of the Microdistrict Polyclinic and Hospital USSR*

Specialty	Number of Medical Positions by Specialty	Approximate Number of Hospital Beds by Specialty
Internal medicine (therapy)	2.00	10.0
Pediatrics	1.25	5.4
Surgery	0.90	7.6
Obstetrics and gynecology	1.00	7.2
Ophthalmology	0.25	1.0
Otolaryngology	0.20	0.6
Neurology	0.25	0.8
Phthisiology (tuberculosis)	0.6	4.2
Dermatovenereology	0.4	1.6
Total	6.85	38.4

* Maistrakh, *Organizatsia zdravookhranenia*, 1959, p. 87.

Special attention must be paid to the first two positions listed in this table, those for internal medicine and pediatrics. The term "internal medicine" is perhaps a not quite accurate translation of the Russian *terapiia* (therapy). A better rendition might be "general medicine," or simply "medicine." Physicians who hold this position are, for all intents and purposes, general practitioners or family doctors whose major responsibility is the health of the adult population of the specific microdistrict to which they are assigned. Indeed, in some instances they are designated as *uchastkovye vrachi,* or microdistrict physicians. They must provide the initial medical, diagnostic, and clinical care to those who live in the microdistrict, and they divide their time between seeing patients at the polyclinic and at their home. (As we shall see later, they also spend some time at the hospital.) By the same token, the pediatricians are responsible for the health of the children and adolescents who live in their microdistrict. Furthermore, the population of the microdistrict is encouraged to regard these doctors as "their doctors"—that is, the ones they turn to when they need medical care; and in view of the fact that there is a fair amount of job stability among medical personnel in the Soviet Union (to a greater extent, maybe, than in the United States), it appears that a personal relationship often can be established between patient and physician that tends to counteract (at least to some degree) the kind of impersonality and assembly-line methods which often are the earmark not only of socialized, but to some degree of all contemporary medicine. At the same time, it must be pointed out that in the Soviet case there is no mutual selection of patient and physician, the two being assigned to each other by the system, in just the same way as there is no selection in any army between physician and soldier on sick call. The situation is slightly different, however, with regard to the specialists. In most instances it is, of course, the general practitioner (or therapist) who refers his patient to one of his specialist-colleagues at the clinic or at the hospital; but the patient can request to see another specialist, and he apparently may make an appointment with him even without going through his own doctor.

We mentioned that the therapist also sees patients at the hospital. Up to 1947, there was a sharp separation between physicians who worked in the community and those who practiced in the hospitals, and the community doctor had practically no access to the hospital, an institutional segregation which, incidentally, is also quite marked in England. Since the hospital, nowadays, is the central facility in clinical practice because of its complex equipment and the fact that a great deal of medical research and teaching are usually carried out there, community doctors without access to a hospital are, to an important degree, cut off from the mainstream of medical progress. In 1947, the Ministry of Health, aware of this problem, reformed the organization of the health service by decreeing that all clinics (that is, outpatient institutions) should become parts of hospitals, and ruled furthermore that doctors must divide their time between practice in the community (at the clinic and at the patient's home) and at the hospital. The intent of the reform was sound, but in practice many obstacles arose (for example, the great physical distance often separating the clinic and the hospital with which it was officially affiliated), so that the reform did not accomplish its purpose. Changes were made so that at the present time community doctors spend an agreed upon part of the year working exclusively at the hospital—that is, without being responsible for community services. For example, one doctor might spend two months each year at the hospital, and the rest in the community; this allows him to catch up and keep up with advances in clinical medicine.

On the basis of the present age distribution of the population, it can be estimated then that about three fourths of the microdistrict's population is fourteen years old or older. This would mean that the "panel" of patients is about 3000 adults, or 1500 per therapist. The 1000 or so children and adolescents in such a population would, in turn, be serviced by one full-time and one-quarter time pediatrician, or perhaps by one pediatrician working about seven and one half hours a day. These do not appear, in either case, to be excessive loads. The 100 pregnancies and live deliveries that might be expected at the present birth rate would be attended by one full-time obstetrician-gynecologist who might, of course, also be expected to concern himself with the other gynecological problems of the microdistrict's female population. Other specialists would be expected to devote less than full time to each microdistrict. The neurologist (sometimes called neuropathologist), who also sometimes fulfills the functions of the psychiatrist, would thus be expected to serve the population of four microdistricts of about 16,000 adults and adolescents, since only one quarter-time position is budgeted for each microdistrict in neurology-psychiatry.

The organizational table, whether it applies to the number of staff positions or to the number of general and specialized beds, must, as noted earlier, be seen as a blueprint and as a guideline for medical administrators, and cannot be interpreted as an absolute indicator of the actual situation. The reality, as one can observe, if only fleetingly, on the pages of the Ministry's house organ, *Meditsinskaia Gazeta*, often departs rather widely from the design, because, for example, of population increases without corresponding redistricting, maldistribution of professional personnel (their concentration in the major cities), shortages of specialists, bureaucratic red tape, insufficient hospital beds, and other only too frequent contingencies. The situation is least favorable in the rural districts, where medical progress has proceeded at a distinctly slower rate than in the cities because of poor transportation and inadequate facilities, the shortage of suitable housing for medical personnel, and the reluctance of personnel to practice there.

While the majority of the population receives its initial medical care through the territorial network (the district poly-clinic constituting, so to speak, the patient's portal into the system of socialized medicine), some members of Soviet society receive their medical care through another gate, the "closed" medical network. This must be, in the nature of the case, a re-sidual category, since everybody else is expected to avail him-self of the common or general medical network. In the closed network, it is not so much geographical location that determines the facility to which one will go as one's social situation, which is determined primarily by occupation and status. There are apparently several types and categories of closed networks. First there are the extensive facilities earmarked for the top Soviet political elite, including the Kremlin clinics and hospitals reserved for the members of that elite and their families. Also, presumably, top foreign Communists, as guests of the Soviet government and the Communist party, would be treated in the Kremlin clinics. The Academy of Sciences, a prestigious organization which comprises the top Soviet cultural elite, also has its own superior facilities reserved for its members and other worthies who might be admitted as a special favor. In this respect, access to medical care is related to the Soviet class system and to the differential allocation of incomes and privileges according to rank and position. In addition, members of the armed forces are treated in a health system maintained by these forces, as are the members of a few ministries (communications and internal affairs). However by far the greatest number of people served by a closed network of health facilities are industrial workers. Industrial plants and organizations are obliged to build and maintain health facilities out of their budgetary resources, although health personnel working in these facilities are appointed and paid by the corresponding local health department, thereby providing a certain uniformity with the common network, and giving the health authorities the same kind of over-all supervision they have over other health facilities. In general, the larger the plant or the factory, the more elaborate and diversified the network of health facilities it will maintain for its workers and employees. Indeed, should the industrial facility be particularly large or important, its health network will be placed under the jurisdiction and support, not of the local but of a regional health department. By the same token, the Kremlin polyclinic is directly under the supervision of the Health Ministry USSR. When Stalin was dying, for example, it was announced that his care was the responsibility of the Ministry and, oddly enough, of that eminent medical group, the Central Committee of the Party, presumably to guard against "medical sabotage."

In the factories the shop plays a role somewhat equivalent to that of the microdistrict in the general network; shop workers are the responsibility of one physician and an assistant. The panel may consist of 1000 to 1500 workers (and sometimes their families). In certain of the more important industries the number of workers on the panel may be reduced to 500 (chemicals, mining, and petroleum).

There are also, at least according to reports by former Soviet citizens, separate health facilities in the major cities, towns, and provincial centers where the members of the officialdom receive care apart from the common people. These facilities are available not only to the officials but also to their immediate families. As such, it would be fair to surmise that these accommodations correspond, at least to some degree, to the private wings or pavilions routinely available to Americans who are willing and able to pay for a more luxurious and more private setting when they are hospitalized. The difference lies in the fact that in the Soviet Union access to these hospital services tends to be restricted not so much along income as along occupational and hierarchical lines. Furthermore, loss of official position leads to loss of access to these restricted facilities. Finally, in the Soviet Union care in these facilities is provided at no direct cost to the patient—that is, it is financed from state funds and constitutes, so to speak, an added increment to income and perquisites of rank.

ROLE OF NONMEDICAL ORGANIZATIONS
AND ADMINISTRATIONS

IF, AS Clémenceau once suggested, war is too important to be left to the generals, there is something in the official Soviet theory of health services that suggests that medical care and prevention of disease are far too vital to be left entirely to the physicians or even to the formal health authorities.[6] In accordance with Soviet ideas of the organic nature of a cooperative society, efforts have been made throughout the history of the Soviet regime to have the "people" help in their own medical care by cooperating with, supporting, and backstopping the efforts of health personnel and organizations. This help takes several forms, the most important of which are the following:

1. *The Soviets*: The soviets are the formal governmental or-

gans in the Soviet Union, and in theory, at least, they represent the people through the deputies who are elected to the soviets. In the final analysis, the soviets are the employers of health personnel and are formally responsible for the health services in their areas of jurisdiction, so that one can say, again in theory, that the people hire health personnel to provide health services. This responsibility is usually exercised by a "permanent (standing) health commission" of the soviet, the formal organ within the soviet concerned with health matters. The membership of the commission consists of elected deputies—that is, it is a predominantly lay group, although it usually has a few professionals as members. The commission is, by and large, the link between the executive branch of the soviet and the health authorities. Apparently, the commission is largely advisory, because executive decisions, budgetary provisions, and other administrative matters are in the hands of the executive committees of the soviet. In many areas of the USSR the soviets are also expected to provide health organizations with support not only financial but also in the form of needed goods and services. Thus the soviets (particularly in rural areas) are expected to "assist," "help," or "support" health personnel and authorities by supplying such items as housing for rural physicians, fuel, electric power, and transportation.

Beset as they are with a multitude of tasks and responsibilities, and often lacking the necessary funds or other resources, the soviets are frequently unable to meet the demands (statutory or other) made by health personnel and agencies; for in this area, of course, the health authorities are competing for scarce resources with many other agencies (industrial and educational, for example) and often do not enjoy the kind of priority that would enable them to stand at the head of the line. This lack of "logistic" support, naturally, increases the difficulties under which health personnel must labor and makes it more problematic for them to fulfill the tasks and duties they are responsible for, and in the countryside and other outlying districts (where the need for such personnel is greatest), it increases the turnover of physicians to dangerously high levels, thereby damaging the quality of professional services. Thus, for example, A. N. Syzdanov, Chairman of the Permanent Health Commission of the Kazakh Supreme Soviet, complained in 1959:

> First of all I consider the most important question to be medical personnel in the rural areas. Up to this time we have had a large turnover of rural physicians. During the past seven years, of the several thousand doctors coming in (to practice in the republic) more than one half have left. The main reason for this is the lack of normal housing conditions for public health workers.
>
> Responsible for this, most of all, are the local soviet organs, which are not satisfactorily fulfilling State decrees for improving rural public health care and are not setting up normal living conditions for medical workers. The permanent commissions can cite numerous instances when the executive committees of local soviets have violated and ignored these decisions. . . .[7]

In addition, if we are to believe the Soviet press, another area of frequent failure is the inability or the unwillingness of local soviets to concern themselves with the building, repair, or maintenance of health facilities, such as hospitals and clinics. This is, of course, a central area of concern on the part of health authorities; and the problem is further compounded by the general lack of roofed facilities that has characterized the Soviet Union since the inception of the Five-Year Plans in the late twenties, and which was further aggravated by the large-scale destruction of the Second World War. Sometimes the necessary funds are placed at the disposal of the local soviets for constructing or repairing medical facilities, but because of the scarcity of materials and shortage of personnel, or because of higher priorities in nonmedical areas, the construction or repair does not begin, or if begun it is not completed, and the funds are not expended, or if they are expended, it is for nonmedical purposes. The situation, in this respect, appears to be somewhat worse in the countryside and some of the outlying regions of the country where the Soviet regime has not invested as many resources as it has in Central Russia and in the industrialized and urbanized areas. There are indications that since the middle of 1962 the regime's policy has moved in the direction of improving the living conditions of the peasants and rural population; this may, in turn, lead to an improvement of health services for the peasant population and, hopefully of course, to increased agricultural production.

2. *The Party.* There is probably no aspect of Soviet society that is not affected by the Communist party directly and indirectly. The party is the real retainer of political power and the source of decisions in all fields. As such, it also plays a role of major significance in the administration and operation of the health service, from deciding what proportion of the budget will be allocated for the service to helping unravel bureaucratic red tape in the health administration and to disciplining members who behaved "incorrectly." The proclaimed goal of the party is that of increasing the welfare and the well-being of the population, and, as such, it must concern itself with the nature and the quality of health care. The "functional" aspect of this care, pointed out earlier, makes it also imperative for the party to be concerned with these matters. Over time the party has assumed a series of managerial functions, and its concern with economic production thus also leads to a concern about the health of the producers themselves. While the party itself is not directly involved in medical administration (in terms of carrying out administrative responsibilities), it is involved indirectly and in many ways at all administrative levels. At the highest reaches of the health administration it can be taken for granted that the most important and responsible positions will be given exclusively to members of the party and that lack of membership, while perhaps not crippling in a medical research position, will disqualify an individual from an administrative and managerial position. This ensures party control and supervision. Members of the party within the Health Ministry USSR, it was reported at the end of 1965, form a group of 500 persons, or half of the total personnel of the Ministry.[8] These party members, and the party organization itself, regard it as their responsibility to criticize the work of the Ministry and particularly to attack its "bureaucratic style of work." For example, at a meeting of the Ministry's Party Bureau in 1959, various deficiencies in the administration of the Health Ministry were

discussed and the bureau noted that many bureaucratic practices in the Ministry had not yet been eliminated. One official,
comrade Babaian, complained that "the mass production of
new pharmaceutical preparations is intolerably slow. By the
time these pharmaceuticals are in mass production, often new,
more effective preparations have appeared." The bureau also
noted that some of the officials whose work was unsatisfactory
did not even attend the meeting.[9]

Furthermore, the party often appears in the guise of the
deus ex machina, as a sort of superorganization and problem-
solver that can be appealed to when the formal health organization stands in the way of the performance of needed tasks.
When, for example, bureaucratic procedures (often called "formalism") interfere with services and cause "inhuman" suffering
or deprivation, the party may appear and interfere, providing
the necessary flexibility. The party thus can represent itself in
the role of the protector of the people against the petty bureau-
crats and is sometimes able to obtain action by cutting through
the red tape and other administrative blocks. The influence of
the party reaches down to the local level as illustrated from the
case of Dr. Titov.

> A letter was received at the Health Ministry about the irregular
> actions and the amoral behavior of the chief physician of the
> Yeniseisk District Hospital of the Krasnoyarsk region, Dr. Titov.
> . . . The behavior of Dr. Titov was discussed at the bureau of
> the Yeniseisk district committee of the party. Doctor Titov re-
> ceived a party reprimand and was dismissed from his job as chief
> physician at his hospital.[10]

It is difficult to assess with any degree of certitude the effectiveness of party control and interference within the health
service. It is clear that in many instances, this interference is
purely symbolic and the underlying situation that caused the
party to interfere remains basically the same. In other cases,
given the authority of the party and the diffuse power inherent
in party membership, such intervention may be more effective.
It may be presumed that the party will concern itself primarily

with those aspects of the health service that most closely affect the realization of its own plans and programs—that is, production, and particularly industrial production.

3. *Social Security.* While there is no ministry of social security (or social welfare) at the all-union level comparable to the Health Ministry USSR, there is such a ministry at the republican level. The organs of social welfare have certain medical functions to perform, deriving primarily from the fact that the ministries provide permanent disability (as well as old age) pensions to Soviet citizens, and are involved in such tasks as determining the degree of infirmity, devising prosthetic devices and providing and fitting them to invalids, maintaining and medically supervising old pensioners, and other similar activities. In general, it may be said that the medical activities and facilities of the organs of social welfare are of a limited type, but that even at this limited level it could be argued that the medical functions that go with rehabilitation, for example, are medical and should be in the hands of the medical organs. It may be interesting to note, in this respect, that in Poland the ministries of health and social welfare have been merged into a single authority on the assumption that this would insure better treatment and handling of patients.

4. *Industrial Ministries, Factories, State and Collective Farms.* We have seen that medical services can be made available to individuals on the basis of their occupation, and as such industrial ministries and large factories, plants, industrial organizations, and mines, for example, are expected to provide medical installations in the form of clinics, hospitals, convalescent homes, and other facilities. What seems to happen, however, and quite frequently, is that while these ministries and factories or other industrial organizations, after some prodding from the health authorities and the trade unions, set aside funds for the construction and maintenance of medical buildings, the construction does not proceed, or if it does, it is not completed, or completed only after long delays. In this situation availability of funds again is not enough to guarantee fulfillment of tasks, particularly in view of the scarcity of manpower and materials and of higher priority commitments confronting the managers

of industry, such as the fulfillment of the production plan. As the late Health Minister Kurashov complained in 1960: "During the last three years the amount of building of hospitals in large new industrial enterprises and especially in distant localities has decreased remarkably." Kurashov also suggested that in recent years some industries had been relieved of their responsibilities to build medical installations, and he suggested that this responsibility be returned to the industries.[11] At any rate, the same problems exist when the industrial ministries and plants are themselves responsible for medical construction.

In the last few years an attempt has also been made to stimulate medical construction in the rural districts by having the state farms and particularly the collective farms, build medical institutions out of their own funds and labor resources. The rationale for this is presumably the extremely slow development of medical construction (and maintenance or repair) in the countryside under the responsibility of the rural district health departments (in some places, as we have seen, these departments have been replaced by the district hospital) and the hope that the farmers themselves would be more diligent in the construction of the facilities that, in the end, would improve their medical welfare and health. It still remains to be seen whether a transfer of responsibility for medical building to the farms will lead to a real improvement of the medical services in the countryside.

5. *Labor Unions.* Soviet labor unions encompass almost the totality of salaried employees and workers in the USSR. (The collective farmers are not members since they are not salaried.) These unions are instrumentalities of the regime and in essence they are the equivalent of company unions as they are known in the West, with the difference that the "company" is the state. The unions have been entrusted in the USSR with a multiplicity of functions, some of which are concerned with the welfare, living conditions, working conditions, and health of the workers. The labor unions, for example, are responsible for the administration of social security funds—that is, compensation for workers who are temporarily disabled at work. Upon the recommendation of a physician and his signing of an illness cer-

tificate, the disabled or sick worker is enabled to receive part of his salary (depending on seniority). As such, the labor union plays a role in controlling the disposition and dispensation of the funds for sickness compensation and in seeing that no abuses take place (for example, the issuance of certificates in unjustified cases). The union thus employs physicians whose work is to check on the work of their colleagues in general practice. In addition, as representatives of the workers and of their interests, the labor unions are expected to urge industrial management to meet its obligations in the construction, maintenance, and operations of the health facilities located at the plant or the factory. Their concern also extends to the installation of safety and health protecting devices at work, and in seeing that the collective agreements reached by the labor union local committees and the factory management are observed, particularly as they apply to workers' welfare and medical facilities. In other words, the labor unions are urged by the regime and by the labor union administration constantly and actively to promote the welfare of their members through "interference" with management, visits to the hospitals and medical facilities, and suggestions. The evidence, as can be gathered from the Soviet press (particularly the medical press) is that more often than not the labor union reaches a kind of *modus vivendi* with management, particularly if its demands were to interfere with production and the fulfillment of planned targets, and local union committees are often taken to task for failing to perform their tasks aggressively. The fact of the matter is that, with the highest priority going to production, the welfare and health of the workers tend to get secondary priority.

6. *Red Cross and Red Crescent Societies.* The Red Cross and Red Crescent Societies belong to the realm of so-called public, voluntary organizations. They are, thus, not part of the official health bureaucracy, although many of their activities are in support of, and in cooperation with, the Health Ministry and its subordinate organs. According to G. A. Miterev, Chairman of the Societies, the membership exceeded fifty million in 1963;[12] it should be recognized that in many cases this membership must be nominal, since it does represent close to one fourth of

the total Soviet population. The function of the members of the Red Cross and (in Moslem areas) the Red Crescent Societies is to assist the health authorities in the performance of such tasks as educating the public in hygiene and accident prevention, distributing pamphlets and health literature, teaching first aid, inspecting living quarters and workshops in order to detect conditions injurious to health, improving public places (parks and railroad stations, for example), helping patients who have been discharged from the hospital (particularly those who do not have families to care for them), collecting blood for transfusions, and other activities of this nature, including the provision of relief funds and equipment to populations outside the Soviet Union who are victims of natural catastrophes. Finally, the Red Cross and Red Crescent have a paramilitary function: to cooperate with the medical services of the armed forces, particularly in times of war.

7. *Voluntary Groups.* In 1918, the first Health Commissar, N. S. Semashko, declared:

> The forms of the participation of the population in medical-sanitary activities and the form of its initiative must be radically altered: the widest participation in this activity of the organized masses and the village poor is indispensable.[13]

Ever since then efforts have been made by the regime to involve the population in so-called voluntary programs in support of the activities of the health authorities. Over time, these activities have taken diverse forms: street committees for the maintenance of cleanliness, councils of cooperation to ensure liaison between the hospital and the community, the promotion of Days, Weeks, or Months of Health, assistance to the Health Ministry in eliminating or decreasing certain diseases, and other projects designed to support the formal efforts of the health authorities and to provide auxiliary services that otherwise would not be performed. The questions that arise, of course, are the degree to which these activities are "voluntary" and the degree to which they help or are integrated with more formal health activities. From what is known of so-called voluntary activities in the Soviet Union, it may be assumed that in many instances they are voluntary in name only, and that in reality they are the results of pressures and persuasion applied to certain members of the population who have been selected to carry out such activities. In addition, it appears that even if people volunteer at first, in time the degree of support decreases, particularly since these activities cut further into the relatively small amount of free time left the Soviet citizen after work. Furthermore, it can be presumed that as medical care becomes more complex and more technical, untrained (even though enthusiastic) volunteers may tend to interfere with the performance of professional or semiprofessional tasks. Nonetheless, for its own reason the regime is interested in maintaining the belief that popular support for its activities is available and necessary.

We have reviewed, in this chapter, the main lines of the organization and administration of the health service. We began with an examination of the formal health structure, the Ministry of Health and the health organizations that are subordinate to it. We then shifted our attention to other organizations and authorities that play a significant role in the provision of health services to the population. We are now ready to turn our attention to the people involved in the service: health personnel.

Chapter 6

Health Personnel

THE EFFECTIVENESS of a nation's health service depends, in most general terms, on its particular combination of three basic ingredients: material resources and facilities (which we shall examine in subsequent chapters), a body of knowledge and techniques (which we assume in most instances to be common to medicine and public health the world over and to which we shall not pay any special attention, except in the chapter on research), and a group of specialized individuals. These individuals, whom we designate as "health personnel," will be the subject of this chapter.

It would be fair to say that in no other area of health services have the Soviets claimed, and with considerable justification, greater progress than in increasing the size of their contingents. Considering for the moment quantitative growth indices alone, the accomplishment has been extremely impressive. It may account, to a noticeable degree, for the improvement of the population's health levels—for example, the doubling of life expectancy at birth, an index of primary importance to a country's economic development. True, similar improvements have taken place in the world's other industrial nations and the health service alone is not responsible for such improvements, but this does not for a moment detract from the Soviet accomplishment, particularly if one remembers the major social traumas that have been a part of Soviet history. It may be pointed out that at the present time the Soviet Union graduates annually about as many physicians as there were in the whole of the Russian empire at the time of the Revolution (a graduation rate, incidentally, about three times larger than that of the United States) and that more than one in every five doctors in the world today is a Soviet physician.

It is possible to delineate, with a fair amount of accuracy, the size and the composition of the Soviet health contingent from statistics recently published by the government. While physicians are the more important and professionally the best-trained members of the "health team," they do not by any means constitute the majority of those engaged in the various phases of the health service. Physicians require the services and collaboration of many others, from nurses to hospital employees, whose activities make the operation of the health system possible.

At the time this book was completed, the latest general figures were for early 1965. More detailed data on health personnel were available for early 1964.

The estimated total population of the Soviet Union on January 1, 1965, was 229,100,000.[1] This population was serviced by 463,000 physicians, 21,000 stomatologists (dentists with an advanced degree), and 39,000 dentists without an advanced degree. Soviet statistics most often lump together physicians and stomatologists and sometimes add the dentists (in Russian called dental physicians), so that it was possible for Soviet sources to claim they had 523,000 physicians of all specialties at the beginning of 1965. But even without these last two categories, the figure is impressive, particularly when translated into number of physicians per constant unit of population as we shall do later, and when it is pointed that these figures exclude medical personnel working in the armed forces.

By the end of 1963 or early 1964, for a population of 226,200,000, there were about four million persons employed in all phases of the Soviet medical and health protection (*zdravookhranenie*) system, representing about 1.7 per cent of the total population and 5.6 per cent of the 70,526,000 persons considered salaried workers or employees (this figure, incidentally, excludes the collective farmers, who are considered members of cooperative organizations). Of the 3,933,000 persons employed in the health service at the end of 1963, 443,300 were physicians (11.3 per cent of the total), 20,200 were stomatologists (0.5 per cent), 37,300 were dentists (1 per cent), and 1,523,400 were semiprofessional health personnel (about 39 per cent). The balance, comprising about one half of those employed in health services, was presumably made up of those who are not employed either at a professional or semiprofessional level (cooks, drivers, cleaners, and the like). As noted earlier, these figures *exclude* medical personnel in the armed forces, so that the total Soviet medical personnel resources are presumably greater than the figures presented here would indicate. However, there are no data indicating the magnitude of the difference (army physicians, for example, are trained in a special medical academy and, as far as we know, there is no peacetime draft of physicians).

The distribution (for the end of 1963) of Soviet medical personnel among the various specialties and of semiprofessional personnel is given in Table 6–1.

PHYSICIANS

FIRST WE SHALL explore in some detail quantitative and qualitative data pertaining to physicians. Then we shall examine in less detail semiprofessional personnel. In order to assess the meaning of the size of the Soviet medical contingent, it will be necessary to compare it with the situation in the period immediately preceding the First World War.

The growth of medical personnel over the years of the Soviet regime may be gathered from Table 6–2 which gives the number of physicians in the half century between 1913 and 1963.

According to these figures the number of physicians has increased twenty-fold since the Revolution, whereas the population has increased by only one third. By mid-1965, the increase

Table 6–1—Health Personnel, USSR, 1963*
(excluding the military, end of year)

Physicians, by Specialization

Therapists[a]	107,300	
Surgeons[b]	47,600	
Obstetricians-Gynecologists	32,700	
Pediatricians	67,100	
Ophtalmologists	12,100	
Otorhinolaryngologists	11,400	
Neuropathologists	12,800	
Psychiatrists	8,600	
Phthisiologists (tuberculosis specialists)	19,500	
Dermato-Venereologists	9,700	
Roentgenologists	19,000	
Specialists in Physical Culture	1,900	
Physicians of the Public Health and Communicable Diseases Groups[c]	34,200	
Nonspecified, Nonspecialized[d]	59,400	
Total Physicians		443,300
Stomatologists[e]		20,200
Dentists ("Dental Doctors")[f]		37,300

Semiprofessional Personnel

Feldshers	364,100	
Feldsher-Midwives	77,300	
Midwives	154,300	
Assistants to Public Health Physicians and Epidemiologists	28,500	
Nurses	684,100	
Laboratory Technicians	58,300	
X-Ray Technicians and X-Ray Laboratory Technicians	19,700	
Dental Technicians	17,200	
Disinfection Instructors and Disinfectors	58,200	
Nonspecified[g]	61,700	
Total Semiprofessionals		1,523,400

Nonprofessional Personnel[h]		1,909,900
Grand Total of Professional, Semiprofessional, and Nonprofessional Soviet Medical Personnel		3,933,000

a. Includes general practitioners, family physicians, physiotherapists, infectionists.

b. Includes surgeons, traumatologists, orthopedists, oncologists (cancer specialists), and urologists.

c. Includes public health physicians, epidemiologists, malarialogists, bacteriologists, helminthologists, and disinfectionists.

d. This represents the difference between the total number of physicians and the total number of those who are reported as having a "specialty."

e. Graduates of a stomatological faculty of a medical institute—that is, a dentist with a professional degree. The designation "stomatologist" will be used here to distinguish this specialty from that of the dentist (see below).

f. In Russian, *zubnii vrach*, or dental doctor, referred to here as a dentist. The dentist does *not* hold a professional degree and is a graduate of a secondary medical school.

g. This represents the difference between the total number of semiprofessional personnel and the total number of those who are reported as having a "specialty."

h. This represents the difference between the total number of those engaged in the health service and the total of physicians, stomatologists, dentists, and semiprofessionals.

* *Narodnoe Khoziaistvo SSSR v 1963 Godu.*, Moscow, 1965, pp. 625, 626.

Table 6–2—Physicians, USSR (1913–63)*
(excluding the military, including stomatologists)

1913	1928	1940	1950	1960	1963
23,205	63,200	141,752	247,340	401,612	463,500

* Zdravookhranenie v. SSSR, pp. 79, 101; and Narodnoe Khoziaistvo SSR v 1961 Godu, p. 742; idem for 1963, p. 626.

was almost twenty-two-fold. Between 1940 and 1963, further-more (a period including the Second World War), the size of the medical contingent more than tripled, giving a *net* average increment of almost 14,000 physicians annually. Even assuming that about 5 per cent of these physicians were actually dentists, the increase is quite sizable.

In recent years the number of graduates from the medical schools has risen significantly, and between 1960 and the end of 1963, for example, the average net increment in the medical profession has been over 20,000 annually. These figures, impressive as they are, acquire even more meaning when they are transformed into numbers of physicians per 10,000 of the population, a widely used index. Table 6–3 provides an indication of changes in this index over the past fifty years.

These figures indicate that since the Revolution the actual supply of physicians relative to the population has increased more than thirteen-fold. At the present time the Soviet ratio of physicians to population appears to be one of the highest, if not the highest in the world, with the exception of Israel (24.3 in 1963),[2] where this rate is artificially inflated by the immigration of physicians trained in Europe. Until recently, Austria could claim a higher ratio than the Soviet Union, but it now has been overtaken (19.7 in 1964).[3] On the basis of estimated Soviet population early in 1965, the number of doctors per constant unit of population was about 50 per cent greater than the cor-

Table 6–3—Physicians, per 10,000 of the Population,
USSR (1913–63)* (excluding the military)

1913	1928	1940	1950	1960	1963
1.5	4	7.2	14	18.6	20.5

* Narodnoe Khoziaistvo SSSR v 1962 Godu, p. 616; idem for 1963, pp. 9, 623.

responding figure in the United States.[4] Furthermore, the American ratio is not likely to rise appreciably in the near future, because the population increase of 1.7 per cent per year may not be matched by a corresponding increase in the number of physicians being graduated from medical schools.

It is thus on the basis of these figures that Soviet officials have claimed, time and again, that the Soviet Union had by 1964–65 more than half a million physicians or one fourth of all the doctors in the world. Of course, this claim should be reduced, because stomatologists and dentists are included in these calculations, to slightly less than half a million and about one-fifth of the world supply of physicians, a respectable figure to say the least. It should also be noted, that Soviet figures must be further corrected downward to account for the presumably large number of physicians employed in the administration of health services, since it is Soviet policy to entrust responsible administrative positions only to physicians.

These rates and indices are purely quantitative and tell us nothing about the quality of the education received by Soviet physicians, which some observers have summarily dismissed as inferior to that in the West. The work performed by Soviet physicians and the utilization of medical personnel (particularly the distribution of such personnel) also have been criticized. We know, for example, that there are wide fluctuations in the rates of physicians to population among the different constituent republics (ranging from 33.5 per 10,000 in the Georgian SSR to a low of 13.9 in the Tadzhik SSR in 1963[5]), and there are similar if not greater discrepancies in the number of physicians per population between rural areas and the large (and middle) size urban centers.

For example, and not surprisingly, the highest ratio of physicians to population is found in Moscow and Leningrad, the two largest Soviet cities and the most important administrative, medical, and research centers. In 1959, the last year for which such detailed figures were available, there were 62.5 physicians per 10,000 people in Moscow, or over three and a half times the national figure, and in Leningrad there were three times as many physicians per population unit as in the nation as a whole.

The supply of physicians falls off rapidly in the provincial centers, the outlying districts, and the countryside in general. Thus, in 1961, while the national figure was 18.8 per 10,000, it was 27.6 for the urban population, but only 9.8 for the rural population. The latter figure, incidentally, included physicians working in city institutions but servicing primarily rural patients seeking treatment there. If only physicians who were actually working in the countryside were considered, then the figure dropped to 5.4—that is, less than one third the national and approximately one fifth the urban figure, as can be seen in Table 6–4.

The uneven distribution of medical personnel and the lack of an adequate number of physicians in the countryside are problems the Soviet Union has not been able to resolve any more satisfactorily than most societies. With the rare exception of men such as Albert Schweitzer, physicians have tended, more and more, to shun rural medical practice, and Soviet doctors are apparently no exception. The problem is particularly acute in the USSR (as it also is in many underdeveloped, largely agricultural countries) because of the immensity of the territory and the absence of an adequate communication and transportation network (particularly during winter and spring) which makes the movement of doctors to patients and patients to doctors and to medical facilities difficult and problematic. From an examination of Soviet sources, there seem to be at least two major sources—one professional-technical, the other sociocultural—for the reluctance of Soviet physicians to work in the village. The first reason is undoubtedly the well-known phenomenon of "trained incapacity," itself the result of the increased sophistication and instrumentation of modern medical practice. This leads to the physician's reliance on auxiliary personnel and facilities available primarily in large municipal hospitals and urban medical centers. Isolated from these resources, the physician often finds himself incapable of practicing a medicine "simpler" than the one he had been taught. Such inability is also compounded by the fact, which we shall explore at greater length, that in most instances the Soviet physician who finds himself assigned to independent work in the countryside is one

Table 6-4—Number of Full-Time Physicians in Clinical-Preventive Services, USSR per 10,000 Population in 1961*

REPUBLIC	URBAN POPULATION			RURAL POPULATION			TOTAL USSR POPULATION
	Inpatient	Outpatient	Total	In city institutions	In rural institutions	Total	
RSFSR	8.3	19.2	27.3	3.8	5.6	9.4	19.4
Ukrainian SSR	8.2	19.4	27.6	5.8	4.7	10.5	18.9
Belorussian SSR	6.5	20.7	27.2	7.0	4.0	11.0	16.7
Uzbek SSR	9.8	19.0	28.8	2.9	5.3	8.2	15.4
Kazakh SSR	8.3	16.0	24.3	2.0	6.5	8.5	15.5
Georgian SSR	7.0	27.0	34.0	6.4	7.1	13.5	22.8
Azerbaidzhanian SSR	8.1	23.3	31.4	4.3	4.3	8.6	19.9
Lithuanian SSR	7.5	22.6	30.1	9.5	2.5	12.0	19.4
Moldavian SSR	8.4	25.3	33.7	3.1	5.7	8.8	14.8
Latvian SSR	8.7	20.7	29.4	11.9	5.2	17.1	24.2
Kirgiz SSR	8.7	16.0	24.7	2.2	8.2	10.4	15.7
Tadzhik SSR	9.5	18.5	28.0	2.7	4.5	7.2	14.4
Armenian SSR	7.1	21.9	29.0	3.4	7.5	10.9	20.4
Turkmen SSR	9.9	19.7	29.6	4.8	3.7	8.5	18.6
Estonian SSR	8.1	22.8	30.9	10.5	4.6	15.1	24.4
Total for Entire USSR Ministry of Health	8.1	19.5	27.6	4.4	5.4	9.8	18.8

* G. A. Popov, "The Problem of Posting and Utilizing Physicians," Sovetskoe zdravookhranenie, No. 10 (1962), pp. 26–33.

who has had practically no clinical experience except the very little available during his formal training.

The second major reason for reluctance to work in the countryside is simply the lack of the cultural amenities and the living comforts (however skimpy they may be) usually available in towns but not in the village. For Soviet physicians, most of whom apparently come from urban communities and from what might be called "middle-class" families and background, an assignment to the countryside—or as it is sometimes called, to the "periphery"—is often considered a kind of exile to be avoided or to be cut short at the earliest possible moment. This may indeed be evidence that the very nature of the industrialization process and its emphasis on urban activities and the importance of the city has produced (or emphasized) a complex of values and attitudes that regards with some contempt anything connected with the village and rural life. As Zile has put it:

> . . . a Soviet citizen has certain intangible bonds with his city, which he is reluctant to sever. These are relationships developed with kinfolk and neighbors and through work, school and play, or just fondness for the city . . . people of such centers as Moscow, Leningrad, Kiev, or Riga, which have comparatively excellent cultural attractions, sporting events and recreational opportunities, are not indifferent to the choice of alternate places of residence and employment.[6]

In theory at least, local soviets are responsible for providing physicians with suitable accommodations. In many instances, however, even these facilities are not forthcoming, either because of lack of resources or initiative or because of other demands with a higher priority.

The net result of these conditions is the reluctance of most physicians to go willingly or voluntarily and the extraordinary turnover of medical personnel once they have gone or been assigned, all of which lead to a shortage of medical people in the countryside. Thus an article in *Sovetskoe Zdravookhranenie* emphasized that "Despite the vast growth of rural facilities and despite the fact that the inhabitants of rural areas can—and increasingly do—turn to urban facilities . . . which serves to equalize the ostensible statistical disparity between city and rural medical facilities, the rural medical problem is still unsolved." The article further elaborates that regardless of the annual increase in the number of physicians dispatched to work in rural areas, the total number of rural doctors remains stable (36 to 37.7 thousand) so that less than 10 per cent of the medical contingent serves about one half the total population. The authors attribute this to labor "fluidity" among medical workers. They give as an example the Riazansk Region, which they consider typical of the general rural-urban dichotomy, where the rural population constitutes 70 per cent of the total, but only 17.5 per cent of the physicians work in the rural districts. Indeed, more than half (55.3 per cent) of all doctors work in the two major regional cities, Riazan and Kasimov, while 27.2 per cent are occupied in other towns. Expressed in numbers of physicians per 10,000 people, this means 22.4 for the urban population and only 2.07 for the village folk. Excluding from these calculations Riazan and Kasimov, the discrepancy becomes smaller—8.12 as against 2.07[7]

A corollary of the situation just described is thus not only a differential in the supply of medical manpower clearly favorable to the urban centers, but also the oversupply of such physicians and frequently their underemployment or unemployment. Thus *Medical Worker* reported in 1962 that in Tbilissi, the capital of the Georgian Republic, the number of "nonworking doctors" was growing from year to year and had already reached the figure of six hundred. About forty young doctors who had graduated the previous year from the local medical school had not even started working.[8] It is, therefore, not surprising that the municipal hospitals seem to be teeming with medical personnel, a situation that rarely fails to amaze Western observers, who often comment on the lavish (if not extravagant, at least in Western terms) use of physicians compared with the situation in Western countries. For example, an English observer, C. Fraser Brockington, reported that in a large hospital in Tashkent (Uzbek Republic) there were 75 doctors for 450 beds and in a children's sanatorium (also in Tashkent), 20 doctors for 265 beds.[9]

This comparatively high proportion of physicians per hospital beds as well as the relatively lower number of auxiliary personnel may also account for the fact, sometimes reported by Western observers, that physicians in Soviet hospitals perform many tasks which in the West are delegated to semiprofessional personnel—to nurses, for example. At the same time, as observers also have reported, it is not unusual for a physician to sit at a patient's bedside and converse with him, a situation that is, unfortunately, not very common in the West.

In an effort to attract more physicians, differentials in pay and more generous retirement provisions have been offered but apparently they are not sufficient to motivate many physicians to remain and practice in the countryside. It has also been suggested that more medical students be recruited from among rural youths and that they be bound to return and practice in their home districts.[10] Because of this situation, and despite official disclaimers, the feldshers continue to play an important role in the Soviet medical system, which we shall explore in greater detail in our treatment of semiprofessional personnel.

It may seem strange on first blush, considering the nature of the Soviet regime, that the health ministries and departments are unable to use their administrative power and general authority to achieve the desired deployment of health personnel for the "good of the service" and the "national interest." Some degree of coercion is, in fact, applied to physicians to ensure an adequate allocation of personnel, particularly between town and country. When medical students complete their studies, they are assigned for two or three years to work in the countryside at the discretion of health authorities. This assignment is considered not only an obligation on the part of the newly minted physician, but also a means of repaying the government and the "people" who financed his education in the first place, since such an education is tuition-free and a stipend is given the student. After this service, which is obligatory for all except a small minority who are retained for immediate graduate work, the physician has more latitude in choosing a place of work and in deciding on the next step in his career (for example, specialization or research work). But despite this system of forced allocation, apparently the Ministry's plans rarely are fulfilled. Indeed, the evidence suggests that a variety of loopholes and escape valves permit many physicians to choose where they will practice; these seemingly account for the bunching up of physicians in the cities and the excessive turnover of doctors in the countryside. It must be remembered that the Ministry of Health and its subordinate organs are large bureaucracies and that it is often possible to manipulate these bureaucracies, through legitimate or nonlegitimate means, to escape undesirable assignments or to obtain transfers. For example, a married woman doctor has certain rights in refusing assignments that might separate her from her spouse, particularly if his post is so important that it would be difficult or impossible for them to move. On a slightly different but related subject, a question might be raised about the wisdom of assigning "green horns" to work in the countryside, particularly where the young physicians must assume responsibility for peoples' health without having had much or any practice and without easy access to colleagues for con sultation, advice, or assistance. In one sense, he serves his apprenticeship by learning at the expense of the rural population. It should be added that there is no formal internship parallel to the American system, although the sixth year of the Soviet medical curriculum is, in essence, mostly a "clinical" year involving work in medical facilities and with actual patients. The logic of the situation would seem to dictate the assignment of seasoned physicians to carry out this work, but apparently this is not possible or practical in many instances. This allocative mechanism probably strengthens the young physicians' instinctive "ruralophobia," by increasing their anxiety at the idea of assuming medical responsibility so early in their careers, and contributes to their trying to escape such assignments.

Another element that must be considered in assessing the utilization of Soviet medical manpower and comparing it with other countries (the United States in particular) is the regulated nature of the physician's employment, common to systems in which doctors are salaried employees and are expected to work only a set number of hours per day or week. The Soviet physician's official workday is 5.5 or 6.5 hours per day, six days a week (depending on the nature of the job), and unless the physician takes another position or, what is more common, a half-time position, he is free to do whatever he wishes and is not, in the usual sense of the work, "on duty." General observations from Western physicians who have visited the Soviet Union is that many of their Soviet colleagues, particularly those in community practice, may not work as many hours per day or week as physicians in similar, usually private, practice in the West whose time commitment must, perforce, be more "elastic." But perhaps more important in a comparative assessment of Soviet and other types of medical system and the use of medical personnel is the sex composition of the medical contingent. Indeed, in view of the over-all personnel shortages in the economy and the high priority commitment to industrialization and to tasks *directly* relevant to this process, it may be fair to say that the impressive increases in the size of the medical group could not have taken place without the large-scale employment of women in medicine. Their percentage among physicians has constantly increased from year to year, until at the present *three quarters* of all Soviet physicians are women, compared with 10 per cent in 1913 (Table 6–5). There has been a tendency for that percentage to recede from its high watermark of 1950, and discussions in the Soviet Union indicate that at the present time entering classes of medical students have a greater percentage of males than in the past, so it is possible that in the

Table 6–5—Women in Medicine, USSR (1913–1963)*
(excluding the military, including the stomatologists,
end of year)

Year	Number	Percentage of Total
1913	2,800	10
1940	96,300	62
1950	204,900	77
1958	294,600	76
1960	327,100	76
1962	361,900	75
1963	374,200	75

* Narodnoe Khoziaistvo SSSR v 1963 Godu, p. 625.

future the figure will gradually come closer to the halfway mark. For example, the percentage of women students training in higher specialized institutes in the three related fields of health, physical culture, and sport has decreased from 62 per cent in the academic year 1958–59, to 56 per cent in 1960–61, and 53 per cent in 1963–64.[11] While we have not been able to find data that would bear only in medical students, the trend is quite visible, and this particularly in view of the fact that medical students constitute, by far, the greater majority of all students in these three areas. At the present time, however, medicine, particularly at the community level and in general practice, is, for all practical purposes a female profession in much the same sense as secondary- and elementary-school teaching in the United States. This is confirmed through personal observations of out-patient clinics in different areas of the Soviet Union, where almost without exception the entire staff, professional and semi-professional, was female. The top positions, however, whether in administration, research, or clinical medicine, tend to be held disproportionately by men. So far, there has been only one woman who has served as Health Minister for the USSR, M. D. Kovrigina (between 1954 and 1959), and there is only a very small minority—under 5 per cent—of women among the members of the prestigious Academy of Medical Sciences—not to be confused, however, with the Academy of Sciences USSR.

It may then be held that the factor of sex composition of the medical contingent has something to do with the number of "medical hours" available to the society, in view of the fact that many women doctors, under Soviet conditions, must combine professional and domestic duties which are often quite onerous and time-consuming. We are referring to such activities as shopping, at best a lengthy and tedious process, the care of the household in the absence of domestic servants or the appliances usually taken for granted in the West, cramped living conditions in apartments (kitchen and other facilities often must be shared with other families), and finally the care and supervision of children. Under these circumstances it is quite evident that many women doctors, once they have spent their specified time at the clinic or the hospital, will have to devote themselves almost exclusively to domestic cares and chores and will have little time or energy left for professional-medical matters.

Education and Professional Training. Space does not permit us to examine in great detail the training of Soviet physicians. So we will focus on highlights, stressing aspects that significantly differ from the situation in the United States. Professional training of physicians consists of six years at a medical institute with studies beginning upon completion of secondary schooling, usually at the age of seventeen or eighteen. In this respect the Soviet system resembles the European pattern. It may also be inferred that of the six (or five and a half)[12] years, the first two would, roughly speaking, correspond to a premedical course in college. This means that the Soviet physicians complete their formal medical training at about the age of twenty-four (except for those whose education was interrupted because they had to spend two years at "productive work" before being allowed to proceed to university or professional training), rather than the typical twenty-six in the United States (or later if internship and residencies are taken into account). This also means that the graduating physician is not a *doctor* in the strict sense of the word and that his degree corresponds more to a Bachelor in Medicine (as in England) than a Doctor in Medicine.

Professional training is given either in a medical institute independent of a university or in the medical faculty of a university. By far the largest number of medical schools are in the first category (80 of 85 in the academic year 1963–64). At that time, there were about 180,000 medical students training in five general areas or "faculties"—medical, pediatric, public health, stomatologic (dentistry), and pharmaceutic. A medical institute thus may consist of one or more faculties. In 1956, the last year in which detailed data of this type were made available, there were 77 medical institutes with a total of 141 faculties and 152,767 students distributed as seen in Table 6–6. In 1956, there were in addition four correspondence branches in pharmacy faculties, with 1,438 students enrolled.[13] In 1963, the number of medical faculties had risen to 176, including 75 in medicine, 33 in pediatrics, 21 in public health, 29 in stomatology, and 18 in pharmacy.[14] It may be interesting to note that compared with 1956 there was in 1963 a higher proportion of stomatologic, or dental, faculties, whereas the proportion of the faculties of medicine and public health decreased, an indication, presumably, of increased concern about dental health.

Table 6–6—Medical Faculties and Students: USSR, 1956*

Faculty			Number of Students	
Medical	65	46%	95,442	63%
Pediatric	25	18%	23,364	15%
Public Health	22	16%	18,438	12%
Stomatologic	12	9%	5,675	4%
Pharmaceutic	16	11%	9,848	6%
Total	141	100%	152,767	100%

* *Zdravookhranenie v SSSR*, p. 152.

In recent years, and in conjunction with the emphasis under the Khrushchev regime on the importance of practical work and studies, evening faculties for semiprofessional personnel who wish to upgrade their qualifications without interrupting their work and eventually become physicians have been established. According to the report of an American mission which visited the Soviet Union in 1963, there were 63 such evening faculties (49 in medicine, nine in pediatrics, one in public health, three in stomatology, and one in pharmacy).[15] According to data (valid for 1963) brought back by the same delegation, between 30,000 and 32,000 new students were accepted in the five faculties annually, and about 25,000 had been graduated from these faculties that year.[16] The magnitude of these figures thus accounts for the sizable yearly increments noted earlier, particularly in view of the fact that the supply of newly graduated physicians and other medical specialists considerably surpasses the attrition in the medical contingent due to death, retirement, and other causes and furthermore outdistances the natural increase of the population.

The general opinion of Western specialists who know something about Soviet medical education seems to be that the training received by Soviet medical students may not be as good as that of American students,[17] particularly because the classes are somewhat larger; students therefore are more likely to watch laboratory work and clinical demonstrations than to participate actively in them.[18] Whether this judgment is justified or not, we are not prepared to say, except to note that under Soviet conditions it does make sense to train a great many physicians in view of the immensity of the territory, the urgency for a minimal level of health protection, and the size of the population. Under those circumstances such a commitment is more logical than the high quality training of a small number of physicians.

At the same time, it must be assumed (and vital statistics seem to bear this out) that these quantitative increments must result in qualitative improvements in the total health level of the population. A rate of about 21 physicians per 10,000 people is likely to be better than a rate of 20 or less if only in terms of the sheer availability of medical care, even if the care is not of the highest quality and there are maldistributions of medical personnel and the amount of medical work hours may be smaller than an equivalent rate would imply in a different health service in another society. Finally, what is known of the quality of Soviet education in general and in science and technology in particular, leaves no grounds for blanket complacency here either.

Specialization and Refresher Courses in Medicine. One of the prominent characteristics of contemporary professional occupations is the increasing trend toward specialization, a trend visible in medicine too. In the Soviet Union the present philosophy is to train physicians in one of three basic specialties (general medicine, pediatrics, or public health) but usually to postpone further specialization until after graduation from a medical institute and, in most instances, after the young physician has "repaid his debt to society and the people" by working for three years in the countryside, or the "periphery." Upon completion of that assignment the physician has, in theory at least, some latitude on whether he will remain a "general practitioner" with the possibility of refresher courses later, become a specialist, or enter academic medicine. One means of becoming a specialist is through a residency, or *ordinatura,* which entails several years' work in a clinic or hospital under the supervision of senior physicians. Another and quite important instrument for specialization are the Postgraduate Institutes for the Advanced Training of Physicians (of which there are 13) and three medical faculties for postgraduate training. After three years of study and clinical experience there, a physician usually is eligible for official certification as a specialist; in some cases more time is needed. In addition, shorter courses are also available to enable physicians to learn certain techniques, and in some instances these courses are combined with correspondence work.[19]

Since medicine is a fast-moving and ever-changing discipline, it is necessary to have a mechanism that will keep the clinical practitioners abreast of new developments, techniques, and practices. This is particularly true of practitioners who work in the community rather than in the large teaching urban hospitals (the source, most often, of advances in medicine and their application). The problem is compounded when the community is isolated and distant from urban centers, as it often is in the Soviet Union. Soviet health authorities hence have instituted a program of refresher courses which also are offered by the Postgraduate Institutes. Courses and practical instruction are available to physicians who have been practicing a number of years. The aim is to provide a two-month refresher course every three years for physicians in rural practice and one every five years for city practitioners. The idea of these refresher courses, and the intent to expose physicians in community practice to them at regular intervals, is fundamental to modern practice; as far as we know, however, this is still a goal. For example, a rural health department, unable to spare a physician or unable to find a replacement, may simply refuse to send him to such a training course. A recent Soviet survey underscores the fact that refresher training seriously lags behind formulated plans. Thus a questionnaire directed at 1,973 of the Uzbekistan Republic's general practitioners (therapists) revealed that of physicians who had been in practice more than five years, less than two thirds (61,7 per cent) had had some specialization or refresher-course exposure. Among those who had been in practice less than five years, only 16 per cent had had such exposure. Equally important was the fact that among the physicians in the first group, one quarter had completed their last specialization or refresher course more than five years previously. In reworking these figures, it was possible to estimate that of all the physicians queried, less than two fifths had had any kind of specialization or refresher course, a situation the author deplored as "undoubtedly lowering the quality of the medical attention to the population if for no other reason than that approximately 40 per cent of all patients turn first to a general practitioner. . . ."[20]

Academic Degrees. A rather sharp differentiation exists within the medical profession between those who are and remain in clinical practice, and those who choose to go into research and teaching (although physicians in practice are constantly urged to engage in research work, and are reminded of the Marxist injunction that theory and practice go together). The latter form a distinct group, particularly as they obtain higher academic degrees and professorial ranks and sometimes (this is the highest and most prestigious distinction) election either as corresponding or full members of the Academy of Medical Sciences. There are two such academic degrees: the Candidate of Medical Sciences, corresponding very roughly to a Masters degree in Medical Sciences, and the Doctor of Medical Sciences, the highest degree in medicine. These degrees are usually acquired when the individual is fairly well along in his career, and the requirements for their award are rather stiff, making them important and meaningful—and prestigeful. They also open the way for a professorial appointment which, in the Soviet Union, not only has prestige value, but also places the doctor-professor in a social and economic bracket many times higher than that of the ordinary practitioner.

Election to the Academy of Medical Sciences either as a corresponding or a full member, the highest professional accolade that can be bestowed upon physicians in academic medicine (with the exception of election to the Academy of Sciences), is reserved for only a very small number of the profession.

SEMIPROFESSIONAL PERSONNEL

WE HAVE DEALT, up to now, primarily with physicians. But equally impressive gains have been registered by the Soviets with semiprofessional medical personnel, who play an increasingly important role in contemporary medicine. Table 6–7 traces the growth of such personnel in the half century between 1913 to 1963. Comparing the figure for 1963 with that for 1913, the increase of Soviet semiprofessional medical personnel has been thirty-three-fold; comparing 1963 with 1928, the increase has been thirteen-fold, and with 1950 more than two-fold.

Table 6–7—Semiprofessional Medical Personnel, USSR (1913–63)* (excluding the military)

1913	1928	1940	1950	1960	1963
46,000	113,700	476,000	719,400	1,338,300	1,523,400

* Narodnoe Khoziaistvo SSSR v 1961 Godu, p. 745. The 1950 figure is taken from Zdravookhranenie v SSSR: Statisticheskii Sbornik, Moscow, Gosstatizdat, 1960, p. 112; Narodnoe Khoziaistvo SSSR v.1962, p .618; idem for 1963, p. 626.

Because the population has also increased, a more meaningful measure of the growth of semiprofessional ranks can be obtained by comparing the number of such personnel with constant units of population. In such terms the growth, although less impressive, is significant enough. For example, that index increased twenty-one-fold between 1913 and 1963, and 70 per cent between 1950 and 1963.

Table 6–8—Semiprofessional Medical Personnel per 10,000 of the Population, USSR (1913–63)* (excluding the military)

1913	1928	1940	1950	1960	1963
3.3	7.7	24	40	65	68

* Narodnoe Khoziaistvo SSSR v 1961 Godu, p. 745. The 1950 figure is taken from Zdravookhranenie v. SSSR: Statisticheskii Sbornik, Moscow, Gosstatizdat, 1960, p. 112; Narodnoe Khoziaistvo SSSR v idem 1962, p. 618; idem for 1963, p. 626.

Another way of looking at these figures is to relate the number of semiprofessionals in medicine to the number of physicians. In most countries the trend has been toward an increase in auxiliary personnel relative to physicians, which permits doctors to service more patients and do it more effectively.

For example, in the United States, the number of nurses increased seven times between 1910 and 1962, and the number of medical and dental technicians rose from the first statistical record of 4000 in 1920 to 44,154 in 1950 and 87,944 in 1960, while the number of physicians merely doubled between 1910 and the early sixties.[21] In Soviet Russia the number of nurses also increased about seven times for the same period. It may also be interesting to note that before the First World War the number of physicians in Russia and the United States far exceeded that of nurses (for example, in pre-Revolutionary Russia there were more than two times as many nurses as physicians and in the United States more than two and a half times as many). In the early sixties, there was more than one and a half nurse to each Soviet physician, and there were almost two to each American physician.[22]

The increase of Soviet semiprofessional medical personnel has also been made possible by the massive influx of women into these occupations. Thus the percentage of women in the health system (when *all* levels, including professional, semiprofessional, and nonprofessional, are considered) amounted to 86 in 1963, whereas the percentage of women among all those working or employed in the national economy for that year was 49. While three fourths of the physicians were women in 1963, more than nine tenths of all semiprofessional medical personnel were women.[23] The health service is thus largely a female operation. Furthermore, because many more women than men continue to enter schools training semiprofessional personnel (but the percentage of women entering medical schools apparently is decreasing), one can assume that for the near future most "medical workers," with the possible exception of physicians, will continue to be women.

The problem the Soviets face in staffing the countryside with medical personnel has already been mentioned. Given the size of the territory and the reluctance of physicians to practice in rural areas, other measures had to be devised to provide some modicum of medical assistance for the rural population. It is in this connection that the role of the feldsher comes into focus as a possible solution and perhaps as a model worthy of examination and emulation by other societies facing the same general problem.

The feldsher is a semiprofessional health worker, officially known as a physician's assistant. Feldshers (from the German *Feldscherer,* or field barber or company surgeon), originally introduced into Russian armies by Peter the Great in the seventeenth century, served primarily in the military. In the nineteenth century civilian feldshers, mostly retired military feldshers, began to practice in the countryside, where they provided the bulk of medical attention available to the peasantry. While the Soviet regime intended to eliminate feldsherism (in essence a second class of medicine), this has not proven possible or practicable because of the demands for medical personnel and particularly the shortage of physicians in rural areas. Staffing the countryside with feldshers apparently does not pose the same problems as trying to use physicians. Many feldshers are of peasant origins themselves and therefore are not too reluctant to return to the village with the added prestige of the educated person. Openings for feldshers are more limited in the cities, since there already are enough, and sometimes too many, doctors. Moreover, the general educational system is such that it tends to channel rural youths into feldsher schools rather than into the medical schools, because the medical schools require the kind of secondary education not as easily available in the countryside as in the cities.

In theory, of course, the feldsher is only a doctor's assistant, and Soviet health authorities emphatically deny that he is entrusted with medical functions and medical decisions. The fact of the matter, however, is that under conditions where there is no physician around, or when no physician is available, the feldsher will fulfill many medical functions, except perhaps for routine surgery. A complaint often voiced in the Soviet medical press is the presence of feldshers in positions demanding doctors. In some respects the feldsher's functions in rural districts resemble those of the public health nurse in the more isolated districts of the United States.

Education and Training. Semiprofessional personnel are trained in secondary medical schools and are usually required to have an intermediate education of seven or eight years before admission. For the academic year 1963–64, there were 560 secondary medical schools with about 220,000 students.[24] The length of training varies from two to three or more years, depending on the specialty involved. Nurses, for example, study for two and a half years; feldshers, midwives, and certain technicians for four years. And, as mentioned earlier, semiprofessional personnel may study and become physicians.

Living Standards and Conditions of Health Personnel. Because there are no detailed studies of health personnel income and expenditure patterns, it is difficult to make categorical statements about standards of living. Such statements, furthermore, would have to be differentiated according to category of personnel, for there exists a rather wide spread among categories, even among those who are physicians.

At the top of the hierarchy of medical personnel one can find those who hold responsible and managerial positions in administration, research, and clinical work. Ministers of health, directors of large medical institutions, and professors of medicine enjoy a standard of living and prestige several times greater than that of physicians who are in ordinary clinical practice. A professor's salary and other perquisites are considerably higher than those of an ordinary practitioner. A professor of medicine might earn from four to eight times the base pay of a physician, while an academician might earn from three to five times or even more than a professor.[25] Salaries for ordinary physicians as well as for other semiprofessional and junior medical personnel are, to say the least, modest, particularly when compared to the price of most commodities and when the minimum wage level has been pegged at about 45 new rubles a month ($49.50 at the current rate of exchange).[26] Table 6–9 gives the latest detailed information available on medical salaries, although it should be noted that a new draft law, proposed by Khrushchev in midsummer 1964 and enacted later that year, raised the salaries of medical personnel by an average of 23 per cent (17 to 26 per cent for physicians, 40 per cent for semi- and nonprofessional health

Table 6–9—Salaries, Health Personnel in New Rubles, per Month, USSR (1955–64)*

I. Physicians in Medical Establishments

	SENIORITY			
	Less than 5 years	5 to 10 years	10 to 25 years	25 years and over
1. a) Physicians in medical establishments of towns and workers' settlements	72.50	80.00	95.00	108.00
b) Microdistrict physicians and pediatricians, all physicians of public health and preventive establishments, and medicolegal experts in towns and workers' settlements	74.00	85.00	102.00	110.00
c) Physicians of medical establishments in rural locality	75.00	83.00	98.00	108.00
d) Physicians of public health and preventive establishments and medicolegal experts in rural locales	77.00	85.00	102.00	110.00
2. Physicians—heads of departments, laboratories, medical offices, sections, medical stations (which are parts of public health installations):				
a) Including those responsible for up to six medical staff positions including that of the head	77.00	95.00	105.00	115.00
b) Including those responsible for more than six medical staff positions including that of the head	77.00	100.00	110.00	120.00

Independent of Seniority:

3. Physicians—managers of public health establishments in charge of		
a) Number of medical staff positions	up to 10	120.00
b) Number of medical staff positions	from 11 to 35	130.00
c) Number of medical staff positions	from 36 to 75	150.00
d) Number of medical staff positions	from 76 to 125	160.00
e) Number of medical staff positions	from 126 to 200	180.00
f) Number of medical staff positions	above 200	200.00

The official pay scale for physicians who are assistant supervisors of public health institutions is established as 15 per cent lower than that of the supervisors of these establishments.

Table 6-9—Salaries, Health Personnel in New Rubles, per Month, USSR (1955-1964) (cont'd)

II. Semiprofessional and Nonprofessional Personnel in Medical Establishments

	Up to 5 years	5 to 10 years	10 to 25 years	25 years and over
1. Feldshers, midwives, head nurses, with a secondary medical training	50.00	57.50	62.50	70.00
2. Other semiprofessional medical personnel:				
a) With secondary medical training or training in biology	45.00	52.50	60.00	67.50
b) Without specialized secondary training	37.50	42.50	50.00	55.00
3. Heads of establishments (departments, medical stations, laboratories of establishments, detachments), dentists	55.00	60.00	67.50	75.00

The official pay scale for semiprofessional medical personnel who are in charge of children's day nurseries is higher:

By 10 per cent in nurseries keeping children twelve hours a day
By 15 per cent in nurseries keeping children sixteen hours a day
By 20 per cent in nurseries keeping children around the clock

4. Nonprofessional medical personnel and service personnel (orderlies, aides, and the like)	35.00	37.50	41.00	45.00

* B. F. Konnov, *Pravovoe Regulirovanie Truda Meditsinskikh Rabotnikov* (*Official Regulations of Work of Medical Personnel*), Moscow, Gosiurizdat, 1960, pp. 17—21. Figures converted to new rubles. Scale set up by law of August 12, 1955.

workers). This increased, for example, the minimum payment for a physician with less than five years of practice from 72.50 to 75.00, to 90 to 105 rubles a month; and a physician with the same seniority in a rural hospital has moved from 75 to 100 or 105 rubles a month. The most highly qualified physicians, those with 25 years of rural service or 30 years of urban service, now receive from 195 to 200 rubles a month.[27] The pay of feldshers has correspondingly been increased from a range of 50 to 70, to 65 to 110 rubles. Nurses now receive from 60 to 110 rubles instead of 45 to 67.50. The pay of nonprofessional medical personnel has moved from the 35 to 45 range, to 45 to 50 ruble range.[28] Although rents in the Soviet Union are nominal and medical care is, of course, free, the prices of most commodities, food and clothing in particular, are high enough to permit the average physician and medical worker only a life of genteel poverty. For example, using prices for 1962, the following may indicate the standard of living afforded by these salaries: white bread .60 r. per kilogram (a kilogram equals 2.2 lbs.; all food prices are in kilograms); beef (rib roast), 1.60 r.; butter (salted), 3.60 r.; sugar, 0.89 r.; tea 7.60 r.; eggs, dozen, 0.96 r.; and milk, 0.27 r. per liter or quart. Consumer goods such as clothing and appliances weigh quite heavily on the budget of the Soviet citizen. For example, a rayon street dress costs about 29 r.; women's shoes, leather oxford, 23 r.; nylon stockings, 3.20 r.; a man's cotton shirt, 6.00 r.; a suit, wool, single breasted, 110 r.; men's shoes, leather oxford, 24.50 r.; 20 cigarettes, superior quality, 0.30 r.; and a fifth of vodka, 4.05 r.[29] A bicycle costs from 45 to 60 r., a good radio receiver about 40 r., a popular wrist-watch 50 r. A car costs at least over 3000 r.,[30] and the customer must wait several years for delivery.

Some physicians can increase their income by taking on additional jobs, and professors and those in academic life can supplement their earnings through consultation, writing, lecturing, and other similar activities. But in general it appears that the health authorities frown on this practice and tolerate it only as long as there are not enough physicians to fill certain budgeted positions. Because most medical positions are official state jobs and these jobs have specific salaries assigned to them, the "bill" Soviet society pays for its medical services can be limited and adjusted to a degree that would be impossible in a system under which most physicians engaged in private practice and determined their fees largely at their own discretion.

In this chapter, we have examined very briefly Soviet health personnel. We have provided statistical materials indicating the rapid growth of such personnel, whether physician, semiprofessional, or nonprofessional, since 1913. We have pointed to the important role played by women in the health service. We also have examined the education of health personnel and specialization and have given some indication of their standard of living. In the next chapter we turn to clinical services and facilities.

Chapter 7

Clinical Facilities and Services

WHETHER a nation's health care is adequate depends, in large part, on the existence of facilities and instrumentalities—from a general hospital down to an aspirin tablet—in which and with which personnel can practice their healing arts. These facilities, in turn, depend on the availability of economic resources, that is, on budgetary provisions for their purchase or construction. The manner in which economic resources are allocated to the health system will be discussed in Chapter 10. Here we shall take up the major clinical facilities and services available to the Soviet population.

With the explosion of knowledge and technology the world has witnessed in the last hundred years, medicine and medical practices, along with science and technology, have become more sophisticated, more heavily instrumented and more expensive; the locus of medical services has tended to shift, gradually, from the patient's sickbed and the community to specialized settings, that is, to medical facilities. The hospital, naturally, is the prototype in the public imagination and the highly dramatic symbol of such settings (with its constant tug of war between life and death). There is, however, a whole range of equally important though not so dramatic other medical institutions—the outpatient clinic, for example—where medical care is available to ambulatory patients, that is, patients who do not require room and board or the "hotel" services of hospitals.

Here again, Soviet progress has been impressive, although perhaps not so impressive as the increase in health personnel noted earlier. We shall review, very briefly, this progress by examining medical facilities and services for the general population as well as for certain designated groups. We shall, first, consider the situation in the urban sector (even though in some instances the Soviet data do not distinguish between urban and rural medical facilities); then we shall examine the situation of the rural population and its special problems.

GENERAL FACILITIES AND SERVICES

MOST SOVIET CITIZENS, in the city and the countryside, have access to socialized medicine either through the "general" or the "closed" network. This means that residence or occupation determines the medical facility the individual must use and the physicians who will treat him. Usually, as we have seen, the individual is registered (and his records will be kept) according to his microdistrict at the district polyclinic serving his area of residence or his plant, and he must go there initially except in case of emergency. The number of urban microdistricts rose from 17,114 in 1955 to 26,163 in 1961, and there were in addition 6000 industrial medical stations, the occupational equivalent of a residential microdistrict. As a result of the increase in these microdistricts, the average number of adults in each dropped from 3,900 in 1955 to 3000 in 1961,[1] and presumably even less in the midsixties. As we have noted earlier, the microdistrict physician, whether general practitioner or specialist, operates from an outpatient facility called the district polyclinic (*raionnaia poliklinika*). The physician sees patients either at the polyclinic or, if the patient cannot come to the clinic or should not come (because he might spread an infectious disease), at home. The physician therefore divides his time between work at the polyclinic and house calls. Most clinics are open thirteen hours a day and thus employ two full shifts of physicians; sometimes arrangements are made to provide for an on-duty physician at night, when the clinic is closed.

We noted, earlier, that the polyclinic constituted the portal of entry of the individual into the system of Soviet socialized medicine. Because of the demand for services this portal is likely to be crowded, and waiting is often the order of the day (as it is in most clinics or even private physicians' offices the world over.) The physician is thus likely to be busy; official norms issued by the Ministry of Health indicate that he must see ("process" might perhaps be a better term) a patient every twelve minutes, or five patients per hour. The general norms of office visits for different specialists at the clinic, as issued by the Health Ministry, are as follows:

Table 7-1—Work Norms for Soviet Physicians in Urban Outpatient Clinics (1960)*

Specialty	Norm of Visits per (Clinic) Hour
Therapy (general medicine)	5
Surgery	9
Pediatrics	5
Obstetrics-Gynecology	5
Ophtalmology	8
Otolaryngology	8
Neuropathology	5
Phtisiatry (tuberculosis)	5
Dermato-Venereology	8
Stomatology (dentistry)	3

* Vinogradov, *Organizatsiia Zdravookhraneniia v SSSR*, 2nd ed., 1962, p. 254. By-laws of July 20, 1960, Nr. 321 (Health Ministry USSR).

It must be understood that these are norms issued for planning and accounting purposes, and do not mean, for example, that the therapist sees each patient for exactly twelve minutes; some patients will be coming in for a procedure or a certificate or renewal of a prescription that may take only a few minutes; others (particularly first visits) will require more time. In addition, as is true everywhere in medicine today, but even more pronounced in a bureaucratized system of the Soviet type, the physician must cope with an enormous amount of paper work —endless forms and reports—and is likely to spend a fair amount of his allotted time on that kind of activity. In some clinics the physician may be fortunate enough to have a nurse to take over some of the paperwork.

An examination of the conditions under which clinic personnel work suggests that harassed doctors, facing long lines of waiting patients, often do not have the time, the patience, and the energy to give each and every one the optimum amount of careful attention. But, although the physician might have a tendency to deal as quickly as possible with patients who do not seem to be very sick, he must be careful lest his behavior antagonize those who come to the polyclinic. As a state employee and a public official, the physician is fair game to those dissatisfied (or even paranoid) patients who feel they have been wronged and have the right to lodge a formal complaint against the doctor; and such complaints can be quite unpleasant, particularly if health and other officials want to show to the population that they are watching over their interests and are ready to punish physicians who are negligent or "inhuman." The tension and sometimes mutual antagonism that arise from these conditions of medical work thus tend to neutralize the advantages that, according to some, derive from the fact that there is no cash nexus in the patient-doctor relationship in a system of socialized medicine. Not only must the physician take care of everyone waiting in the antechamber, but also he often must hurry because he must vacate the office for the next physician and *his* quota of patients.

The physician who makes house calls is allowed one half hour per patient, but this includes transportation time. Some clinics have a service car placed at the disposal of medical personnel; otherwise the physician walks or uses public transportation. House calls are arranged either by telephoning a special nurse who takes down the particulars, and ascertains whether a house call is justified, or by dropping a slip with the name and address of the patient in a special box at the clinic. But a patient who calls a physician when he obviously is not very sick, and could just as easily get to the clinic, will certainly not endear himself to his microdistrict physician.

The whole issue of the doctor-patient relationship tends to

be further complicated (some might say poisoned) by the question raised by official sickness certificates,[2] a question we have treated at length elsewhere and which we can only mention here. The physician is in the position of issuing certificates of illness to those individuals whom he considers sick. These certificates (*bulleteni*) are quite important in Soviet society, for they not only officially absolve the individual from the penalties for unauthorized absenteeism, but they are necessary for him in order to receive sick pay or other benefits. Pressures are often put on physicians by persons who are not, in the strict sense of the word, "sick," but who need, for any number of reasons, the relief provided by the certificates. The state, of course, places counter-pressures upon the physician in order to reduce his latitude in these matters and to minimize the economic costs or losses caused by these excuses. While unexcused absenteeism is not punished as harshly now as it was under Stalin's regime, it is still very much frowned upon officially and exposes the individual to disciplinary and financial sanctions. As a rule physicians are not allowed to give a certificate good for more than three days. After three days the patient must be seen again and the excuse may be renewed, but not for more than ten days altogether. Should additional absence on medical grounds be necessary, the patient then must be referred to a commission of two or three physicians who examine him and decide what his further treatment should be or whether he should "return to duty." The physician thus must be (as a military doctor usually is) constantly on the lookout for malingerers or others who would use the medical excuse for their private ends. This situation is, in itself, not conducive to the best relationship between physician and patient.

The polyclinic, with its complement of specialists and with the equipment at its disposal, provides a wide range of clinical, diagnostic, and other medical services on an outpatient basis. In addition to the general polyclinics there are more specialized institutions, the dispensaries and consultations, where special types of patients and/or disease conditions are treated. It seems clear that in the large cities there are many separate medical institutions, but that in the smaller areas and towns most medical services available will be at one outpatient institution. There are dispensaries for patients suffering from tuberculosis, venereal and skin diseases, cancer, and mental illness. Of perhaps greater importance and interest are the "consultations"—that is, medical-social service institutions where advice and care are given to mothers and their children. We shall return to these later.

There is little doubt that the great majority of patients who come to see physicians can be served on an outpatient basis—that is, without being hospitalized—whether the treatment takes place at the patient's home or at the physician's office or at a polyclinic. According to Soviet information only 17 to 20 per cent of all patients who need medical care at any one time are hospitalized; the rest are treated entirely within an outpatient setting.[3] In 1961, there were 38,707 outpatient medical institutions of all types. However, this figure is not broken down between urban and rural institutions, although it is according to republic (Table 7–2).

Table 7–2—Outpatient Medical Installations, USSR (1961)*

Republic	1961
RSFSR	21,340
Ukraine	6,937
Belorussia	1,379
Uzbekistan	1,612
Kazakhstan	1,993
Georgia	1,394
Azerbaidzhan	924
Lithuania	476
Moldavia	417
Latvia	521
Kirghizia	338
Tadzhikstan	304
Armenia	417
Turkmenistan	469
Estonia	286
TOTAL USSR	38,707

* BME, 2nd ed., Vol. 30, Col. 1088, Table 49.

In 1961, there were more than one billion patient-visits at the outpatient institutions maintained by the Health Ministry USSR and over 88 million house calls—an average of about 5.5

outpatient visits and house calls for every person.[4] The average number of such visits and calls was, however, considerably higher for town dwellers (8.8 in 1961, with slight variations for the different republics).[5]

We have been dealing so far with outpatient facilities available to the general public. Reference should also be made to the medical services available to industrial workers—that is, to those who belong or are assigned to the closed or occupational network rather than the general or residential one.[6] Several factors—plant location, type of production, and particularly work-force size—determine the nature of the medical facilities maintained for the industrial worker. The smallest facility in industrial medicine is the aid-station, of which there are two types: the medical aid-station and feldsher aid-station, the first manned by a physician, the second only by a feldsher. A feldsher aid-station is designed for factories employing between 300 and 800 workers; a medical aid-station must be set up when there are 800 or more workers (500 in the coal, oil and mining industries). Workers in smaller factories presumably use the residential network.

The number of feldsher aid-stations has increased steadily since 1940 (by almost 400 per cent); the number of medical aid-stations, on the other hand, has increased more slowly (slightly over 200 per cent between 1940 and 1961; Table 7–3).

Table 7–3—Medical and Feldsher (Industrial) Aid-Stations, USSR (1940–61)*

Type of Station	Number of Stations				
	1940	1950	1955	1960	1961
Medical	4,287	6,575	7,498	8,952	8,303
Feldsher	5,652	8,824	14,013	18,626	20,413

* BME, 2nd ed., Vol. 30, Cols. 1091, 1092, Table 53.

Although no explanation has been offered, it may well be that medical aid-stations represented an uneconomical use of medical personnel, and that some of them have been downgraded to the level of a feldsher aid-station.

For purposes of health administration and planning, industrial facilities for workers are divided into units called shop microdistricts, corresponding to the microdistricts of the general network. Groups of workers become the responsibility of a shop microdistrict physician. The shop microdistrict physician must see to it not only that his patients receive the necessary care, but also that their health is protected through his efforts to improve working conditions and industrial safety. Thus the physician is expected to "go to bat" for the workers before management and to work to reduce health hazards. Actually, many of his efforts are frustrated because the measures he advocates often are expensive and may be rejected by cost-conscious management.

In the larger industries employing 1000 or more (2000 in the coal, oil, mining, and chemical industries), the plant is expected to maintain outpatient and sometimes inpatient medical facilities, such as clinics, hospitals, sanatoria, and so on. Shop physicians are attached to these facilities if such are available; if not, they are attached to the clinics of the territorial network. The larger the plant and the number of workers, the greater and the more diversified the facilities it is expected to maintain. An industrial plant's medical organization is called a "Medical-Sanitary Section"; in 1961, there were, under the supervision of the Health Ministry USSR, 1,063 such sections, nine tenths of them located in the RSFSR and the Ukraine, the two most industrialized and populous republics.

An idea of the size of the industrial medical network can be gathered from the fact that in 1961 there were 918 hospitals with a bed capacity of 125,000 in the medical-sanitary sections of the Soviet Union. These sections maintained 1,086 medical aid-stations, 3,926 feldsher aid-stations, and other facilities of a medical and preventive nature, and had to fill more than 37,000 medical staff positions. In recent years, most sanitary-medical sections have developed into diversified health centers with not only the standard medical facilities, but also such refinements as dietetic dining rooms and children's crèches.

Dispensarization. Another important service, one largely of a preventive nature, is the program of dispensarization, or the systematic observation and periodic examination both of patients with an identified condition and of healthy groups. The program is designed to catch incipient forms of disease and to stop disease before it has had a chance to develop too far. In theory at least, dispensarization implies not only medical and preventive measures in the narrow sense of the term, but also steps to improve the individual's environment, whether at home or at work. We say "in theory" because the realities of Soviet social and economic conditions often make taking such steps quite difficult, if not impossible. The categories of healthy members of the population which are under dispensarization are the following: children (from the moment of birth), adolescents, students in intermediate and higher educational institutions, pregnant women, and certain types of workers exposed to more than normal health hazards. In addition, persons suffering from chronic medical conditions such as tuberculosis, cardiovascular diseases, gastrointestinal diseases, cancer, and others may be placed under this program. The importance of dispensarization is bound to increase with time, particularly because medicine has now been able to deal effectively with most infectious diseases and has, by prolonging life, increased the number of candidates for chronic and degenerative conditions. According to Soviet figures, in 1961, more than 40 million persons (above 20 per cent of total population) were given preventive examinations, the majority being school students (Table 7–4). There also are special examinations aimed at uncovering a specific disease condition at an early stage. In 1955, for example, 17.4 million persons were examined to detect cancerous and

Table 7–4—Number of Persons Undergoing Medical-Preventive Examinations, USSR (1955–61)*

Group Examined	NUMBER EXAMINED (IN THOUSANDS)		
	1955	1960	1961
Workers in Industrial Enterprises (in cities)	4,738.9	6,537.4	6,723.5
Workers in Communal, Food and Children's Institutions	4,934.9	5,768.7	5,889.9
Workers on State Farms and Repair-Tractor Stations	1,962.4	2,287.3	2,371.8
School Children	19,518.4	23,742.3	25,670.0

* BME, 2nd ed., Vol. 30, Cols. 1093–4, Table 54.

precancerous conditions; in 1961 this number had grown to 38.3 million.

Emergency Medical Care. A system of emergency care also has been developed in the Soviet Union. Anyone who has visited Soviet cities has probably seen the vehicles of the *skoraia meditsinskaia pomoshch* (rapid medical assistance) with their red-crosses, hurrying on calls. Emergency medical care may be obtained by dialing 03 on the telephone, and an ambulance with physician and nurses or feldshers will, in most instances, be dispatched to the emergency site. In 1961, there were 2,131 emergency medical care stations that were either independent or component parts of medical institutions. According to published data over 25 million calls were made in cases of accident or illness. Frequently, the emergency service is requested when medical care is unavailable from the regular district polyclinics (at night, for instance, although some polyclinics have a physician on duty when the clinic is officially closed). In 1961, there were almost 8,000 ambulances attached to the system of emergency medical care, or one ambulance per 15,000 of the urban population (the figure was one per 26,000 in 1955.)[7] In the countryside, sparsely populated settlements, and outlying districts, emergency medical care is sometimes the responsibility of stations of sanitary aviation (*stantsii sanitarnoi aviatsii*) which are attached to regional, provincial, and republican hospitals. Physicians of 171 such stations gave (1961) emergency assistance to 1,221,500 persons. We shall later examine some other specialized medical services, but we turn now to the backbone of the medical system, the hospital, where the more serious conditions are treated

Hospital Facilities. According to Soviet statistics, there were about five times as many hospitals in 1963 as in 1913, again with wide variations in the growth rate between the different republics (Table 7–5). The increase in the *number* of hospitals is, however, a very crude index of growth, because the figures do not tell us anything about the hospitals themselves (whether they are general, specialized, psychiatric), nor, more importantly, do they tell us the number of beds in these hospitals. This number is a critical item of information; it is generally agreed that very small

Table 7–5—Number of Hospitals by Union Republic, USSR (1913–63)* (excluding the military)

Union Republic	1913	1940	1955	1960	1963
RSFSR	3,149	8,477	13,515	14,259	14,010
Ukraine	1,438	2,498	4,754	5,043	4,971
Belorussia	240	514	867	991	1,042
Uzbekistan	63	380	748	1,122	1,149
Kazakhstan	98	627	1,479	1,719	1,799
Georgia	41	314	610	677	694
Azerbaidzhan	43	222	459	625	697
Lithuania	44	77	276	309	269
Moldavia	68	109	325	343	359
Latvia	50	89	279	269	243
Kirghizia	6	112	219	261	281
Tadzhikstan	1	121	205	244	252
Armenia	6	96	226	269	268
Turkmenistan	13	99	232	313	272
Estonia	40	58	236	224	212
Total USSR	5,300	13,792	24,430	26,668	26,545

* BME, 2nd ed., Vol. 30, Cols. 1077–8, Table 40; Narodnoe Khoziaistvo SSSR v 1963 Godu, p. 627.

hospitals cannot give very good or specialized care because they cannot afford the complicated equipment and specialized personnel for complex and up-to-date medical care. We know, for example, that before the Revolution 26 per cent of all hospitals in Russia had five beds or less, 53 per cent had from six to twenty beds, and only 21 per cent had more than twenty beds. The fact that four fifths of all hospitals in Russia before the Revolution had fewer than twenty beds indicates that the supply of good hospital care was quite inadequate.

In the half century between 1913 and 1963, the supply increased faster than the number of hospitals; in 1963, there were more than *nine* times as many beds as before the Revolution (Table 7–6). But since the population also increased during this period, an even more accurate measure of the supply of hospital beds can be obtained by translating these figures into rates—that is, the number of hospital beds per constant unit of population. If we do this, we see that the number of beds per 10,000 people increased almost seven times for the period indicated (Table 7–7). It will also be seen that while this increase took place in the country as a whole, it was by no means uniform from

Table 7–6—Hospital Beds, by Republic, USSR (1913–63)*
(excluding the military, in thousands)

Republic	1913	1940	1950	1955	1960	1963
RSFSR	133.4	482.0	609.8	761.7	990.9	1,145.5
Ukraine	47.7	157.6	194.2	248.1	343.8	403.4
Belorussia	6.4	29.6	32.0	41.5	55.9	71.1
Uzbekistan	1.0	20.3	32.0	40.2	74.2	84.6
Kazakhstan	1.8	25.4	35.5	55.4	81.3	107.5
Georgia	2.1	13.3	19.4	23.9	30.3	35.0
Azerbaidzhan	1.1	12.6	17.0	20.5	27.4	35.3
Lithuania	2.2	8.9	10.8	15.9	21.4	24.7
Moldavia	2.5	6.1	10.8	15.3	22.0	27.1
Latvia	6.2	12.0	14.0	18.8	23.0	25.3
Kirghizia	0.1	3.8	7.1	9.3	16.3	21.0
Tadzhikstan	0.04	4.5	6.8	9.2	14.2	18.2
Armenia	0.2	4.1	6.5	9.3	13.2	15.9
Turkmenistan	0.3	5.6	7.5	9.9	13.5	15.6
Estonia	2.5	5.1	7.3	9.9	11.5	13.7
Total USSR	207.6	790.9	1,010.7	1,288.9	1,739.2	2,043.9

* BME, 2nd ed., Vol. 30, Cols. 1079–80, Table 42; Narodnoe Khoziaistvo SSSR v 1963 Godu, p. 627; idem for 1962, p. 619.

Table 7–7—Supply of Beds to Population, USSR (1913–63)*
(excluding the military, number of Beds per 10,000 population)

Republic	1913	1940	1950	1955	1960	1963
RSFSR	14.8	43.3	59.2	67.8	82.2	91.9
Ukraine	13.6	37.7	52.2	62.4	79.8	90.4
Belorussia	9.3	32.6	41.2	52.9	68.0	84.1
Uzbekistan	2.3	30.2	49.8	54.9	84.4	86.2
Kazakhstan	3.2	39.4	52.0	66.7	79.3	90.4
Georgia	8.0	36.0	54.6	61.7	72.1	79.4
Azerbaidzhan	4.8	37.8	57.8	60.7	69.1	80.5
Lithuania	7.7	30.0	42.1	60.2	77.5	84.8
Moldavia	12.2	24.6	45.1	57.6	72.3	83.5
Latvia	24.9	63.0	71.7	93.0	107.3	114.0
Kirghizia	1.2	24.1	40.3	48.4	73.1	84.2
Tadzhikstan	0.4	28.6	43.9	50.8	67.7	77.5
Armenia	2.1	30.1	47.6	58.6	69.6	76.9
Turkmenistan	2.7	41.6	61.3	72.5	82.9	86.8
Estonia	26.2	47.7	66.1	85.2	94.1	108.8
Total USSR	13.0	40.2	55.7	65.1	80.5	90.3

* BME, 2nd ed., Vol. 30, Cols. 1079–80, Table 42; Narodnoe Khoziaistvo SSSR v 1963 Godu, p. 628.

republic to republic, nor is the ratio the same in all republics. Again, the rate of increase was the greatest in republics which had the smallest number of beds relative to population before the Revolution. A limiting case would be, of course, a situation in which a republic had had no beds at all in 1913, so that the establishment of even one bed would give an increase that mathematically would be expressed as infinity (1/0). While this was not the case in any republic, the increase in Tadzhikistan which had only four tenths of a bed per 10,000 (or four beds per 100,000) was almost 200-fold between 1913 and 1963, or 20,000 per cent, a rate of increase more than 28 times the average rate for the nation as a whole. The republics of Central Asia, because they were so poorly supplied before the Revolution, have registered the greatest percentage increase. On the other hand, at least two of the Baltic Republics (Latvia and Estonia) which were the best supplied before the Revolution have registered increases smaller than the national average.

About one fifth of Soviet hospitals are municipal hospitals (city hospitals), but they contain almost one third of all the hospital beds, with an average of about 120 beds each (Table 7–8). As such, these hospitals have an average size definitely smaller than the regional hospitals, of which there are only 163, but which have 455 beds each on the average. Almost half of all hospitals are rural, although they have only between one sixth and one seventh of all hospital beds, and the average number of beds is extremely small, about 22 per hospital; this gives rise to certain problems with respect to the quality and comprehensiveness of medical care in the countryside.

Another measure of the medical system is the distribution of the total number of hospital beds according to specialties. While such a breakdown is unavailable for the pre-Revolutionary period, data have been published for the period 1940–63 (Table 7–9). It will be seen from Table 7–9 that while the total number of beds more than doubled in the twenty-year period, in some categories the increase was much greater (as much as fifteen times for oncological or cancer beds), while in other categories the increase was somewhat less than average, and in one type of beds, general beds, the number actually decreased from

119,700 to 65,900, indicating a trend toward more and more specialized beds and presumably a better quality of hospital care.

The health authorities have been concerned for several years with the existence of very small rural hospitals (some with as few as five beds), and a campaign has been underway to eliminate these so-called dwarf facilities (*karlikovie*) and to transform them into outpatient clinics. Thus, according to orders of the RSFSR Health Ministry, beginning in 1960 it was forbidden to build microdistrict hospitals with less than fifty beds.

The preceding figures again are purely quantitative and tell us very little about the nature and the quality of medical services available to the Soviet citizen. And yet the sheer magnitude of these facilities, even though they may be crowded and some-

Table 7–8—Hospitals, by Type and Number of Beds, USSR (1961)* (excluding the military)

Type of Hospital	Number of Hospitals	Number of Beds (in thousands)	Average Number of Beds per Hospital
Regional	163	74,200	455.2
Municipal	4,949	590,500	119.3
Special Hospitals (pediatric, infectious, tuberculosis, and others)	1,663[b]	178,000	107.0
District (in urban settlements and rural localities)	3,159	305,100	96.6
Microdistrict (rural)	12,888	282,900	21.95
Inpatient units of outpatient clinics[a]	2,291	110,500	48.2
Inpatient units of Scientific-Research Institutes and Clinics of Higher Educational Institutes	148	37,500	253.4
Maternity Homes (except collective farm maternity homes and maternity divisions in general hospitals)	955	67,800	71.0
Neuropsychiatric Colonies and Inpatient Units of Neuropsychiatric Clinics	464	175,000	377.2
Other Hospital Institutions	132	23,900	181.1
Total	26,812	1,845,400	68.8

a. Includes antituberculosis, oncological, dermatovenereal diseases, and others, but excludes neuropsychiatric.
b. Of these, 994 for children, and of these, 808 for noninfectious.
* *BME*, 2nd ed., Vol. 30, Cols. 1081–2, Table 44.

times poorly equipped, is a significant improvement over the pre-Revolutionary situation. There are indications, as we have seen, that the health authorities intend to concentrate on building larger hospitals which can be better equipped and better staffed; this will necessitate, at the same time, better transportation facilities so that patients from rural districts and other outlying regions can get to these facilities. At the present time such transportation cannot always be taken for granted because of poor road conditions, particularly in the spring and the winter.

Services for Women and Children. Pregnant women and children are given medical services in specialized institutions (mostly in the cities) which cater exclusively to their needs, on the premise that this will permit medical personnel to provide better quality care for them.

Table 7–9—Beds by Specialty, USSR (1940–63)* (in thousands)

	1940	1950	1955	1960	1963
Medical	102.3	173.7	256.6	361.7	416.7
Surgical[a]	99.4	135.1	170.6	236.7	270.6
Oncological	1.7	12.2	16.9	24.2	30.6
Gynecological	33.6	42.2	56.0	91.3	109.4
Tubercular:	34.0	75.8	109.8	157.2	225.1
For Children	5.3	10.2	17.2	20.9	28.1
For Adults	28.7	65.6	92.6	136.3	197.0
Infectious Diseases:	94.3	125.6	148.8	166.6	174.7
For Children	31.9	43.8	67.9	75.3	79.5
For Adults	62.4	81.8	80.9	91.3	95.2
Children's Diseases (noninfectious)	52.5	77.2	105.5	163.9	211.9
Eye	13.4	15.8	21.9	30.3	33.7
Otolaryngological	6.0	8.8	12.2	20.0	26.6
Dermatovenereal	15.4	30.0	28.4	31.0	33.6
Psychiatric	82.9	70.9	106.5	162.5	196.0
Neurological	10.0	14.1	18.9	30.5	39.9
Maternity (in maternity homes and hospital departments)	113.5	122.2	144.9	175.3	188.5
General Beds	119.7	73.2	57.0	67.9	65.9
Total Number of Hospital Beds	790.9	1,010.7	1,288.9	1,739.2	2,043.9

a. Includes beds for neurosurgical, traumatological, urological, and stomatological patients. For each year the total number of beds by specialty is less than the grand total of all beds given. The difference may well consist of beds not controlled by the Health Ministry.
* *BME*, 2nd ed., Vol. 30, Cols. 1081–2, Table 43; *Nar. Khoz. SSSR* v. 1962, p. 620; *idem* for 1963, p. 630.

Let us, by way of illustration, briefly examine these institutions and the services they provide. When a woman realizes (or suspects) she is pregnant, she is told to report to a so-called women's consultation (*Zhenskaia Konsultatsiia*), a kind of gynecological outpatient clinic. (The clinic also provides contraceptive advice and information.) Once the pregnancy is established, the woman has the choice of proceeding with it, in which case she is registered for care, supervision, and instruction, or, if she does not wish to bear the child, of requesting an abortion.[8]

The staff of the clinic (particularly visiting nurses) see expectant mothers at the clinic and at home and help women with newborns. They treat women with gynecological diseases and problems and provide a modicum of social and legal assistance. A few years ago, and presumably to some extent today, the consultations were busy teaching the psychoprophylactic method of natural childbirth which was based on Pavlov's teachings. In recent years, however, much less has been heard about this method.

The major inpatient facilities in this field are the following: the maternity home (to which women's consultations are usually attached); obstetrical-gynecological departments of hospitals; and in the countryside, in addition to these, maternity homes belonging to collective farms (and built at their expense) and feldsher-midwife as well as midwife stations. In the countryside the main burden of gynecological and obstetrical services falls on the maternity houses of collective farms and on the feldsher-midwife stations. It must be remembered that in the rural areas the midwife still plays a major role in these matters and provides the bulk of obstetrical services to peasant women. When the Soviets list the number of beds available for pregnant women, they may lump together "medical" beds, where physicians are in attendance, and "midwife" beds, where midwives and feldshers are working. Table 7–10 gives the number of obstetrical beds of both types, by republics. Here again quantitative indices show extremely impressive progress over the prerevolutionary period; indeed, the number of maternity beds for the country rose about thirty times in the fifty years between 1913 and 1963.

According to a decree passed in 1956, women workers who

are members of labor unions are entitled to 112 calendar days of leave with pay in case of pregnancy, and in case of twins or more children, or complications, the postdelivery period may be extended from 56 to 70 days. Those who do not belong to the unions (an extremely small minority) receive smaller benefits. Should a mother want more leave, without losing her job, she has the right to take an additional three months off, but without pay. In addition, women can maintain their seniority status for a year after the birth of the child, an important provision since seniority determines the size of welfare benefits in case, for example, of temporary absenteeism due to illness. The provisions for women in the countryside, on the other hand, are less generous; according to the general regulation for collective farms, women collective farmers are freed from work for one month before and one month after the birth of a child.

There is a wide range of facilities that provide medical care and supervision for children: children's hospitals with outpatient clinics called "child-polyclinic-consultations," pediatric divisions of general hospitals, children's sanatoria, crèches-kindergartens,

Table 7–10—Number of Beds (Medical and Midwife) for Pregnant Women, USSR (1913–63)* (in thousands)

Republic	1913	1940	1950	1955	1960	1963
RSFSR	5.5	90.7	82.7	92.3	112.3	119.2
Ukraine	1.2	35.0	33.7	41.4	48.9	50.4
Belorussia	0.3	5.4	4.4	5.0	6.7	7.4
Uzbekistan	0.06	2.8	3.5	4.8	7.8	9.6
Kazakhstan	0.03	4.3	4.9	7.8	11.9	13.8
Georgia	0.1	1.9	2.5	3.2	3.9	4.3
Azerbaidzhan	0.04	2.0	2.1	2.5	3.3	4.0
Lithuania	0.03	0.4	1.7	2.2	2.4	2.4
Moldavia	0.03	0.6	1.7	3.1	4.2	4.3
Latvia	0.15	0.8	1.1	1.6	1.7	1.6
Kirghizia	0.01	0.8	1.0	1.5	2.6	3.1
Tadzhikstan	—	0.6	0.8	1.0	1.4	1.9
Armenia	—	0.7	1.2	1.6	2.2	2.4
Turkmenistan	0.01	0.8	0.9	1.4	1.7	1.8
Estonia	0.06	0.3	0.8	1.0	0.9	0.9
Total USSR	7.5	147.1	143.0	172.4	213.4	227.1

* BME, 2nd ed., Vol. 30, Cols. 1115–16, Table 76; Narodnoe Khoziaistvo SSSR v 1963 Godu, p. 621.

school hygiene divisions of sanitary-epidemiological stations, as well as medical stations in schools.

The central position in the system of protecting children's health belongs to the child-polyclinic-consultation (*Detskaia Konsultatsiia*), whose mission, generally speaking, is to watch over children's health and development from birth to the end of the eight-year general school, that is, until the child is fifteen or sixteen. This system, incidentally, is also part of dispensarization which, as we have seen, is said to cover almost the entire child population, including nursing infants, although it is doubtful that the coverage is that extensive in the countryside and in some of the less-developed Central Asian republics. The child-polyclinic-consultation among other functions, sends visiting nurses to homes and supervises the child's health education. In 1963, there were 319,500 hospital pediatric beds and over 67,100 pediatricians.[9] The growth of the network of pediatric beds by republic between 1940 and 1961 (when the number of such beds more than tripled) can be traced in Table 7–11.

Some degree of cooperation is said to exist between the

Table 7–11—Number of Pediatric Beds in Hospitals, USSR, by Republic (1940–61)* (in thousands)

Republic	1940	1950	1955	1960	1961
RSFSR	57.4	87.4	122.0	156.2	165.5
Ukraine	15.1	19.7	31.4	45.9	50.0
Belorussia	2.0	2.5	4.5	6.2	7.0
Uzbekistan	2.6	4.5	5.6	10.4	11.7
Kazakhstan	5.6	4.8	8.1	12.2	13.4
Georgia	1.0	1.8	2.6	3.6	3.7
Azerbaidzhan	1.7	2.6	3.0	4.0	4.3
Lithuania	0.5	1.0	2.1	2.8	3.3
Moldavia	0.3	0.9	2.0	4.2	4.8
Latvia	0.9	1.6	2.3	2.8	2.9
Kirghizia	0.5	0.7	1.4	2.9	3.3
Tadzhikstan	0.7	1.0	1.1	2.0	2.2
Armenia	0.5	0.9	1.5	2.2	2.6
Turkmenistan	0.7	1.0	1.4	2.0	2.2
Estonia	0.2	0.8	1.6	1.9	1.9
Total USSR	89.7	131.2	190.6	259.3	278.8

* BME, 2nd ed., Vol. 30, Cols. 1119–20, Table 78.

school system and the health authorities with respect to children's health problems. While dispensarization applies to children until they reach school age, a comprehensive medical examination is scheduled yearly after the summer recess. Children found to have a weakened condition or an illness are placed on a special list for systematic treatment. Here again, the system probably works best in the city schools, and the statistics we have on the results of such examinations apply only to urban school children. In 1955, for example, 1,157,000 children were examined, and in 1961, 1,803,000 prior to entry into first grade.[10] (Since, at the beginning of the academic year 1961–62 there were 8.7 million children enrolled in grades 1 through 4 of the urban schools, and if we assume that the 8.7 million were about evenly distributed among the four classes, then approximately 83 per cent of the first graders were given the medical examination.)

There are, in addition, a series of other institutions, perhaps not medical in the strict sense of the word, but which contribute to the building and the maintenance of children's health: crèches, kindergartens, homes for children, pioneer camps of the sanatorium type, and children's sanatoria. Most of these institutions, although not necessarily under the supervision of the Health Ministry, have medical personnel supervising the children's regimen. During the summer and particularly during harvesting season, temporary arrangements are made to supervise farmers' children while their parents are in the fields.

SPECIAL PROGRAMS

IN ADDITION to the facilities outlined above, the Soviet health service maintains several programs for the treatment and prevention of specific disease entities. We can only mention them briefly here.

Cardiovascular Diseases. As infectious diseases are brought under control, and as the life span of the population increases, heart and circulation conditions do become more widespread and require special attention and treatment. Soviet health authorities have devised, and are still in the process of devising, methods and programs to handle such conditions. The most important of these programs is dispensarization, or the systematic examination of groups to which we referred earlier, and which often permits the early discovery and more effective handling and treatment of cardiovascular conditions. Among the groups systematically examined for such diseases are students, adolescent workers, workers and employees in industry.

Tuberculosis. Tuberculosis, still an important medical and public health problem in the Soviet Union, is aggravated by the extraordinarily crowded conditions under which most of the people live. A special network of antituberculosis facilities, both of the inpatient and outpatient type, has been established. Beds for tubercular patients are available either as part of specialized beds in general or specialized hospitals and in antituberculosis sanatoria. Outpatient care is available either in outpatient clinics or in specialized antituberculosis dispensaries as Table 7–12 shows.

Table 7–12—Antituberculosis Institutions and Tuberculosis Specialists (Phtisiatrists), USSR (1940–61)*

	1940	1950	1955	1960	1961
Outpatient Institutions	1,687	4,132	5,622	6,177	6,340
Dispensaries	554	722	1,118	1,377	1,448
Number of tuberculosis hospital beds, in thousands	34.0	75.8	109.8	148.9	164.9
Number of beds in antituberculosis sanatoria, in trousands	78.8	124.4	142.5	150.6	153.6
Number of tuberculosis specialists	3,867	9,402	13,200	16,461	17,350

* BME, 2nd ed., Vol. 30, Cols. 1101–2, Table 62.

The distribution of tuberculosis beds in the different republics and changes since 1940 are shown in Table 7–13. The number of beds for tuberculars had risen to 225,100 in 1963.[11] The major preventive measure is vaccination of children against tuberculosis. In 1961, it was reported that over 16.5 million Soviet children had been vaccinated, a number triple that of

1950 and twenty times that of 1940. As a result the 1961 morbidity (illness) rate for tuberculosis was claimed to be 47.2 per cent of the 1950 figure, and the mortality about one fifth of what it had been in 1950 (but no rates were given, a good indication of the still unsatisfactory status of the tuberculosis situation). Apparently, antituberculosis measures adopted were most effective among children. In 1960, a program was outlined for the liquidation of tuberculosis; this is to be accomplished primarily through an increase in the number of TB beds (to reach a total of 450,000 by 1966), the goal being to hospitalize all those with the disease until recovery.

Cancer. Just like cardiovascular diseases, the rate of cancer increases in a population in proportion with its life expectancy. There is a special network of anticancer institutions consisting (on January 1, 1962) of 19 institutes, 253 dispensaries, and 1,930 anticancer units in clinics and in hospitals. The development of anticancer facilities, and particularly of the number of beds for cancer patients, has been particularly rapid since the end of the Second World War. While there were only 1,700 such

Table 7–13—Beds for Tubercular Patients by Republic, USSR (1940–61)*

Republic	1940	BEDS 1960	1961
RSFSR	18,270	68,362	76,436
Ukraine	7,945	39,727	42,625
Belorussia	1,110	4,472	5,125
Uzbekistan	870	9,325	9,827
Kazakhstan	1,067	7,666	8,703
Georgia	286	2,288	2,438
Azerbaidzhan	382	2,292	3,042
Lithuania	1,277	2,526	2,617
Moldavia	220	2,755	3,353
Latvia	1,800	2,190	2,290
Kirghizia	—	1,942	2,401
Tadzhikstan	215	1,987	2,349
Armenia	181	920	895
Turkmenistan	220	1,281	1,468
Estonia	166	1,128	1,373
Total USSR	34,009	148,861	164,942

* BME, 2nd ed., Vol. 30, Cols. 1103–4, Table 63.

beds in 1940, the number rose to 12,224 in 1950, 26,381 in 1961, and 30,600 in 1963. The increase in such beds for the different republics between 1950 and 1961 is charted in Table 7–14. We

Table 7–14—Beds for Cancer Patients, by Republic, USSR (1950–61)*

Republic	1950	1960	1961
RSFSR	5,915	12,781	13,861
Ukraine	4,211	6,361	6,777
Belorussia	401	739	825
Uzbekistan	250	835	885
Kazakhstan	180	866	1,051
Georgia	149	375	410
Azerbaidzhan	264	365	440
Lithuania	178	315	326
Moldavia	95	270	270
Latvia	280	519	623
Kirghizia	—	197	272
Tadzhikstan	51	80	85
Armenia	55	120	145
Turkmenistan	35	203	226
Estonia	180	180	185
Total USSR	**12,244**	**24,206**	**26,381**

* BME, 2nd ed., Vol. 30, Cols. 1105–6, Table 66; 1963 figure from: *Narodnoe Khoziaistvo SSSR v 1963 Gadu,* p. 630.

have mentioned programs of mass examination to detect incipient disease. The Soviets report that in 1961, 38 million persons were examined; 39,000 were discovered to have a cancerous condition and 373,000 precancerous condition, or a rate of one person with cancer and ten with precancerous conditions for each 1000 examined. The usefulness of such an examination is that in many instances measures can be initiated to treat the patient, and these measures tend to be much more effective than those taken later, after the disease has been allowed to proceed unchecked. Apparently, the urban population is examined more frequently and systematically than the rural population.

Venereal Disease. Measures against skin and venereal diseases are also undertaken by specialized institutions. In 1961, there were 6,075 specialized centers for the treatment and prevention of these diseases (outpatient dispensaries, stations, divisions, or offices); in 1963, there were 33,600 beds, as well as 9,700 specialists in these matters.[12] Among the measures taken for the elimination of these diseases are the compulsory registration of patients, active search for sources of infection (and their treatment), investigation of all persons having had contacts with the patient, mass examinations of those groups of the population who might have become infected through nonsexual contacts, and active treatment until cure. Published figures indicate that rates of active syphilis decreased almost 17 times between 1950 and 1961 (from 24.7 cases per 100,000 of the population to 1.5), while acute gonorrhea decreased, in that same period, from 81.6 cases per 100,000 to 55.4.

Mental Illness. The main focus of the treatment of mental illness appears to be outpatient psychiatry rather than hospitalization, with an effort to maintain, insofar as possible, the patient in the community and working, even though at a reduced level. The model institution is the outpatient neuropsychiatric dispensary, of which there were 167 in 1961. In 1963, the number of hospital beds for psychiatric patients was 196,000 and the number of psychiatrists (including neuropathologists) was 21,400. It may be added in passing that whereas in the United States about one half of all hospital beds are for mental patients, in the Soviet Union the proportion is about one in nine or ten. This difference may not be due as much to the difference in amounts of mental illness in the two societies (as the Soviets claim) as to a shortage of beds and their utilization for other, more pressing conditions. The Soviets are planning to increase their supply of hospital beds for psychiatric cases until the rate of such beds per constant unit of population equals about half that of the United States. In the meanwhile, Soviet psychiatrists have gathered valuable experience in maintaining patients in the community and in developing workshops where ex-mental patients are trained for industrial work.[13]

Sanatoria and Houses of Rest. One must also consider, as a component of the Soviet medical system, the network of sanatoria, health resorts, and houses of rest, although in many instances these sanatoria appear to be indistinguishable from luxury hotels, and their medical functions seem to be quite peripheral. In 1961, there were about 330,000 beds in the 2,098 sanatoria and houses of rest under the supervision either of the labor unions, the republican health ministries, or other authorities.

The labor unions maintain and supervise sanatoria and houses of rest (roughly one third of all available beds) for their members, a certain proportion of whom receive passes either free of charge or partially covering costs, usually on medical indications, but sometimes as a reward for a good production record, regardless of health needs. Most sanatoria "owned" by the health ministries are for patients suffering from tuberculosis: 1,160 sanatoria with 150,422 beds, of these 742 sanatoria with 85,535 beds for children (1961).[14] These sanatoria are on the state budget and the treatment is paid entirely from state funds.

Services for the Rural Populations. We have mentioned at several points the rural population's special medical and health problems. For a variety of reasons, primarily political and economic but also geographical, the establishment of the network of medical institutions and services for the peasant population has lagged considerably behind that of those available to the urban population. The emphasis, for example, on industrialization and urbanization as areas of primary priority, and the general policy of extracting from the countryside a great part of the capital necessary for the development of the country, has led to a policy of underinvestment in the countryside and of exploitation of the peasantry. It would not be fair, however, to state that the situation in the countryside has remained completely stagnant. In 1913, there were 56,300 hospital beds in the countryside and 4,500 feldsher and midwife stations; by 1961, there were close to 700,000 beds and 82,182 feldsher, feldsher-midwife, and other health stations. The situation in the rural areas with respect to hospitals and beds in 1961 was as shown in Table 7–15.

In spite of substantial improvements over the pre-Revolutionary situation, many members of the rural population still receive at least their initial health and medical care and attention from medical personnel other than physicians. Thus the

Table 7-15—Hospital Beds, Rural Population, USSR, 1961*

Type of Hospital	Number of Hospitals	Number of Beds	Average Number of Beds
Regional	163	74,160	455
District	3,159	305,112	96.6
Specialized	218	11,565	53.1
Inpatient Units of Outpatient Clinics	307	10,090	32.5

* BME, 2nd ed., Vol. 30, Col. 1124, Table 83.

average number of visits to medical and semiprofessional personnel by the rural population for 1961 was 4.9 per capita, but of these, less than half (2.2) were to physicians. The others were to feldshers, midwives, and other semiprofessional personnel.

In recent years, as was noted earlier, there has been a trend against building small rural hospitals because they are unable to provide diversified and specialized medical services to patients. At the present time a campaign is on for collective farms to build larger facilities, and for several collective farms to establish larger hospitals (of 50 to 75 beds) to provide better care for their members. In addition, with more free time and better transportation, a greater proportion of the rural population is beginning to receive hospital attention in urban areas. Thus, statistics indicate, for a series of medical facilities in

7-16—Percentage of Admissions to Nonrural Medical Facilities That Were from Countryside, USSR (1950–61)*

Type of Facility	1950	1955	1960	1961
Regional Hospitals	33.9	44.1	49.4	49.0
Municipal Hospitals	8.9	12.5	12.1	12.7
Rural District Hospitals in Population Centers	40.3	51.2	51.5	50.7
Specialized Hospitals	12.2	13.2	13.8	14.0
Maternity Homes	8.0	12.7	12.0	11.4
Clinics of Medical Institutes	15.2	20.8	21.8	19.4
Inpatient Units of Scientific-Research Institutes	16.4	19.3	23.7	22.7
Inpatient Units of Outpatient Clinics	36.2	49.1	48.1	47.8

* BME, 2nd ed., Vol. 30, Col. 1125–26, Table 86.

urban areas, that the percentage of admissions from the villages is steadily increasing (see Table 7–16).

As a result of this use of urban medical facilities, Soviet health authorities indicate that the difference in, for example, the number of available hospital beds per constant units of the population between urban and rural population is constantly on the decrease and eventually will disappear, as shown in Table 7–17.

Table 7–17—Supply of Hospital Beds, Urban and Rural Populations, USSR (1950–61)* (including psychiatric beds)

| | NUMBER OF HOSPITAL BEDS PER 1,000 | |
	Urban Population	Rural Population
1950	8.9	3.2
1955	8.6	4.8
1960	9.5	6.7
1961	9.9	6.8

* BME, 2nd ed., Vol. 30, Cols. 1125–6, Table 87.

In spite of such undoubted progress (at least as expressed in statistical tables), the general impression remains that there is much to be done to improve the health services available to the hitherto somewhat neglected population in the countryside, and that the goal (defined on the basis of the ideology) of the elimination of all differences between the countryside and cities is still a long way off.

We have, in this chapter, examined the major dimensions of the clinical and health facilities and services available to the Soviet population, and have found that, compared with the situation before the Revolution, impressive quantitative progress has been made. The one major area that is still quite deficient is the countryside where, for a variety of reasons, health progress has not kept up with the advances made in the urban centers. There is ground to believe, however, that in the future the discrepancy between urban and rural services will slowly recede.

Chapter 8

Preventive Health Services

TO STATE THAT, in theory at least, the Soviet medical system is oriented toward prevention would be redundant. Prevention is considered the touchstone of the edifice of Soviet medicine, and most Soviet writers on the subject echo Pavlov's sentiment that preventive medicine (or hygiene, as he called it) is *the* medicine of the future. In the regime's early years Lenin himself complained that not enough attention was being paid to prevention when he declared: "Sanitation—this is all, this is the prevention of all diseases; we like very much to treat patients, we feel very sympathetic and pity those who are dying and (yet) we do very little to prevent illness and premature deaths."[1]

Before proceeding any further, it should be noted that in some instances the strict distinction between preventive and clinical services is difficult to make and that many, if not most, of the clinical services described in the previous chapter embody preventive elements. This is, of course, most true of the programs of mass examinations (particularly dispensarization), but it also applies to the daily work of medical personnel, particularly the microdistrict physician and especially the pediatrician. In addition, it must also be recognized that, in principle at least, a system of socialized medicine should promote prevention since the financial obstacles that interpose themselves between patient and physician are eliminated, permitting the individual to see a doctor at an early stage of illness, when medical intervention is often most effective. Because of the central importance attached to the official Soviet view of prevention, it will be necessary, in this chapter, to return briefly to certain theoretical and ideological considerations.

The basic ideological inspiration for the emphasis on prevention is found in the Marxist view that interprets illness as the result of defective social conditions, particularly (under conditions of capitalism) the shameless exploitation of the workers for the benefit of the owners of capital. This critique was perhaps most vividly stated in Engels' *Conditions of the Working Class in England,* in which he described the atrocious conditions under which the workers lived in the first half of the nineteenth century. Crowded in substandard slums, without an adequate water supply or waste disposal system and badly overworked and undernourished, the urban proletariat was an easy prey to disease and a candidate for early death. With the advent of the Revolution in 1917, still according to this theory, the elimination of private ownership of the means of production and of the exploitation of man by man was expected to usher in, in the area of health as in many others, a period of prosperity, well-being, and absence of disease. Just the opposite happened. Nevertheless, it is interesting to note that in the regime's early years the ideologically determined belief that a change in the social structure meant that disease was automatically on its way out led some physicians prematurely to predict the withering away of clinical medicine, as some had predicted the withering away of the state or the family. In practical terms, such an attitude implied that health authorities could relax, safe in the knowledge that only an improvement of the external milieu would have an impact on disease whereas actually it was precisely the massive measures taken to industrialize that were found to cause many conditions hazardous to health and limb, thus necessitating treatment facilities and personnel. The assumption of the withering away of clinic medicine, taken seriously in at least some circles influential in the Health Commissariat, led to an ideologically (though not realistically) determined tendency to neglect clinical medicine and therapy as such, and to concentrate efforts on prevention alone. Such a policy, given the regime's post-1928 program of forcible industrialization and urbanization, with its concomitant extreme crowding of people in urban centers without adequate municipal services, could only lead to a decrease in the health authorities' effectiveness in dealing with illness. The policy had to be drastically altered. Emphasis on prevention at the expense of clinical services received in due time the epithet "mechanism and menshevizing idealism," and the groups of physicians who held these ideas were dissolved. And, as Vinogradov informs us, "a devastating critique in *Pravda* of June 4, 1932 destroyed the 'theory' of the withering away of therapeutics and the transformation of therapists into organizations of 'socialist productive process.'"[2]

Nevertheless, and taking these adjustments into consideration, the official line remains that prevention is the central concern of the health authorities and that the "greatest advantage of socialist public health care over capitalistic (even where the latter is state controlled) is that the principle of prophylaxis is built into the social system itself, in socialistic economics."[3] Furthermore, the official view is that the Marxist-Leninist ideology permits the only "rational" approach to illness and its prevention because it is derived from "the scientific understanding of the mutual relationship of the organism and its environment, both of the recognition of the decisive importance of social conditions for the maintenance and the strengthening of health and for the limitations of the sources of disease."[4]

Since illness is, according to this view, the result of unfavorable social conditions, it stands to reason that under socialism of the Soviet type, illness should decrease and eventually disappear once full communism has been established. The distinction between socialism and communism helps, of course, to explain why there still is illness in a society from which, according to Soviet ideology, the exploitation of man by man has been eliminated. Soviet medical ideologists further declare that the *preconditions* for the elimination of illness already exist, and we have, at an earlier point, touched on these: The health service and prevention are functions of the government, and the organization of measures for prevention thus can be centrally directed from one headquarters; they can be planned and coordinated, and the financing can be assured by revenues from the state. In addition, special legislation can be promulgated to protect the public health and prevent the spread of illness.

SOME HISTORICAL CONSIDERATIONS

TO MAKE OUR presentation more meaningful, a few historical references are in order.

It was in industrializing and urbanizing Europe of the nineteenth century that the first stirrings of a systematic program of disease prevention, in the form of public health, hygiene, and sanitation measures, took place. These measures, at first often taken empirically, reflected, of course, the increasing concern of the authorities and the medical profession about the ravages that infectious diseases and epidemics wreaked upon the working population. While the English, whose country had been industrialized earliest, led the way in public health, similar progress was registered on the Continent, particularly in France and Germany. The situation, however, was quite different in tsarist Russia. Compared to the rest of Europe, Russia in the nineteenth century was a country largely in a state of suspended animation. Predominantly rural, with a small urban population and an autocratic regime, the government's concern for public welfare, medical services, and public health, as we have seen, was necessarily of a limited nature. It should be recognized, at the same time, that the degree of industrialization and consequent urbanization was so modest that they did not pose the same kinds of problems faced by the English workers in the British Midlands. On the other hand, the sorry state of the Russian peasantry and the almost complete absence of rural health services were a heavy human and economic liability. Responsibility for public health measures and prevention was divided among different authorities and administrations, thereby making a coordinated national program impossible. For every

ruble spent for medical services in those years, only 5 kopecks
went into public health and prevention. The First World War
and related events highlighted rather than attenuated the medical and public health unpreparedness of tsarist Russia.

DEVELOPMENT OF SOVIET PREVENTIVE SERVICES

THE SOVIET REGIME came to power against the background
of a deteriorating health situation, and the activities of the Soviet health authorities in the early years of the regime were oriented primarily toward stemming the tide of epidemics that
threatened to engulf the new regime. Efforts of the health
authorities (even before the formation of the Health Commissariat RSFSR) tended, at first, to be concentrated at the local
level. Public health-communicable diseases subdepartments were
formed in the public health departments of the executive committees of the soviets. When the Health Commissariat RSFSR
was formed in 1918, it included a public health-communicable
diseases section. There was, however, very little of a preventive
nature that the Health Commissariat could do, particularly between 1919 and 1922, when the epidemics raged and the resources of the new state were at their lowest point. With the
return of more normal economic and political conditions under
the New Economic Policy, the Commissariat began taking more
energetic steps in the direction of a preventive organization. A
decree of the Council of Peoples' Commissars, dated September
15, 1922, established a central organization for public health
and formally determined the rights as well as the obligations
of public health authorities. The New Economic Policy gave
way to the massive programs of industrialization launched in
1928. The transfer of large masses to the cities made the work
of the public health organs more difficult and important; the
new conditions of crowding and insufficient municipal services
threatened the health of the population.

The regime and the health authorities began to take more
active measures to insure preventive work by organizing, in

1933, a Public Health Inspectorate (*sanitarnaia inspektsia*) whose main purpose was to improve the state of public health and particularly to protect the population through a closer supervision both of the food-processing industry and public eating places. Later, public health inspectors were established in the republican health commissariats; these inspectors were given the rank of first deputy commissars of health. At the local level, inspectors were appointed in the health departments with broad powers to bring violators (whether enterprises, institutions, or individuals) to court for violation of health codes or regulations, as well as to impose fines or even to order the closing of enterprises for such violations. While these measures were intended to improve the situation, there is considerable indication that in many if not in most instances the inspectors were powerless to act, given the high priority accorded industrialization and the ways and means whereby industrial managers could evade if not the letter, at least the spirit of the regulations. For example, a manager might find it much easier and more convenient to pay fines than to undertake costly alterations that would eliminate the conditions for which the fine had been imposed. Dissatisfaction with the work of public health inspectors led, in 1935, to still another reorganization, which created an All-Union Public Health Inspectorate subordinate this time not to health commissariats but directly to the Council of Peoples' Commissars, with a Chief State Public Health Inspector who was given broader powers, appointed by the council and reporting directly to it. The inspector also had the right to propose new legislative measures to the council. Later on, however, the inspectorate was reincorporated into the structure of the Health Commissariat. Before the Second World War,

> Soviet health protection had a ramified State Public Health Inspectorate with centralized direction, embracing all aspects of preventive and particularly of the current health surveillance, managing the public health antiepidemic activities of all medical institutions, combining controlling and organizing functions and leaning on the self-generated activities of the population.[5]

From the evidence available, the organs of public health were equal to the tasks that confronted them during the war, at the front and at the rear; at least there are no indications that there were widespread epidemics of the type that accompanied the First World War and the postwar period, or if there were, they were kept in check and did not threaten the population as had been the case previously. After 1945 activities of the public health organs were expanded, to maintain constant surveillance over possible foci of disease and to take measures against epidemics. Yet, amazingly enough, given the nature of Soviet health administrative philosophy and its condemnation of the uncoordinated nature of public health efforts before the Revolution, public health and prevention often were hindered precisely by a lack of coordination and integration. The proliferation of institutions, laboratories, persons, and units working either independently of each other or in ignorance of each other, resulted in waste, confusion, and needless duplication of efforts in some cases and often inaction in others. Until 1948, alongside Public Health Communicable Diseases Stations there were public health laboratories, stations, squads, and other institutions, each having different standards and autonomy in their functions, a situation that hindered effective and coordinated work in this area. This was remedied by making the stations the basic preventive and coordinating agencies at all levels, and by incorporating into them other preventive organizations and institutions.

THE FORMAL ORGANIZATION OF PREVENTIVE SERVICES

AT THE PRESENT TIME the protection of the public health and the prevention of epidemics as well as related activities are the province of the public health organs of the Ministry of Health USSR, and the First Deputy Health Minister always holds the position of chief inspector. There are three broad areas that the public health organization of the Ministry deals with: (1) public health (environmental conditions—industrial health, school hygiene, food handling, water supply, waste disposal, and so on); (2) epidemics—measures to control, prevent, and eliminate epidemic diseases; and (3) dangerous infectious diseases. A similarly structured organization exists within the republican health ministries. The chief instrumentality is the so-called Public Health (Sanitary) Communicable Diseases Station or SES (*Sanitarno-epidemiologicheskaia stantsiia*), an institution serving as headquarters for all preventive activities in its designated area. Such stations are found at the republican, regional, municipal, and district (rural) levels, and are headed by chief public health inspectors. Included in the make-up of the SES are various public health, bacteriological, and antiepidemic institutions, as well as laboratories, bureaus, antimalarial and antitularemial stations, and other related organizations and personnel. As such, the SES is said to be a diversified and multifaceted public health center, in charge of measures to protect and improve the population's living, working, and recreational conditions, to carry out measures against communicable diseases, and to effect constant surveillance of conditions presenting health problems. Since 1940, the number of such stations has more than doubled, from 1,943 to 4,832 in 1961.[6] While in the cities the station is an independent entity with its own budget, in the countryside the station has become a division of the district hospital which has, it will be remembered, supplanted the rural district health department. This is an attempt, at least at that level, to coordinate and unify clinical treatment, public health, and preventive measures. The number of physicians employed in public health work has increased from over 12,000 in 1940 to almost 34,200 in 1963.[7] The size and the functions of the stations depend on the territory they serve and the particular health problems in that territory. The Moscow City (Sanitary) Public Health-Communicable Diseases Station (presumably a model and large institution) has the following departments:

1. Department of General and Municipal Hygiene and Sanitation
2. Department of Industrial Hygiene and Sanitation
3. Department of Hygiene and Nutrition and Food Sanitation

4. Department of Hygiene of Children and Adolescents and of School Sanitation
5. Department of Communicable Diseases and Microbiology
6. Department of Parasitology
7. General Laboratories
8. Organizational-Methodological Department
9. Administrative-Economic Department

In smaller localities, the station is correspondingly smaller, and its structure is simpler, but its functions are essentially the same: to watch over the conditions that might cause illness and to stop the spread of communicable diseases. Administratively, the station and the organs of public health in general have a dual subordination. They are subordinate both to their immediately superior public health organ in the hierarchy of such organs *and* to the health ministry or department to which they are attached. Presumably, the first provides the *modus operandi*, and the latter the general mandate as well as financial and logistic support.

Physicians who are staff members of the stations also have the status, rights, and privileges of public health inspectors (that is, they can impose fines or take violators to court), and their directives and decisions are, in theory, mandatory and can only be repealed by their superiors in the inspectorate. This virtual independence of the public health officer helps to preserve his freedom of action and (in theory, again) ensures that public health measures are instituted without interference. In practice this is not, by far, always the case. In addition, decisions of inspectors may be repealed by the USSR Council of Ministers or the republican councils of ministers.[8] Head physicians of stations are simultaneously state inspectors of the area serviced by the station.

In the last few years most efforts of the public health organs have been directed at improving urban living conditions, an area that had been neglected and had deteriorated as a result of the influx of people into areas that did not have appropriate municipal services (running water, piped gas, sewerage, waste disposal, air purification, town planning, and so on).

Communicable diseases control work involves not only the elimination of existing epidemic diseases, but also the prevention of such diseases and the limitation of their spread. Vaccinations and other injections are said to be widely used. Soviet health authorities report, for example, a 72.6 per cent decrease of poliomyelitis from 1959 to 1961, which they attribute to the use of a live-virus antipolio vaccine given in 1960 and 1961 to about 78 million persons (slightly more than one third of the total population).

In spite of the elaborate nature of the system of preventive measures, there is ample evidence that while progress has been impressive, a great deal remains to be done. Thus, in 1960, the government and the party indicated that the tasks of the health organs should be, in the near future, to eliminate such diseases as diptheria, tularemia, poliomyelitis, and syphilis, as well as diseases of a more local significance (malaria, trachoma, and so on), and to reduce sharply the amount of certain other infectious diseases. Articles, speeches, and resolutions on the subject are apt to emphasize again that all of the "preconditions" for the elimination of many such diseases exist in the Soviet Union at the present time, but that the authorities are not making proper use of these possibilities. Minister of Health Kurashov (who died in 1965) noted in 1960, for example, that the health authorities must in the next three years conduct a broader attack on infectious diseases to completely eradicate some and greatly reduce others. He pointed out there was hope for a complete elimination of trachoma, but that the struggle against intestinal diseases was not satisfactory. To do this, he added,

> . . . the organs of health protection need the daily assistance of the local soviets and, in the first place, the organs of municipal economy which must in the shortest order put in order the water supply, sewage, and the cleaning up of areas in cities and regions that have a high illness rate.

In addition Kurashov indicated the geographical regions where corrective measures were most needed: Central Asia, the Northern Caucasus, and the lower Volga.[9] For example, the Health Minister of the Armenian Republic complained, in 1960, that they had been unable to achieve a significant decrease in intestinal infections because of poor public health work, the unsatisfactory conditions of public places, and deficiencies in the water and sewage systems and in the cleanliness of public buildings.[10]

A problem, which comes up frequently, is the lack of *effective* control by the public health organs over conditions that might be prejudicial to public health. For example, in the construction of new plants whose operations affect the atmosphere, the water supply, and the soil, very often a compromise—that is, half measures—are agreed upon by the public health and industrial authorities. In the same way, health standards and regulations are simply by-passed or ignored by these in charge of building apartment houses. They then face the public health organs with a *fait accompli*. For example, the Health Minister of the Estonian Republic complained in 1960:

> In the last few years, the public health service has not dictated norms to the *Gosstroi* (State Trust in Charge of Construction), but on the contrary, the construction of one-room apartments with the entrance into the gas equipped kitchen through the living room was decided by *Gosstroi*. Such planning is not compatible with public health requirements. And yet we acquiesced to it.[11]

A few words, finally, should be said about the prevention of industrial accidents. Dr. Ekk, in an article published in Russia toward the end of the nineteenth century had stated that "except for accidental deaths," man could live up to one hundred. Whether this is true or not, the fact remains that accidents are an important cause of mortality and crippling injuries and invalidity. This is a particularly important problem in the industrial society, with its widespread use of heavy and powerful machinery. It may be presumed that, in the early phases of industrialization and specifically of Soviet industrialization, concentration on the rapid accumulation of manpower drawn from the countryside made the application of industrial safety measures difficult insofar as they would slow down construction and add costs the planners were not willing to bear. The situation may be improved today, particularly because capital has become much cheaper than human beings, although the Soviet medical press reports cases after case where objections of physicians and other health personnel to health and safety hazards were overruled or simply ignored by industrial and state organizations. In theory, of course, the health authorities must pass on every construction project, new building, addition to existing productive installation, ventilation system, and so on that might affect the health of workers and population. But, given the complicated bureaucratic nature of the Soviet state, and given the priority of industrial tasks over all others, things rarely work out as planned.

Preventive Services and the Clinic. In addition to the formal organization of preventive services, Soviet public health theory insists that preventive work also be the function of medical personnel in clinical practice, and particularly the therapists who are in charge of the microdistrict population and the pediatrician who takes care of the children. It is thus part of their mandate to be responsible for the general health level of their area and to take measures that will prevent illness from arising or from spreading. Indeed, as we have seen, the ideal often proclaimed after the Revolution was that there would be no difference between treatment and prevention, though it appears that in actual practice the physicians are so overburdened with the task of providing clinical services that they have little time and energy (except in the most formal manner) to give to prevention, and they feel that this task belongs exclusively to those working in the SES stations. Dr. T. F. Fox, the editor of *Lancet*, after a visit to the USSR in 1954, concluded that despite well-meaning statements and slogans most efforts of Soviet medicine and medical personnel were directed toward the treatment of illness rather than its prevention.[12]

At the same time it must be recognized that clinical medicine is more glamorous, dramatic, and perhaps interesting than preventive medicine. The former often presents emotionally charged crises, problems to be solved, daring operations to be performed. Preventive medicine consists of routine efforts intended to prevent crises and, by comparison, suffers. As one article in *Soviet Estonia* put it:

> Physicians pay more attention to new methods of treatment than to measures to prevent diseases. The population is more interested in the therapeutic action of novocain than in the preventive characteristics of morning calisthenics.[13]

As the infectious diseases gradually recede under the impact of preventive measures (whether these be vaccinations, the purification of the water supply, draining of marshes and swamps, or the use of antibiotics), and people are saved from early death as the result of the efforts of preventive medicine, they become candidates for other illnesses, often called the degenerative diseases. In the United States, for example, heart disease and cancer are the leading causes of death, not so much because the incidence of cancer and heart disease has increased per se, but rather because people live longer and become prey to these conditions. The task of preventive medicine becomes more complicated as a result of this phenomenon, and ideally, a medical checkup at regular intervals for the entire population would permit a reduction of morbidity and mortality. The Soviets are attempting to deal with this problem through the dispensarization system discussed in Chapter 7. Implementation of a true program of preventive examination covering the entire population would require a much higher ratio of doctors to population than presently exists in the Soviet Union. Health Minister Kurashov said in 1961 that implementation of the Program for the Building of Communism endorsed by the Twenty-second Party Congress would require, in the area of health, twice as many physicians as the 400,000 then available in the Soviet Union.[14]

VOLUNTARY AND EDUCATION WORK IN PREVENTION

WE ALREADY HAVE mentioned the importance Soviet health authorities attribute to the participation of the "people" in the enacting, enforcing, and carrying out of measures to prevent ill-ness and promote health. It is probably in the area of prevention that popular participation is most significant, since it can be assumed that many steps taken to prevent illness require less technical knowledge and professional skill than the clinical treatment of such illnesses. Over the years, attempts to involve the public in health measures have varied as the health author-ities have sought better and more effective ways to utilize their services in support of health activities. Volunteers can perform such tasks as cleaning up yards, visiting dwellings, helping bed-ridden patients, reporting violations of health regulations, and the like. They also can be used to instruct the population, for example, not to call physicians needlessly, because such calls decrease the amount of time the doctor has for patients who really need medical assistance.[15] At the present time, one form of such activity is the "Council of Cooperation" formed in hos-pitals, outpatient clinics, and other medical institutions. The membership of the council consists of professional personnel from the medical facility, representatives of the labor unions, and representatives of the population serviced by that facility. In addition, the Red Cross and Red Crescent Societies, which number many millions of members, cooperate with the Health Ministry and health organs, teach first aid, and help in the pre-vention of disease.

One of the serious obstacles to a system of illness prevention is general ignorance in matters of health as well as personal hygiene. This was certainly one of the factors in the disastrous situation before the Revolution and particularly during the First World War, and the Soviet regime and health authorities felt impelled, soon after they had seized power, to embark upon a massive program of health education and propaganda.

The Soviet regime, Lenin once had said, rests on a balance of persuasion and coercion. In the area of prevention the work of persuasion is called "public health enlightenment." The func-tion of this enlightenment and education is to change the habits and to introduce new health practices in line with contemporary knowledge in preventive medicine. In 1918, a Department of Public Health Education was established within the Commissariat of Health, and corresponding subsections of health education were created in provincial and railroad health departments; exhibits on these matters began to be shown in specially designated Houses of Health Education. At the present time, health education is directed primarily from the Moscow Institute of Health Education through Houses of Health Education (of which there were 348 in 1961), the use of posters, the preparation of materials, and the carrying of special campaigns on certain health problems.[16] It may be interesting to note, at the same time, that there continues to flourish in the Soviet Union, as in most Western countries, a certain amount of quackery and charlatanry, particularly in the rural districts, which exists alongside "rational" medicine. By this we mean a range of popularly held superstitions, beliefs, and practices about health that are exploited by quacks who prey on such gullibility. This, of course, is particularly true of the conditions against which medical science is still powerless. The Soviet Union has its share of individuals, for example, who claim they have a cure for cancer. A few years ago, the Central Committee of the Communist Party felt compelled to publish a long letter in which it disqualified itself as an expert in the matter of a cancer cure (which means that representations had been made to the party) and refused to intervene either with the Academy of Medical Sciences or the Ministry of Health, which had declared the method worthless.[17]

Every physician, as part of his professional and social duties, is expected to devote some time to public health education, either by giving lectures, organizing evenings of questions and answers on health, writing articles for the local press, or giving talks on the radio or television. The press is also used to disseminate information about health. A magazine called *Health* had a circulation of about 800,000 in 1961; similar magazines have begun publication in some of the republics. Some local newspapers regularly print articles and special inserts of questions on health and its protection. Special courses given by so-called "Universities of Health" are aimed at increasing the population's competence in these matters.

Recently, the name of the official organ of the Health Ministry USSR has been changed from '*The Medical Worker*' (*Meditsinksii Rabotnik*) to '*The Medical Gazette*' (*Meditsinskaia Gazeta*), in line with a change of editorial policy toward broadening of the readership. The aim is to reach not only professionals but also semiprofessionals and other individuals who have some responsibility for the care of the sick, to give information of a nonspecialized nature regarding the treatment, and particularly the diet, of patients with various disabilities. As the editorial comment on the change of name stated:

> . . . the broad public hygiene and social problems of the protection of health will be more extensively treated on the pages of the paper. Labor and health are inseparable. We must more actively invade the various areas of economics, labor and life, where prevention determines the outcome of the struggle for the health of man. . . . The circle of our authors will now include not only medical scholars, doctors, nurses and feldshers, but also midwives, public health and pharmaceutical workers. The pages of the paper will reflect this broad circle—workers in Party, soviet and trade union organizations, workers in *Gosplan*, the economic councils, medical industries, trade, public catering and domestic services, district militiamen, architects, engineers, scientists, construction workers. . . .[18]

As the nature of the health and medical problems change, so does the nature and content of public health education. In recent years particular attention has been concentrated on such areas as the prevention of cardiovascular diseases, cancer and infectious illnesses, the protection of children's health, and the promotion of healthy working, living, and recreational conditions.

We have, in this chapter, reviewed the main aspects of the preventive efforts of the Soviet health system. We have examined some of the ideological tenets of prevention, the development of preventive services, and the present organizational structure of these services, and we have briefly reviewed efforts in the health education of the population which have a preventive character.

Chapter 9

Medical Research

MEDICAL RESEARCH AND IDEOLOGY

ANY SCIENCE worthy of the name, and a profession and the professional practices based on that science and its applications, cannot remain static. Their dynamism is, to a certain extent, imparted by the search for new knowledge, the discovery of hitherto unknown regularities, relationships, and laws, and the improvement of practices. In this respect, medicine, which is to a very great extent the application of scientific knowledge to problems of disease and injuries, is not very different from other scientific fields. As such, medical research, wherever a "rational" medical system exists, is very much part of the "medical enterprise." In essence, the nature and the role of Soviet medical research are not different from what they are in other societies: a constant inquiry carried out by qualified personnel, and financed or suported by special allocations, since research is a costly activity and the researcher is part of the division of labor.

And yet, given the nature of Soviet society and values, and the special place that science occupies in that society and the ideology on which it rests, medical (as well as other scientific) research bears some Soviet characteristics that deserve attention.

In most official statements, for example, a relationship is established between science and Marxism. Thus, former Health Minister Kovrigina had this to say on the subject of medical research in 1957:

> Like all other branches of knowledge, medical science is developing in our country on the basis of dialectical materialism and the Marxist-Leninist conception of the world. The strength of our scientific medicine lies in its close bond with practice and life.[1]

Such a statement can be meaningfully interpreted in the light of our knowledge of the importance of the fundamental ethos of Soviet society, its basic philosophy and *Weltanschauung* that derive from the Marxist ethic and philosophy. According to that philosophy, there is (or there should be) no knowledge only for the sake of knowledge; to learn about nature is to act upon nature. It is only in a class society, according to the Marxist analysis, with one class exploiting the other, that a distinction arises between intellectual work (carried on by the oppressing class) and manual work (done by the exploited class). This distinction makes it possible for many intellectuals to lead a "parasitical life at the expense of the toilers," and to engage in "pure" science, as an intellectual pastime and diversion, rather than in an attempt to solve "real" problems. Therefore, there are two characteristics of Soviet science: one is the stated disappearance of the distinction between theory and practice, and the other is the planning of scientific activities at the national level. While this approach to science and to research does not reject theory as such (indeed, Soviet science must present its findings in such a way that they will harmonize with Marxist theory), theory and practice must be in essence utilitarian—that is, they must not be divorced from the needs of society, and scientists must contribute to the solution of the problems faced by society rather than involve themselves in research that, while intellectually satisfying to them, is sterile from the point of view of the practical needs of the moment. As academician Vinogradov wrote: "Generous is the aid and concern of our government for the development of medical science. The duty of honor and conscience of the Soviet scholar is to swiftly embody in the practice of public health all that which is gained in the scientific institutions, in the clinics, and not to be content with this but to move forward to ever higher goals.[2]

From the propaganda viewpoint, the regime likes to indulge in comparisons both with the tsarist period and contemporary capitalistic countries. Under tsarism, the Soviets claim, the state with its "bourgeois class organization of health protection was not interested in the wide application in practice of the successes of medical science. In the USSR the same science is placed at the service of the toilers."[3] The same kind of criticism is applied to capitalistic countries. There, we are told, in many scientific research institutes the work very often is quite "removed from questions of the protection of the health of the large masses of the population and serves the aims of oppression and the strengthening of the exploitation of the toilers."[4] By contrast, Soviet medical and scientific research may be characterized as

> . . . permeated with a spirit of humanism, directed at the prevention of illnesses, at their maximal decrease, at the strengthening of the health of the population, lengthening of its life (expectancy) and an increase in its work capacity. In their work, the scientific-research institutes of the USSR are directed by Marxist-Leninist methodology, in contrast with the institutes of the capitalistic countries which carry out a bourgeois ideology and advance theories inimical to Marxism-Leninism, including some of a mankind-hating character.[5]

This stress on practicality tends to affect the regime's approach to the organization and the financing of medical science and research: The activities of physicians and other scientists engaged in medical research should be oriented to the tasks that are of the greatest concern to the regime. If, furthermore, the problems the regime faces in the area of health can be identified, then an understanding of the nature of Soviet medical research and its general direction will emerge. Insofar as one of the regime's main goals lies in industrialization (and in production in general), the aim of medical research must be, first and foremost, to reduce, minimize, mitigate, and neutralize the impact of illness (and injuries) upon the working or productivity potential of the population, particularly industrial workers. This is, as we have seen, to an important degree the task of the clinical and preventive organizations of Soviet health services. And yet, to the degree that insufficient or inadequate knowledge about the etiology, course, and treatment of pathological conditions hinder the health authorities, then it is up to medical science to fill in the gaps.

The stress on the importance of the practical aspects of research and science is particularly significant in such a field as medicine, given the strategic significance of health and working capacity. Improvement in medical care means not only lives saved, but a prolongation of life expectancy, a reduction in suffering, a decrease of incapacity and disability, and important economic savings. At the same time, it should be noted that of all types of research, medical research is probably one of the least "classified" ones, so that it is possible, at least in many areas, for physicians in clinical practice to utilize results of scientific medical research achieved elsewhere. Western visitors to the Soviet Union have usually noted the familiarity of Soviet scientists with the foreign literature and achievements in their fields. There is, for example, an institute in Moscow, employing a large staff, whose task is to translate and disseminate the results of foreign scientific research.

Historical Development. The first medical research institutes appeared in Russia toward the end of the nineteenth century. While the first is said to have been the Bacteriological Institute of the Kharkov Medical Society, which was founded in 1887, Mechnikov, in 1886, had organized a public bacteriological station which later served as the base for the Odessa Scientific Research Institute of Epidemiology and Bacteriology named after him. One of the most important and famous research institutes of pre-Revolutionary Russia was the Institute of Experimental Medicine (1890) in St. Petersburg, where Pavlov did a great deal of his work. In 1895, the Moscow Bacteriological Institute, based originally at the New Catherine Hospital, was established. In addition, bacteriological laboratories and stations were established in some of the larger cities of the Russian Empire.

The first medical research institutes established after the Revolution reflected, of course, the health authorities' fundamental preoccupation with the problem of epidemics—for example, the Saratov Institute of Microbiology and Epidemiology in the Struggle against the Plague (1918), the Institute of Experimental Medicine and Control of Sera and Vaccines (1919), the Central Smallpox Institute (Moscow, 1920), and others. Gradually, institutes concerned with theoretical questions of medicine, nutrition, and professional diseases were founded. In 1932, there was established, on the base of the pre-Revolutionary Institute of Experimental Medicine, a coordinating center for medical and biological research called the All-Union Institute of Experimental Medicine (VIEM). This institute was destined to become the nucleus of the Academy of Medical Sciences USSR, which was founded in 1944.

MEDICAL RESEARCH INSTITUTIONS

IN 1960, there were 273 medical research institutions (in addition to medical schools and institutes for the postgraduate education of physicians) employing more than 33,650 scientists.[6] Just like the medical system itself, medical research not only is planned, but also tends to be centralized, directed, and carried out at several distinct hierarchical levels. This permits the application of the principle of pragmatic research and, in theory, prohibits the dissipation of efforts and personnel on problems that, from the viewpoint of the regime, have no practical and immediate significance. It must, however, be recognized that there *is* a fair amount of dissipation of effort—much more, indeed, than would be apparent from the blueprint alone, perhaps because of the bureaucratic nature of research support.

At the present time, scientific research institutes can be grouped into five distinct levels, depending on the nature, national significance, and importance of the work they are doing. In this definite hierarchy of research institutes, the more prestigious ones are involved in general theoretical and basic problems, the less prestigious in more mundane matters (such as specific illnesses), and others in the application of research to medical problems.

While in the realm of medicine and health protection the most important research is that done by the institutes affiliated with or subordinate to the Academy of Medical Sciences, some research of medical and theoretical significance is carried out in institutes associated with the Academy of Sciences USSR (not to be confused with the Academy of Medical Sciences). These institutes constitute, therefore, the first and highest level of medical research. They are concerned with theoretical problems and basic research in medicine and in biology. In addition to the institutes that are part of the structure of the Academy of Sciences, there are a few "central" research institutes placed directly under the jurisdiction of the Health Ministry USSR, in which concrete and practical problems of clinical significance and of national importance are investigated, such as diseases of the eyes, ears and throat, mental illness, plastic surgery, and the like. These also belong to that first level.

The second rung of institutes consists of those placed under the supervision of and financed by the Health Ministry USSR, primarily through the Academy of *Medical* Sciences, which could also well be called the specific research arm of the Health Ministry. Since this Academy plays a fairly critical role in medical research, we will examine its origins and functions as soon as we complete the enumeration of the levels of research.

The third levels consists of research institutes maintained by the republican health ministries (they are the most numerous), whose field of interest is more limited. They, for example, might study certain disease conditions peculiar to the area for which the health ministries are responsible; or they might investigate such problems as malaria and dysentery. These institutes are closely tied to their supporting ministries and to the specific departments and tasks of these ministries (for example, medical-preventive assistance to the urban population, public health and antiepidemic services, assistance to mothers and children). The institutes receive assignments and problems from the republican ministries and attempt to solve them. Some of these institutes are also "head" institutes and supervise and assist the work of lower level institutes of the same specialties and the corresponding departments of the medical institutes (schools) of the republic.

The fourth level consists of the regional, provincial, and municipal research institutes which, in addition to research, are also concerned with the organization of health services and raising qualifications of medical personnel in their area. The result of the work of these more local institutes may, of course, then be applied to other areas as well as the entire country. This, for example, is true of the work of the Moscow Institute of Emergency Care named after N. V. Sklifasovskii, which has done pioneer work in the use of cadaver blood for transfusion.

Finally, the fifth level consists of institutes that are under nonmedical auspices but still carry out work of some medical significance. Some, for example, are under the supervision of the Ministry of Social Welfare RSFSR, such as the Central Institute for Prosthesis and Prosthetic Appliances. Others, under the aegis of the Ministry of Higher Education, are concerned with such problems as physical education and sports.

THE ACADEMY OF MEDICAL SCIENCES

BY COMPARISON with the Academy of Sciences, which dates back to the eighteenth century, the Academy of Medical Sciences is a relatively new institution, established toward the end of World War II in 1944 by decree of the Council of Peoples' Commissars. The base for the Academy was, as we have seen, the All-Union Institute of Experimental Medicine. One of the important reasons for the foundation of the Academy was presumably the unsatisfactory nature of medical research in the Soviet Union and the deficiencies that were uncovered as a result of the war, deficiencies that to some extent were the result of the regime-imposed isolation of Soviet medicine from world trends and of medical-scientific personnel from foreign colleagues. As pointed out in a recent monograph on the subject, the major problems were in the areas of medical technology, surgical instruments, and drugs. There is reason to believe that contacts with and help from Western physicians and medical authorities during the war drew attention to the relative backwardness of Soviet medicine, medical technology and research.[7]

According to its constitution, the Academy of Medical Sciences is "the highest scientific institution in the field of medicine in the USSR, organizing the most outstanding scientists in the country." Until Stalin's death, the Academy was subordinate to the Health Ministry and functioned strictly as a research department of the Ministry. Since then the Academy has gradually emancipated itself from the tutelage of the Ministry and functions more or less autonomously.

The fundamental purpose of the Academy, as stated in its constitution, is to solve questions in the theory and practice of medicine, to contribute to the continued growth of medical sciences in conformity with the needs of public health, to solve problems of medical hygiene, to make provisions for the defense of the country, and to carry out the assignments of the Ministry of Health and higher governmental agencies. The planning of medical research is usually on a "priority" basis, determined by the severity of the different problem areas to be attacked and to be resolved. For example, I. V. Davydovskii outlined in 1957, in an ascending order, what he felt were the important and priority problems faced by the Soviet Union, and to which the Academy of Medical Sciences should pay attention:

1. The lowest priority order belongs to those diseases that have already disappeared or will do so in the near future. They do little harm and no longer constitute an item of governmental concern: plague, cholera, smallpox and typhus.
2. The second consists of the diseases in which the outlook is optimistic. This includes such conditions as whooping cough,

diptheria, poliomyelitis and brucellulosis. Malaria, although it
is practically eradicated, and tuberculosis can also be included
in that category.
3. The next level is that of diseases that are not only clearly
   resistant, but may even be increasing. In particular geriatric
   problems, as well as grippe (flu), angina, rheumatism; all
   streptococcicosis, staphylococcicosis and pneumococcicosis infections belong in this category, as well as cancer and cardiovascular diseases.
4. And finally, radiation illnesses which, though not very important at the present, are likely to become so in the future.[8]

There is little doubt that in Soviet medical research the Academy of Medical Sciences is the directing and "tone-giving"
institution, even to those institutes and other research organizations that are not directly subordinate to it.

As the central agency for medical research, the Academy
has as one of its important functions the maintenance of liaison
and communications with Soviet and foreign research institutions in order to keep abreast of developments, coordinate,
standardize, and avoid duplication. Within the Soviet Union
this means contacts with the Academy of Sciences of the USSR,
the academies of sciences of the republics, and scientific institutes and societies. The Academy of Medical Sciences is also
the main channel for the establishment of liaison with foreign
scientists and scientific institutions. In certain specific and important instances the Academy will join with another scientific
institution for the investigation and discussion of major theoretical and practical problems. One of the more famous of these
was the Joint Session of the Academies of Sciences and Medical
Sciences in 1950, whose task was to place the teachings of
Pavlov at the center of medical, physiological, and biological
research, a sort of enshrinement not unlike that of Lysenko
carried out earlier by the Academy of Agricultural Sciences.

Finally, many of the institutes of the Academy are also
called "head institutes" in the sense that, in addition to working
in their assigned fields, they also direct, coordinate, and supervise the work of subordinate republican institutes working in

the same area, helping them to set up plans for research, providing them with advice, consultation and information.

MEDICAL RESEARCH AND NATIONALISM

FROM AN EXAMINATION of the main characteristics of Soviet medical research the following emerges. Medical research, and the amount of attention, personnel, and resources devoted to it, do not appear to be items of primary priority, given the emphasis on industrialization, production, and science. The results of Soviet medical research have been singularly unimpressive; not one scientist of Pavlov's stature has emerged, nor has any Nobel prize in medicine or physiology been awarded to a Soviet scientist since 1917. It may well be that in the early phases of a massive industrializing drive the best brains and talents are attracted by the sciences and technology rather than by medicine. There are, however, certain other factors that may account for this rather poor showing. One is the general disruption of higher training and medical education that followed the Revolution and which lasted several years and was complicated, of course, by poor economic conditions and the general disruptions accompanying the implementation of the Five-Year Plans and the collectivization of agriculture. It may be surmised that, under these circumstances, a generation of medical scientists received poor training which is reflected in their performance today. In addition, isolation from the West has kept Soviet medicine and medical scientists somewhat outside of the channels of world medical developments and contributed to the isolation and parochialism of much of Soviet medicine. For it is not enough to have access to the literature. It is important for scientists to meet, visit each other, and work side by side in laboratories and clinics. A small window to the West was opened during the Second World War, but was immediately shut tightly by Stalin after the end of hostilities. Between 1945 and 1953, the isolation was almost complete, and the medical scientist who cited Western studies would often be accused of kowtowing to the West and denying the priority and superiority of Russian and Soviet medical science. A quick glance at the Soviet medical literature between, say 1947 and 1954, will reveal the officially imposed obsession of Soviet medical scientists with the questions of priorities of Russian science, and since 1950, the enshrinement of Pavlov as the godhead of Soviet medicine, which as some Soviet scientists acknowledge today, hindered not only medical research but also clinical medicine.[9] The priority campaign aimed, it will be remembered, at proving that every invention that had benefited mankind was a product of Russian genius and had been stolen by the West and mendaciously claimed by its savants. This was extended to the field of medicine, where busybodies occupied themselves for years in glorifying "national" or "patriotic" science and villifying Western scientists or Soviet scientists who had anything favorable to say about Western scientific advances.

In its extremes of narrow-minded chauvinism the priority campaign went as far as to rename surgical interventions after the Russians who supposedly had originated them or in some cases only "proposed" them. This campaign, as repugnant as it must have seemed to genuine scientists, undoubtedly did a great deal of harm to medical research. The insistence that all of medical research and practice conform to Marxist tenets and Pavlovian theories only created a restricted and narrow framework within which orthodoxy, but not genuine science, could flourish. It should be noted, however, that even under those conditions genuine scientists learned to live with the regime, and that ritual obeisance, at the beginning and the end of a book, to Marxist theorists (including Stalin) and Pavlov was sometimes enough to get the book past the censorship. In other instances the campaign had more tragic results, particularly when the positions of certain scientists were coveted by less qualified but ideologically correct scientists, or pseudoscientists. But, in general, medicine (even with such a person as Lepeshinskaia with her theory of the nonorganic origins of organic cells) did not suffer as much as genetics under Lysenko. At the present time, the damages caused by the Stalin period are being repaired, but not all traces of dogmatism have been removed. While we no longer find statements to the effect that "Stalin's brilliant ideas have been and forever will remain the basic principles of medical scientific activities in our country,"[10] one can still find traces of the old obsession with the "priority of Russian Soviet science." Thus, as late as 1960, an article in *Meditsinskii Rabotnik* complained that an operation proposed by a Soviet physician in 1928 in a dissertation had been buried in some institute, as a result of which the "priority was ascribed to the American surgeon, Dr. Femister in the foreign literature."[11] In psychiatry, to cite but one example, the blanket condemnation of Freudian psychology has removed a whole range of problems from effective investigation.

MEDICAL RESEARCH—A BUREAUCRACY

A SECOND important aspect of medical research is its bureaucratization. Bureaucratization allows, of course, for the degree of centralization, dictation, and control desired by the regime to ensure that its investments in research are the most productive and are directed to the most important problems of medicine *as the regime sees them*. Ideally, and in theory, this would allow for the existence of an extremely efficient system: The regime would identify the problems that concern it most (industrial absenteeism, for example, caused by upper respiratory diseases); it would then direct its research arm (or arms)—from the Academy of Sciences to the Academy of Medical Sciences and down the line—to concentrate their efforts on finding ways and means to reduce absenteeism caused by these conditions. Actually, the situation is quite different. There is a great deal of paperwork and many decisions and resolutions, but often the work does not get done. Bureaucratic infighting may reduce the effectiveness of the research enterprise; and very often, creative scientists do not put their best foot forward when they are forced, so to speak, to work on a problem. Frequently, official pronouncements are apt to emphasize that it is the duty of medical scientists to work for their country and to solve the most important problems that affect the welfare of their country, rather than to investigate subjects which are of great interest to them but relatively unimportant or irrelevant to the nation's health. Sometimes topics or themes are assigned to medical scientists and clinicians without prior consultation or the consent of the researchers, or without taking their experience into account.[12] Those who have made the assignment can then report to superior officials that the research is being done. "Bureaucratically" the task has been done; in fact, very little has been accomplished.

A complaint that frequently crops up in the literature is that the general level of instrumentation, its repair and maintenance, is so low that it often hinders scientific and investigative work.[13] Expensive equipment purchased from abroad is frequently left unused because no one knows how to operate it. Finally, researchers sometimes are saddled with heavy teaching schedules and cannot pursue their research effectively. This appears to be particularly true of the so-called peripheral institutions where physicians teach or have a heavy clinical practice and yet are under severe pressure to carry out research, particularly on assigned themes. They simply do not have the time to do the research, or to do it well.[14]

Dr. Fox, who visited (or rather revisited) the Soviet Union shortly after Stalin's death, reported that some of the institutes he had seen were splendidly equipped and their staff clearly of high quality, but he added:

> I cannot believe that they will play their full part in the development of medicine until their research-workers are able to work without looking over their shoulders. The very essence of science is that facts are facts . . . and Russian investigators will remain under a grave handicap so long as those who accept Western discoveries or ideas know they are liable to censure as "lackeys of bourgeois science" or worse. The Soviet Union, like the rest of us, will sooner or later have to choose between science and chauvinism.[15]

Dr. Fox wrote these words in 1954. Since then the situation of Soviet medical research has undoubtedly improved. The priority campaign has been, to a great extent, dismantled and ideological controls have lessened. Soviet medical scientists have been able to travel more frequently abroad and to stay there longer, and more Westerners have been able to go to the Soviet Union—some have even worked in Soviet laboratories. These are good omens. At the same time it is possible that, as the industrialization drive and heavy investment into producers' good decrease, the regime will have more resources (in personnel and particularly capital) to invest in medical research and that a higher priority will be given such research. Up to the present time, however, Soviet medical research has been unimpressive (particularly when compared with research in other scientific areas), and certainly the Soviet Union has not become in medicine the mecca that Vienna, Paris and London were in the nineteenth century or the United States in the twentieth, especially since the end of the Second World War. In other words, there have not been, as far as we know, medical breakthroughs equivalent to the *sputniks* and *luniks*. And yet, from what we know of Soviet space achievements and the quality of higher education, there is no fundamental reasons why there should not be in the future, provided the regime assigns medical science the same order of priority given the physical sciences.

We have, in this chapter, reviewed the major dimensions of Soviet medical research. We have examined the official, Marxist, attitude toward research, the history of medical research in Russia and the Soviet Union, the nature and organization of this research, and certain of its characteristics. In the next and last chapter we turn our attention to the financing of the health system.

Chapter 10

The Financing of
the Health Service

ONE OF TODAY'S most burning and controversial social questions, at least in the United States, is that of financing medical costs. As medicine becomes more complex and as it begins to rely more and more on highly qualified personnel, operating delicate and expensive equipment located in more costly and complicated facilities, the economic cost of medical and health services steadily increases.

Medical science, progress, and technology have thus outstripped yesterday's physician with his horse and buggy, his little black bag, and his uncertain knowledge and techniques. By the same token, the fee-for-service payment, which in its ideal form was essentially a private transaction between patient and doctor, tailored to the patient's ability to pay, is fast becoming obsolete. The physician is thus less and less able to cope with medical indigency on a sliding scale, as he could in the small community of yesterday. And, at any rate, the major medical expenses today are those incurred for costly services performed when the patient is hospitalized. If we assume that costs of medical services must somehow be met, and if, furthermore, the patient is increasingly less and less able to meet them from savings, current income, and mortgage on the future, other ways must be devised. Failure to do so can only impair the functioning of the health system and of the population and be detrimental to society as a whole.

Two major devices exist to meet these needs: insurance and public funds. In an insurance scheme a group of individuals pay a certain fee into a fund; when any of them needs medical services the fund pays the bills. This is another version of the ancient Chinese system in which people pay physicians as long as they are well and are treated free of charge when they fall ill.

The other means is to have the costs of medical care covered by public funds—from the state treasury. This is essentially the way Soviet health services are financed. It is one of the Soviet Union's proudest and loudest boasts that medical services are provided "free" to the population. In other words, the individual patient need not pay directly the doctor, hospital, or clinic for medical services, with the exception of drugs prescribed for outpatient use (the Third Party Program promises the elimination of this direct cost). And it is true that in Soviet medical institutions, whether hospitals, clinics, or institutes, one would be hard put to find a cashier's window or accounting office where patients would settle the bills they had incurred. And yet it is quite clear that nothing in this world, not even in the Soviet Union, is "free"—that is, without an economic cost—and certainly not medical services, whose costs, as we have just seen, have a constant tendency to rise. Hospitals are expensive to build and to maintain, and medical personnel do not live on fresh air and on the dewy-eyed gratitude of the patients whose lives they tirelessly save. Medical personnel must be paid for their time—their labor—and their training must, somehow, be financed. Thus, for example, it is estimated that the training of one physician costs the Soviet state 74,652 rubles (pre-1961) or about 8000 American dollars and probably more today. Someone must foot the bill, and the total bill is likely to be high.

In the Soviet Union it is, of course, the state that directly pays. But the state itself does not produce money; funds are derived, eventually, from the wealth produced by labor. The

Soviet citizen thus pays for his medical services indirectly, in the form of taxes. These taxes are then channelled into the state treasury and reallocated to the health sector as well as to the other sectors of the economy, whether they be national defense, education, or industrial expansion. There are three major sources for such funds: (1) payments made by industrial organizations from their profits, or the difference between the cost of production (including salaries) and the value of the output; (2) the income tax, which is a minor source of revenue, and, as Khrushchev had indicated, is to be eliminated in the future; this will not, however, mean an elimination of taxes, since governmental revenues will be then derived, from (3) the turnover tax. The turnover tax, essentially a sales or excise tax applied to all consumer goods in the Soviet Union, is the major source of revenue. It is a regressive tax, since it affects the purchasing power of the lower income groups much more drastically than middle or high income groups, and it is a hidden tax. The customer is not aware of how much of the price he pays for bread or clothing or any other item consists of the economic cost of producing, processing, distributing, and retailing what he buys and how much is tax (that is, enforced savings, or a decrease in the ability to effect an economic demand for goods and services). If, let's say, it costs the Soviet consumer 20 kopecks to buy a loaf of bread, and if it has cost the state 11 kopecks to produce and transport the grain and bake and sell the bread, the 9 kopecks difference (or profit) will be channelled back into the state treasury, and combined with millions and billions of other transactions, will then provide the funds necessary to pay a doctor's salary, build a clinic, purchase equipment, or finance *sputniks*, subways, or steel plants.

By the same token, industrial enterprises turn over a certain percentage of their profits to the state treasury and to their social insurance fund which provides, among other things, for partial or full payment to workers who have been officially declared sick or injured. Soviet sources (echoed by Sigerist in his book on Soviet medicine) claim that contributions made by the factories to the state, for medical services and compensation are *not* deductions from the workers' salaries, but rather additional benefits given the workers. Writes Sigerist: "Contributions (by the plants, factories, etc.) are in proportion to the wage bill and cannot be deducted from wages; they are additions to wages, a part of the socialized wages of workers." These are brave but empty words. For the workers have, by their work, *earned* their salaries but have nothing to say concerning the amount deducted from the earnings of the factory. But by both controlling wage earnings and operating the health system, the regime maintains control over the flow of resources into the medical area—to a much greater degree than would be possible in a mixed system of private and public medical care, as in the United States, for example. Thus the Soviet state does not *give* medical and other health services out of the goodness of its Communist heart. Rather, it extracts as it must from the population, in one subtle way or another, the necessary funds to pay for the aggregate of these services. And given the nature of the Soviet system, there is, of course, no other way of financing the health service. It may also well be, in the long run, not only a fairer, but also more effective a way to provide health services to the population of a country. What is, however, not clearly explained to the population is the nature of the financing. It is presented in a special way in order to show the "concern of the regime for the people." Here, for example, is a Soviet statement on the subject culled from a textbook for medical students:

> Expenditures are another item in which the USSR state budget differs radically from that in the capitalistic countries. In those countries the budget is used to enslave the workers and progressively lower their standard of living, whereas in the Soviet Union the budget reflects the basic economic law of socialism, which aims at the maximum satisfaction of the steadily growing material and cultural needs of society as a whole. The budget in capitalistic countries is fundamentally military in preparation for a new world war. For example, American military expenditures make up about 80% of the total budget, with scarcely 1% devoted to public health.[1]

There is no point in refuting this statement, and particularly its distortion of percentages, since most public health expenditures in the United States take place at levels below that of the federal government.

ALLOCATION OF FUNDS

ONCE THE FUNDS have been collected by the state treasury (or treasuries), the question of their allocation arises. In contrast with, let's say, the industrial ministries or organizations that create wealth and resources by production, the Health Ministry and related ministries and departments are essentially in the "business of spending"—that is, they are allocated budgets and credits which they use to purchase the services (personnel) and goods or facilities necessary to provide health care for the population. Indeed, in most instances, as we have seen, there is no "settling of accounts" between patient and the clinic, hospital, or industrial doctor who has treated him. The establishment of the national and local budget itself is a complicated process. The total budget reflects, of course, the main orientation of the regime and the reality problems it faces. Indeed, one must look at the budget as a dynamic aspect of the regime's operations, and as such it is closely (in theory) integrated with planning, and particularly the planning of the national economy. Planning of health expenditures starts, in most instances, with estimates of future requirements and the general expansions (or contractions) projected by the regime. It also takes into account data on the age, sex, and occupational make-up of the population, as well as illness rates and the nature of the local economy, climate, and geography. It is at this point that the general norms of medical services we have examined earlier come in handy for planning—that is, they are used as an accounting device. On the basis of past experience and of population statistics it is therefore possible to make an estimate of personnel needs within, of course, broad limits.

The estimates are then reviewed by the health department or the ministry and then submitted to the source of funds for approval or for revision. Once approved, they become binding on the health department and their affiliated institutions.

In the total budget for the Soviet Union expenditures for the health service fall under the rubric of "social-cultural" measures, which embrace, in addition to health and physical culture, education, social welfare, social insurance, and assistance to mothers with large families or no husband. Approximately one third of the Soviet budget is devoted to "social-cultural" activities, the largest portion of which is spent on education, followed by social welfare and health, as can be seen from Table 10-1. It can be estimated that at the present time the Soviet expenditure for health services per person is about 23 rubles annually (or about 25 dollars).

Table 10-1—Expenditures for Social-Cultural Measures, National Budget for USSR (1940-63)* (in millions of new rubles)

	1940	1950	1955	1960	1963
Total expenditures of USSR budget	17,435.0	41,323.7	53,953.8	73,126.2	87,000.0
Including: For social-cultural Measures	4,090.3	11,672.5	14,717.2	24,936.7	31,000.0
% of total budget expended for education	12.9%	13.8%	12.8%	14.1%	15.8%
% of total budget expended for health	5.1%	5.1%	5.7%	6.5%	6%
% of total budget expended for physical culture	0.1%	0.1%	0.1%	0.1%	
% of total budget expended for social welfare	1.8%	5.3%	4.7%	8.9%	9.4%
% of total budget expended for mothers with many children or no husband	0.7%	0.9%	0.9%	0.7%	0.5%
% of total budget expended for social-cultual Measures	23.5%	28.2%	27.3%	34.1%	35.6%

* *Gosudarstvennyi Biudzhet SSSR i Biudzhety Soiuznykh Respublik: Statisticheskii Sbornik,* Moscow, Gosfinizdat, 1962, pp. 18, 19, and 20. The national budget includes the union, republic and local budgets; *Narodnoe Khoziaistvo SSSR v 1963 Godu,* p. 655.

It can be seen that an average of about 5 per cent of the total published budget was allocated to health between 1950 and 1955, and that this percentage has tended to increase to about 6 per cent in recent years.

Actually, if one examines the structure of health expenditures, it will become clear that this percentage does increase as one goes down in the territorial-administrative structure, since a great majority of the expenses of maintaining health facilities fall on local budgets rather than on republican or national ones. For example, in 1960 about 40 per cent of the budgets of the constituent republics was allocated to social and cultural measures; the allocation for health was 9.4 per cent. In the local budgets (below the republican level), the percentage that went to health in 1960 was 27.[2]

If we further parcel out the expenses for health within the republics, we can see that of the monies appropriated for that purpose, over three quarters were spent either by the towns or the districts (in rural areas), as Table 10–2 shows.

Table 10–2—Distribution of Health and Physical Culture Expenditures Within the Constituent Republics, USSR (1958)*

	In Million of Old Rubles	As % of Total Budget
Republics (autonomous republics), provinces, regions, and departments	5,068.0	15.7
Towns or municipalities	14,971.0	46.4
Districts	9,599.3	29.7
Workers' settlements	858.6	2.6
Rural areas (villages)	1,798.9	5.6
Total	32,295.8	100%

* *Mestnye Biudzhety SSSR (Statisticheskii Sbornik)*, Moscow, Gosfinizdat, 1960, p. 270. Information for later years not available.

It will be noted that this table lumps together the categories of health and physical culture. Expenditures for the latter are never more than 1 per cent of the budget, and they would not affect the percentage distributions.

On a more concrete level we know, for example, that in 1958 the total budget of Hospital No. 57 in Moscow was 8,517,000 rubles (or about $900,000). Wages to personnel accounted for 54 per cent of the budget; overtime, 3.3 per cent; maintenance expenses, 12.3 per cent; food for patients, 4.0 per cent; medications, 5.6 per cent; equipment purchases, 6.4 per cent; purchases of soft inventory, 6.3 per cent; books, 0.17 per cent; and miscellaneous, 0.13 per cent. The annual cost of maintaining one bed was 19,120 rubles (about $2,100).[3]

It may be of interest to the reader to get some idea of the averages of expense of different categories of goods and services in the health system. This information may be found in Table 10–3.

Table 10–3—Expenditures on Health Goods and Services USSR Constituent Republic Budgets (1960)*

	In Millions of New Rubles	As % of Total Expenditures
Wages	2,063.2	50.8
Special additions to wages	110.8	2.7
Office and other expenses	318.4	7.8
Official travel expenses	15.2	.4
Food (for patients)	495.3	12.2
Drugs and dressings	281.0	6.9
Equipment and inventory	89.9	2.2
Capital investment for construction	161.1	4.0
Soft inventory, uniforms, and linens	118.3	2.9
Capital repairs, buildings, and equipment	137.9	3.4
Total	4,059.6[a]	93.3%[a]

* Gosudarstvennyi Biudzhet SSSR i Biudzhety Soiuznykh Respublik, op. cit., p. 88.
a. Soviet source items do not add up to the given total of 4,059.6, being short by 268.5 million rubles or 6.7 per cent of the total.

In addition to the provision of financial support, there are other arrangements worth mentioning. Thus, industrial plants, factories, and so forth are obliged to provide medical facilities for medical personnel. In general, as seen earlier, the larger the plant or combine, the larger and the more sophisticated or complete its medical facilities must be. The provision of these facilities is dictated by the following norms: for plants that number over 10,000 workers, inpatient facilities are required at the rate of 12 beds per 1000 workers (thus a minimum of 120 beds) and an outpatient facility to handle 150,000 visits a year; in a plant with 5000 to 10,000 workers, a hospital with 75 beds and capacity to handle 75,000 outpatient visits yearly; in a plant with 2000 to 5000 workers, inpatient facilities of 50 beds and facilities for 50,000 outpatient calls; with 800 to 2000 workers, a medical aid station; and in plants of 300 to 800 workers, a medical station manned by a feldsher. The norm for nurseries is room for 12 children per 1000 female workers.[4] The financial responsibility for these facilities is as follows. The industrial organization must provide the buildings and their maintenance, repair, and equipment as well as the transportation, public utilities, and salaries of technical personnel out of its budget or funds. The health authorities, on the other hand, appoint medical personnel, pay their salaries, and purchase medical apparatus and pharmaceuticals. Also, in constructing new plants or renovating or enlarging old ones, medical facilities, day nurseries, and living quarters for medical personnel must be provided. Compensation for disability—that is partial (or total) salary—for workers who are sick or injured is paid upon medical certification, by the labor union organization to the workers. According to a report by the Alts[5] approximately 9 per cent of the wage fund is deposited in the social insurance fund. In addition to these benefits, passes admitting workers to sanatoria are also dispensed by the labor union of the factory.

In the last few years there have been attempts in the countryside to force the kolkhozes to build medical facilities out of their own resources, including district hospitals (this is usually expressed as a result of the "initiative of the kolkhozniks"). In view of the meager income and standard of living of the collective farmers this can hardly be a popular measure, but it is perhaps an indication of the poverty of the resources available to the rural soviets.

It would, however, be naive to assume that the simple allocation of funds and other resources to the medical network guarantees that the installations, or other purposes for which the funds were allocated, will be built, repaired, or fulfilled. In the Soviet Union, as well as in any other system, availability of money must be matched by availability of personnel, materials, and sometimes even good will and cooperation. The evidence is that these ingredients are sometimes lacking, the funds unused, and the work undone. Thus, in 1960, the Health Ministry USSR complained that in the previous three years the Health Ministry RSFSR (the largest of the Soviet constituent republics) had failed to use more than 200 million rubles allocated for the building and modernizing of the medical industry. In 1961, *Stroitel'naia Gazeta* traced a shortage of vitamins to the fact that the construction of a vitamin producing plant had been delayed and sidetracked time and again as materials, funds, and personnel were diverted to other purposes.[6]

One final question which cannot, of course, be answered, is "Does the Soviet Union expend enough financial resources for the medical care of its population?" In one sense, the demand for medical services of all types is practically infinite, and the regime must allocate its resources which are always limited in a way appropriate to its other commitments. Semashko, the First Health Commissar, complained in 1923 that "The Peoples' Commissariat for Finances has defeated the Peoples' Commissariat of Health,"[7] and there is little doubt that such defeats have been inflicted time and again. And yet, the allocation of limited resources into the health service has been such as to maintain an adequate level of health in the population as a whole, consonant with the regime's other needs and other commitments.

We have in this final chapter, examined the manner in which the health system is maintained or financed by the Soviet regime. Health services are considered a public service and financed from state revenues which are derived from taxation.

Summary and Conclusions

THIS SMALL BOOK has examined the main contours of the Soviet system of socialized medicine. Because of its format, only the highlights have been sketched, and this quite briefly. A longer and more detailed study of the Soviet health service is still to come and probably will be available within two to three years. Hence this book is to be considered only as an introduction to the subject.

We began in Chapter 1 with a formulation of the importance of health for any society by pointing to the functional aspects of medical care at the societal level, in addition, of course, to the role that this care plays in the satisfaction of individual needs and emotions. The health system, conceived in its broadest sense as the totality of measures centered around health, conserves, preserves, and extends human life and man's ability to act in the different roles he plays in the course of his daily life and occupation. As such, health may be conceived as a basic strategic *resource* of the society, and the health service or medical system as that general mechanism that services and conserves that resource. It is in this perspective that one can begin to appreciate the contribution made by medicine and public health to the development of Soviet power, and see it as more than merely "socialized medicine" or the expression of the concern of the party for the welfare of the population.

In Chapter 2, we backtracked in time to obtain a better understanding of the historical background and the accumulated fund of medical knowledge and institutions the Soviets inherited at the time of the 1917 Revolution. For this we went back several centuries and traced medical developments up to the time of Peter the Great, whose modernization of Russia also entailed a modernization of medicine and of the medical profession. Medicine developed in post-Petrine Russia under the aegis of the state and under the impetus of its many demands. The nineteenth century also saw the development not only of private medicine and high scientific standards consonant with those of Western Europe, but also the unfolding of a rather new type of medical service—zemstvo medicine—which expressed perhaps the best elements of humanitarianism and dedication to the people (or populism) that was part of the culture of the Russian intelligentsia. We also saw the efforts of the medical profession, as an autonomous association of professionals, to study and propose plans and programs for the improvement of the health services and the population's health levels, particularly the peasantry who lived, for the most part, in wretched conditions. Efforts to implement these plans were made during the short existence of the Provisional Government, but were brought to an end by the advent of the Soviet regime which resumed, in its own way, the development of medicine.

Because ideology occupies such a central position in Soviet society, and since it claims to provide not only an explanation for most social phenomena but also the regime's basic legitimacy, we felt that an analysis of the health system must include that critical aspect of the Soviet *Weltanschauung*. Thus, in Chapter 3 we endeavored to picture the nature and the role of ideology in Soviet society, focusing upon the impact of this ideology on medicine, the control of the health system, and the functions of health personnel.

In Chapter 4 our aim was to trace the history and the unfolding of the Soviet health service against the broad background of events that took place in Soviet society and which affected the nature and the mission of the health authorities. To do this, we used the standard periodization of Soviet history and attempted to relate the major problems of each period to the unfolding, the changes, and the development of medicine.

In Chapter 5 our aim was to describe the formal and official administration of medicine and public health, and to include those institutions and agencies of a nonmedical nature that contribute to the work of the health system. Thus, after a description of the Health Ministry and its different levels, and their relationship to the official structure of the governmental organs, we turned our attention to the role of the soviets, the party, social welfare agencies, industries, labor unions, and voluntary agencies, which function, in one way or another, to "support" the efforts of the health authorities in their work of maintaining the health of the population.

In Chapter 6 we dealt with Soviet health personnel, noting the different types of such personnel, from physicians through semiprofessionals and nonprofessional health workers, emphasizing the significant increases in the size of the health contingent and in the ratio of all health personnel to the population. We pointed out, for example, that the Soviet Union today has one of the highest (if not the highest) ratio of doctors to population in the world, and that plans indicate an even higher ratio in the future. Of particular interest is the fact that three fourths of all physicians and an even greater proportion of all health personnel are women. While we cannot necessarily equate the size of the medical contingent with the quality of medical care or the effective use of medical resources, we feel that the improvement in personnel since the tsarist period has been remarkable.

In the next chapter we examined in some detail Soviet health facilities and services. This meant, first, a look at the health facilities available primarily for the urban population, particularly outpatient clinics and hospitals. We also noted the marked progress, since the Revolution, in the supply of hospital beds. We examined the health services available to the rural population, where the picture is considerably less bright, although we feel that with time, more resources, and increased and improved transportation the range of health services available to the rural population will tend to approximate that of the urban population.

In Chapter 8, devoted to preventive services, we felt the need to go back to the ideological roots of the Soviet system and to developments in Soviet history in order to place preventive services in their correct perspective. While, theoretically, preventive medicine is considered by the Soviets as the medicine of the future, at the present time it still plays a relatively minor role in the totality of efforts expended by the health authorities.

Ideological considerations, particularly the relationship between research and practice, are also important in the medical research enterprise, which we examined in Chapter 9. Our interest was not only in the philosophy of Soviet medical research, but also in the control, centralization, bureaucratization, and administration of that research. We came to the conclusion that Soviet medical research had not been particularly fruitful when compared to medical research in the West, and this for a variety of reasons we suggest in that chapter.

Our final chapter bears on that eternal and unavoidable question, even in the Soviet Union, of costs. Since the health service is generally an expensive enterprise, our interest was on the manner in which the financing of health services was carried out, from the collection of the necessary funds by taxation (primarily the turnover tax), through the planning of health expenses, and the actual disbursements. As a "service," the financing of health care resembles, to some extent, that of the financing of public education in most countries in the world today.

The final question the reader might ask is "Does Soviet socialized medicine work, and how well?" We might counter by another question: "For whom, or what, does it work? For the society as a whole, or for the individual Soviet citizen in particular?" The answer to the first (and undoubtedly from the viewpoint of the Soviet regime the most significant) part of the question is that it has worked and is working. Simply in terms, for example, of a decrease in the death rate, a decrease in infant mortality, and an increase in the life expectancy, all these indices, crude as they may be, indicate substantial if not dramatic improvements in the last fifty years. The Soviet regime has created a comprehensive and national system of health protection and medical services that might well serve as a blueprint for any modernizing nation. Starting with very limited resources in facilities and personnel at the time of the Revolution, the regime proceeded to expand these resources at a rapid rate, but reserved to itself the right to control this expansion and the work of health authorities. In order to do this, it established a sophisticated although sometimes cumbersome system of bureaucratic and financial controls in the Health Ministry and its administratively subordinate organs. There is little doubt that, over-all, the health system has fulfilled its mission satisfactorily, at least on a quantitative basis. There is no doubt, furthermore, that the work of the health authorities and personnel have contributed, directly and indirectly, to the major program that has preoccupied Soviet society since 1928: industrialization. While it cannot be claimed that the Soviet Union is a great power because of its health system, it can be asserted that among the many factors that contribute to that power the health system is a major one, for it helps to keep people working and alive by protecting their health and by decreasing and sometimes eliminating the disturbing impact of physical and mental illness and premature death. Assuredly for good and compelling reasons, the stress has been in the quantitative rather than the qualitative direction, since a qualitative approach under the circumstances of the Soviet regime would have not only have been too costly but also would have been unrealistic. This means that, insofar as the individual is concerned, his needs may, at times, be neglected; he may become the victim of higher priority claims.

Soviet socialized medicine has been one of the more impressive and positive achievements of the Soviet regime, and has probably met with the approval of the great majority of the population. If the population has any complaints, they certainly do not seem to deal with the concept or the blueprint of socialized medicine, but rather with the execution of the program at the local, personal level. But despite many shortcomings (which the regime cleverly attributes not to itself or to its system of socialized medicine, but to the personal negligence of some health personnel), the Soviet citizen finds in socialized medicine at least some evidence of the regime's concern, for *his* health and *his* well-being and the welfare of those who are dear and close to him.

It is a great pity, however, that for reasons of its own the regime has not permitted social scientists to have access to the Soviet population (and particularly to people as patients) so that patient satisfaction (or dissatisfaction) could be measured using the same general types of instruments employed in the West by medical sociologists (questionnaires, interviews, surveys, and the like). More than once I have raised this question with Soviet colleagues, particularly after I had been criticized for using Soviet Displaced Persons in an earlier work as source of information on patient attitudes in the Soviet Union. I proposed, furthermore, that the same types of questionnaires be administered to a sample within the Soviet Union, but was turned down on the ground that such an investigation was unnecessary since the answers were already known from meetings, public discussions, letters to newspapers, and so forth. My inference can only be that this defensive attitude was motivated by a concern that what might come out of such an investigation (particularly if carried out with anonymous questionnaires) might show Soviet medicine in a light not so favorable as the regime might wish. Indeed, my impression is that the Soviet Union will remain secretive and veiled as long as the regime feels that any aspect of its domestic situation has not come up to the standards it has set for itself or claims it has already attained, and/or is inferior to its counterpart in the West.

Despite these strictures, the challenge posed by Soviet socialized medicine to the West, and particularly to the United States, is imposing. There is, first, the obvious challenge of the contribution medicine and public health make to Soviet power and potential by raising the health level, the vitality, and the longevity of the population. Further, at the political and ideological level the challenge might be formulated as follows: In the world situation today, because of the absolute nature of contemporary weaponry and the assurance of mutual suicide in the use of these weapons, the struggle for men's minds, loyalty, and allegiance between East and West takes more and more the form of what each system can offer to the people. It is in this respect that the Soviet blueprint of socialized medicine, dispensed as a public service and financed from taxation, and with its constitutional provision of free and professional medical care to the entire population, has broader ideological appeal, particularly to the underdeveloped countries of the world, than the more sophisticated, mixed private and public American model. As a former Minister of Health for India once expressed it (in a personal conversation): "We simply cannot afford a medical system of the American type; for our needs, and with our resources, the Soviet model is infinitely more relevant." There is no doubt that the underdeveloped countries are impatient to solve their health problems (which slow down their economic and social developments) and that this solution will come primarily from governmental sources with governmental finances, and that, if asked, the Soviets will be glad to assist and advise in these matters.

Equally disturbing (for Americans, at least) is the rate at which physicians are being trained in the Soviet Union, compared with the United States, and the fact that from 20 to 25 per cent of all the world's doctors today are Soviet doctors. The USSR, if it so chooses, soon will be able to export physicians to the underdoctored areas of the world; it has already done so on a limited scale. In the second half of the twentieth century, the medical missionary appears likely to replace his religious colleague of yesterday as a means of peaceful penetration. It may be noted that the United States finds itself in the embarrassing position of having to import large numbers of physicians trained abroad to staff its hospitals, thereby further depleting the already meager medical contingents of some developing countries, such as India.

Finally, I submit that health is too important a matter to allow us to ignore or dismiss almost half a century of accumulated experience in the Soviet Union, even granted that conditions in the West as well as in the different underdeveloped countries of the world are often unlike Soviet conditions. As I have pointed out earlier, the Soviet contribution in this area has certainly not been primarily in medical research and in the generation of new medical knowledge. Rather, and this is a central point, it has been in the critical area of the *application* and *distribution* of already existing knowledge through the organization and the administration of a comprehensive national health service, and the dispensing of health care financed by the state through public funds to a large urban and rural population. I think that the Soviet experiment with socialized medicine must be critically examined and assessed for the lessons it might yield to those concerned with health and the planning and the implementation of medical and related services in their respective countries. Finally, such an examination is important in any comparative assessment of health services in different countries, as well as in any understanding of Soviet society as a fairly stable national social system of the industrialized and urbanized type, regardless of one's feelings about its political system or its ideological foundations.

Notes

Chapter 1—Soviet Society and Its Health Services

1. *A Day in the Life of Ivan Denisovich,* a novel by Solzhenitsin, described one day in the life of a concentration camp prisoner during the Stalin regime. It was published under Khrushchev and is one of the very few Soviet books openly dealing with the fate of prisoners in camps.

2. Joseph Stalin, "The Tasks of Business Executives," in *Problems of Leninism,* 11th ed; Moscow, Foreign Languages Publishing House, 1940, pp. 365–6.

3. Zbigniew K. Brzezinski, *Ideology and Power in Soviet Politics,* New York, Praeger, 1962, pp. 14–20.

4. A. I. Mikoyan, speech delivered on February 17, 1956, in *The New York Times,* February 19, 1956, p. 26.

5. On this, see the discussion "Toward a 'Communist Welfare State?'" in Abraham Brumberg, ed., *Russia Under Khrushchev,* New York, Praeger, 1962, pp. 571 ff.

6. See Raymond A. Bauer, Alex Inkeles, and Clyde Kluckhohn, *How the Soviet System Works,* Cambridge, Harvard University Press, 1961; Alex Inkeles and Raymond A. Bauer, *The Soviet Citizen,* Cambridge, Harvard University Press, 1959. See also Mark G. Field, *Doctor and Patient in Soviet Russia,* Cambridge, Harvard University Press, 1957, and "Former Soviet Citizens' Attitudes Toward the Soviet, the German and the American Medical Systems," *American Sociological Review,* 20 (December, 1955), 674–9.

Chapter 2—A Brief History of Russian Medicine Prior to 1917

1. *Bol'shaia Meditsinskaia Entsiklopediia (Large Medical Encyclopedia;* hereafter *BME*), 2nd ed.; Vol. 10, Moscow, 1959, Col. 768.
2. *Ibid.,* Col. 769.
3. Essentially "sub-physicians." For more details on the *feldsher* see Chapter 6 on health personnel.
4. *Zapiski vracha-obshchestvennika* (1889–1918), Medgiz, cited in *XXV Let sovetskogo zdravookhranenia, (Twenty-five Years of Soviet Health Protection),* Moscow, Medgiz, 1944, p. 5.
5. N. Ekk, *Mezhdunarodnaia Klinika,* Vol. 5 (1886), Nos. 3 and 4.
6. *BME,* 2nd ed.; Vol. 10, Moscow, 1959, Col. 780.
7. *Sorok let sovetskogo zdravookhranenia (Forty Years of Soviet Health Protection),* M. D. Kovrigina, editor in chief, Moscow, Medgiz, 1957, pp. 577–8.
8. N. A. Vinogradov, ed., *Organizatsiia zdravookhranenia v SSSR (Organization of Health Protection in the USSR),* 2nd ed.; Moscow, Medgiz, 1962, p. 32.
9. *Forty Years of Soviet Health Protection,* p. 391.
10. *Narodnoe khoziaiastvo SSSR v 1961 godu: Statisticheskii ezhegodnik (National Economy of the USSR: Statistical Yearbook),* Moscow, Gosstatizdat, 1962, p. 747.
11. Vinogradov, *loc. cit.,* p. 32.

Chapter 3—Marxism and the Ideology of Medicine

1. "For Lasting and Deep Knowledge," *Meditsinskii Rabotnik,* February 10, 1952, p. 1.
2. Karl Marx, *Capital: A Critique of Political Economy,* trans. by Samuel Moore and Edward Aveling from the 3rd German edition, edited by Frederick Engels, revised and amplified according to the 4th German edition by Ernest Untermann, New York, Modern Library, 1906, pp. 291–2.
3. *Ibid.,* pp. 296–7.
4. *Ibid.,* p. 297. Italics supplied.
5. Friedrich Engels, *Conditions of the Working Class in England,* New York, Macmillan, 1958, p. 188.
6. V. I. Lenin, *The Development of Capitalism in Russia,* Moscow, Foreign Languages Publishing House, 1956, pp. 242–3.
7. V. I. Lenin, *Sochineniia, (Works),* 4th ed.: Moscow, Gosudarstvennoe Izdatel'stvo Politicheskoi Literatury, 1949, Vol. 24, pp. 436–9.
8. M. I. Barsukov, *Bol'shaia Oktiabrskaia Sotsialisticheskaia Revo-*

liutsiia i Organizatsiia Sovetskogo Zdravookhraneniia (The Great Socialist October Revolution and the Organization of Soviet Health Protection), Moscow, Medgiz, 1951.

9. M. P. Mul'tanovskii, *Istoriia Meditsiny (History of Medicine)*, Moscow, Medgiz, 1961, pp. 318–19.

10. N. N. Anichkov, "Socialist Humanism of Soviet Medicine," *Meditsinskii Rabotnik*, May 1, 1953, p. 2. Italics supplied.

11. Z. A. Gurevich, *Koronarnaia bolezn' (Coronary Disease)*, Kiev, Gosmedizdat, 1963, pp. 81–82.

12. G. Tsaregorodtsev and S. Petrov, "Crisis Characteristics of Bourgeois Medicine," *Meditsinskaia Gazeta*, July 5, 1963, p. 3.

13. "Vrach," *Bol'shaia Sovetskaia Entsiklopediia, (Large Soviet Encyclopedia)*, 2nd ed.; Vol. 9, 1951, Cols. 238–9.

14. A. Bakulev, "Realization of the Dream of Generations," *Izvestia*, August 24, 1961, p. 3.

15. K. V. Maistrakh, *Organizatsiia Zdravookhraneniia (Organization of Health Protection)*, 4th ed.; Moscow, Medgiz, 1956, pp. 8–9.

16. *Ibid.*

17. *Health Services in the Union of Soviet Socialist Republics*, WHO/PHA/27, p. 4.

18. N. A. Vinogradov, ed., *Organizatsiia Zdravookhraneniia v SSSR (The Organization of Health Protection in the USSR)*, 2 vols., 1st ed.; Moscow, Medgiz, 1958, I, p. 27.

19. Vinogradov, *Organizatsiia Zdravookhranenia*, 1st ed., p. 26.

20. Maistrakh, *Organizatsiia Zdravookhraneniia*, 5th ed., 1959, p. 14.

21. C. Fraser Brockington, "Public Health in Russia," *The Wider World*, July 21, 1956.

Chapter 4—The Development of the Soviet Health Service:
From 1917 to the Present

1. V. I. Lenin, *Sochineniia (Works)*, 4th ed.; Moscow, Gosudarstvennoe Izdatel'stvo Politicheskoi Literatury, 1949, Vol. 30, p. 163.

2. Lenin, *op. cit.*, pp. 375–6.

3. Barsukov, *The Great Socialist October Revolution*, p. 64.

4. Statement by Khirin at the First Ural Regional Congress 1918, in G. E. Gurevich, "Istoricheskii S'ezd," *Sovetskoe Zdravookhranenie*, VI (1947), p. 39.

5. Barsukov, *Fragments of the History of National Medicine*, Moscow, 1962, p. 74.

6. *Ocherki Istorii Zdravookhraneniia SSSR (1917–1956) (Fragments of the History of Health Protection USSR)*, Moscow, Medgiz, 1957, p. 82.

7. *Ibid.*, p. 186

8. *Izvestia NKZ RSFSR*, 1923, No. 1, in *Ocherki*, p. 179.

9. Z. P. Soloviev, Tezisi doklada "Profilakticheskie zadachi lech-

ebnoi pomoshchi," in *Voprosy Zdravookhranenia*, Moscow, 1940, pp. 137–8. Cited in *Ocherki*, p. 180.

10. *Izvestia NKZ RSFSR*, 1922, Nos. 3–4, cited in *Ocherki*, p. 165.

11. E. I. Smirnov, "Triumph of Our Doctrine," *Meditsinskii Rabotnik*, June 23, 1945, No. 35.

Chapter 5—Organization and Administration of The Soviet Health Service

1. Kenneth R. Whiting, *The Soviet Union Today*, New York, Praeger, 1962, pp. 121 ff.

2. *Health Services in the Union of Soviet Socialist Republics*, WHO/PHA/27, p. 5.

3. N. A. Vinogradov, *Organizatsiia*, 1st ed., Vol. I, p. 416.

4. *BME*, 2nd ed., Vol. 10, Cols. 809–10.

5. *Health Services in the Union of Soviet Socialist Republics*, WHO/PHA/27, p. 6.

6. Suggested by Dr. Pierre Rentschnik, *Hippocrate au Pays des Soviets*, Geneva, Médecine-Hygiène, 1958, p. 101.

7. A. N. Syzdanov, speech at the Second Session of the Kazakh Supreme Soviet, *Kazakhstanskaia Pravda*, July 22, 1959.

8. "On the New Frontier," *Meditsinskaia Gazeta*, November 26, 1965.

9. "Improve the Style and Methods of Work of the Apparatus," *Meditsinskii Rabotnik*, November 24, 1959, p. 2.

10. *Meditsinskii Rabotnik*, January 13, 1952.

11. *Meditsinskii Rabotnik*, January 27, 1960.

12. G. A. Miterev, "The Soviet Red Cross and Health Protection in the USSR," *Sovetskoe Zdravookhranenie*, XXII, 10 (1963) p. 3.

13. *Ocherki Istorii Zdravookhranenia v SSSR (Fragments of the History of Health Protection in the USSR)*, Moscow, Medgiz, 1957, p. 87.

Chapter 6—Health Personnel

1. *SSSR v Tsifrakh v 1964 Godu (The USSR in Figures in 1964)*, Moscow, 1965, p. 7.

2. *Israel Government Yearbook*, 5725 (1964/65), published by the Government Printer for the Office of Information (December, 1964), pp. 188, 203.

3. Based on figures in *Oesterreichisches Jahrbuch 1963*, Nach amtlichen Quellen, herausgegeben vom Bundespressedienst, 50, Folge, Wien, 1964, pp. 676, 685, 686, 682.

4. Howard A. Rusk, "Health and the Budget," *The New York Times*, January 2, 1966.

5. *Narodnoe Khoziaistvo v 1963 Godu,* p. 624.

6. Zigurds L. Zile, "Progress and Problems of City Planning in the Soviet Union," *Washington University Law Quarterly,* vol. 1963, pp. 45–6.

7. Ya. I. Rodov and Ya. S. Mindlin, "Medical Cadres—A Pressing Problem of the Medical Service Among the Rural Population," *Sovetskoe Zdravookhranenie,* No. 10 (1964), pp. 7–11.

8. "Papas, Mamas, and Young Loafers," *Meditsinskii Rabotnik,* March 27, 1962, p. 2.

9. C. F. Brockington, "Public Health in Russia," *The Wider World,* July 21, 1956.

10. Ya. I. Rodov and Ya. S. Mindlin, "Medical Cadres—A Pressing Problem of the Medical Service Among the Rural Population," *op. cit.*

11. *Narodnoe Khoziaistvo SSSR v 1963 Godu,* p. 578.

12. Recent information suggests that a curriculum revision would reduce the medical course to five and a half years, but no detailed information is available at this writing. There is, additionally, a move to make eight months of the sixth year (or class) a sort of "on the job" training which would correspond to an internship in Western terms.
A. A. Govorkov and M. N. Khaitov, "Field Experience of Students of Medical Institutes," *Sovetskoe Zdravookhranenie,* No. 9 (1963), pp. 40–42; Seymour Rosen, *Significant Aspects of Soviet Education,* Washington, U.S. Department of Health, Education and Welfare, 1951, OE–14112, Bulletin 1965, No. 15, p. 21.

13. *Zdravookhranenie v SSSR,* p. 152.

14. *Medical Education in the Soviet Union,* Washington, U.S. Department of Health, Education and Welfare, 1904, p. 7.

15. *Medical Education in the Soviet Union,* p. 7.

16. *Idem,* p. 5.

17. For example, "Expert on Russian Medical Education Rates It Far Below U.S. Standards," *New York State General Practice News,* Vol. 11, No. 5, (September–October, 1959), pp. 14–15; and Arnold Lieberman, "Comments on Soviet Medicine," *The New York State Journal of Medicine,* Vol. 61, No. 10 (May 15, 1961), pp. 1771–3.

18. The Americal medical delegation that visited the Soviet Union in 1963 was also surprised at the paucity of cadavers for studying human anatomy. "The increasing acceptance in the United States of the practice of individuals willing their bodies for medical purposes seemed incredible to physicians in the USSR." *Medical Education in the Soviet Union,* p. 23.

19. *Medical Education in the Soviet Union,* p. 15.

20. Professor P. A. Abdullyev, "Improving the Specialization and Improvement of General Practitioners (Therapists)," *Sovetskoe Zdravookhranenie,* No. 10 (1963), pp. 53–5.

21. United States Bureau of Census, *Historical Statistics of the United States: Colonial Times to 1957,* Washington, United States Department of Commerce, 1960, p. 3475; and *Statistical Abstract of the United States,* 1964, pp. 69, 232.

22. *Narodnoe Khoziaistvo v 1963 Godu,* p. 623; *Sorok Let Sovetskogo Zdravookhraneniia,* Moscow, 1957, p. 39.

23. *Narodnoe Khoziaistvo SSSR v 1963 Godu,* p. 480–1.

24. *Medical Education in the Soviet Union,* p. 20.

25. Rita S. Finkler, M.D., "Medical Russia Revisited," *Journal of Newark Beth Israel Hospital* (January, 1960), p. 42.

26. Officially the new ruble is worth $1.11.

27. *Bulletin,* XII (June, 1965), No. 6, p. 15. Institute for the Study of the USSR (Münich).

28. See *Pravda,* July 14, 1964. An English version is available in the *Current Digest of the Soviet Press,* XVI, No. 29 (August 12, 1964), pp. 15–16.

29. *Dimensions of Soviet Economic Power,* Hearings, Joint Committee (Economic) Congress of the U.S., Sec. 5(a) of Public Law 304 Seventy-ninth Congress, December, 1962, p. 403; and *Comparison of the United States and Soviet Economies,* Joint Economic Committee, Congress of the U.S., Part I, Washington, 1960, Table IV, p. 335.

30. Donald D. Barry, "Russians and Their Cars," *Survey* (October, 1965), p. 99.

Chapter 7—Clinical Facilities and Services

1. *BME,* 2nd ed., Vol. 30, Col. 1090.

2. M. G. Field, *Doctor and Patient in Soviet Russia,* Cambridge: Harvard University Press, 1957, particularly Chapter 9, "To Certify or not to Certify"; "Some Problems of Soviet Medical Practice: A Sociological Perspective," *New England Journal of Medicine,* 243:919–926 (May, 1953).

3. *BME,* 2nd ed., Vol. 30, Col. 1088.

4. *BME,* 2nd ed. Vol. 30, Col. 1089, Table 50.

5. *BME,* 2nd ed., Vol. 30, Col. 1090, Table 51.

6. Recent information indicates that over two-thirds of these facilities also service workers' families. "Minister of Health S. V. Kurashov answers questions of our readers," *Trud,* November 19, 1964, p. 3.

7. *BME,* 2nd ed., Vol. 30, Cols. 1093–4, Table 55.

8. The Soviet policy on abortion has gone through four phases, the present policy having been established in 1955, replacing one in force between 1936 and 1955, during which abortions (except for some clear-cut medical indications) were strictly forbidden. Between

1920 and 1936, abortions on "social indications" were legal. Between 1917 and 1920, the tsarist policy of absolute prohibition of abortion was still in force. For more details see Mark G. Field, "The Re-Legalization of Abortion in Soviet Russia," *New England Journal of Medicine*, 225: 421–427 (August 30, 1956).

9. *Narodnoe khoziaistvo SSSR v 1963 Godu*, p. 630.

10. *BME*, 2nd ed., Vol. 30, Col. 1120.

11. *Narodnoe Khoziaistvo SSSR v 1963 Godu*, p. 630.

12. *Narodnoe Khoziaistvo SSSR v 1963 Godu*, pp. 630, 625.

13. See Mark G. Field and Jason Aronson, "Mental Health Services and Work Therapy in the Soviet Community: A Report of two Visits," *Community Health Journal*, Vol. 1, 1:81–90 (Spring, 1965); "Approaches to Mental Illness in Soviet Society: Some Comparisons and Conjectures," *Social Problems*, 7:277–297 (Spring, 1960).

14. *BME*, 2nd ed., Vol. 30, Col. 1113.

Chapter 8—Preventive Health Services

1. Cited in L. O. Kanevskii, *Uchastie trudiashchikhsia SSSR v stroitel'stve zdrovookhraneniia*, (Participation of Toilers of the USSR in the Construction of Health Protection), Moscow, Medgiz, 1957, p. 46.

2. Vinogradov, *Organizatsia Zdravookhraneniia v SSSR*, 1st ed., p. 111.

3. B. Ya. Smulevich, "Toward the Discussion of Social Hygiene," *Sovetskoe zdravookhranenie*, No. 3 (1959), p. 44.

4. *Sorok let sovetskogo zdravookhraneniia*, p. 22.

5. "Sanitarnaia inspektsia," *BME*, 2nd ed., Vol. 29, Col. 207.

6. *BME*, 2nd ed., Vol. 30, Cols. 1129–30, Table 90.

7. *Narodnoe Khoziaistvo SSSR v 1963 Godu*, p. 625.

8. *Health Services in the USSR*, WHO/PHA/27, pp. 19–20.

9. Speech, Sixth Session of Supreme Soviet, *Meditsinskii Rabotnik*, January 27, 1960.

10. Speech by Z. M. Garimanov, "Wide and Clear Perspectives," *Meditsinskii Rabotnik*, December 9, 1960.

11. Speech before a meeting of the most active workers of health protection, in *Meditsinskii Rabotnik*, December 9, 1960.

12. T. F. Fox, "Russia Re-Visited," *Lancet*, October 9, 16, 1954, pp. 748–53, 803–7.

13. "Let's Talk of the Culture of Medical Services," *Sovetskaia Estonia*, October 2, 1960, p. 2.

14. S. Kurashov, "In the Name of the Individual's Health," *Izvestiia*, October 8, 1961, p. 3.

15. See, for example, E. Gorbudnova and S. Abramova, "Strength

of the Social Active," *Meditsinskii Rabotnik,* September 4, 1953, p. 2.

16. For details see *Health Education in the USSR,* Geneva, World Health Organization, 1963, Public Health Papers No. 19.

17. *Pravda,* August 1, 1962, p. 2.

18. "To Our Readers," *Meditsinskaia Gazeta,* November 2, 1962, p. 1.

Chapter 9—Medical Research

1. M. D. Kovrigina, "Toward a Further Rise in Soviet Public Health," in *Meditsinskii Rabotnik,* November 1, 1957, pp. 1–2.

2. "Science for the People," *Meditsinskii Rabotnik,* May 1, 1960, p. 2.

3. *Sorok Let Sovetskogo zdravookhraneniia,* p. 21.

4. "Scientific Research Institutes," *BME,* 2nd ed., Vol. 20, Col. 68.

5. *Ibid.*

6. *Soviet News,* 4233, Friday, March 18, 1960, p. 4.

7. Galina V. Zarechnak, *Academy of Medical Sciences of the USSR,* PHS Publication No. 702, Washington, D.C., 1960.

8. "Questions of the Organization and Planning of Medical Science: A Prospective Plan for the Most Important Problems of Medical Science 1959–1965," *Vestnik Akademiia Meditsinskikh Nauk SSSR,* 13 (7): 46–61, 1958. Translated at the National Institutes of Health, Bethesda, Maryland, p. 8.

9. An interesting and revealing recent criticism of this approach can be found in an article published by V. V. Parin, of the Academy of Medical Sciences (who himself suffered imprisonment under Stalin): "Scientific Heritage and Dogmatism," *Literaturnaia Gazeta,* February 24, 1962. A slightly abridged version in English is available in *The Soviet Review* (August, 1962), pp. 55–64.

10. "Men in Red," *News From Behind the Iron Curtain,* April, 1954, No. 4. Actually, this is a quote from *Contemporanul* (Bucharest) March 20, 1953, but it reflects accurately the official ideology of the times.

11. "Public Assistance is Needed," *Meditsinskii Rabotnik,* February 26, 1960.

12. See, for example, "Formal Attitude to an Important Matter," *Meditsinskii Rabotnik,* June 12, 1953, p. 3, and also an article by Professor B. Bogralnik, Gorkii Medical Institute, in the same periodical, January 29, 1960.

13. See, for example, Ivan D. London, "Instrumentation in Soviet Psychological Research: A Contribution to the Methodology of Tourism," *Journal of Social Psychology,* 1960, 52: 51–65, p. 54.

14. Professor Belenkii, "Druggist and Chemist," *Meditsinskii Rabotnik,* September 27, 1960.

15. T. F. Fox, "Russia Re-Visited," *Lancet,* October 9 and 16, 1954, pp. 748–53, 803–7.

Chapter 10—The Financing of the Health Service

1. K. V. Maistrakh, *Organizatsiia zdravookhraneniia,* 5th ed., 1959, p. 246.

2. *Gosudarstvennyi biudzhet SSSR i Biudzhety soiuznykh respublik: Statisticheskii sbornik (State Budget of the USSR and Budget of the Constituent Republics: Statistical Handbook),* Moskva, Gosfinizdat, 1962, pp. 94–5.

3. "City Hospital No. 57—Board of Public Health, Stalin District, Moscow," WHO Files, Geneva.

4. K. V. Maistrakh, *The Organization of Public Health in the USSR,* 4th ed., 1956, English translation.

5. Herschel and Edith Alt, *Russia's Children,* New York, Bookman Associates, 1959, p. 121.

6. "They said 'No' at the drugstore . . . ," *Stroitel'naia Gazeta,* August 23, 1961.

7. Cited in Lazarévitch, *La médecine en URSS,* Paris, Iles d'or, 1953, p. 50.

Index

Index

District: description of, 88–89; poly-
clinic of, 90
Doctor: *see* Physician
Doctor of Medical Sciences Degree,
124
"Doctors' plot" (1953), 56
"Dwarf" facilities (small rural hos-
pitals), 145

Education work, in prevention, 170–
73
Ekk, Nikolai, on mortality in pre-
Revolutionary Russian population,
24, 168
Emergency care, 141; Moscow Insti-
tute of, 180
Engels, Friedrich, 9, 33, 35, 36, 159
Environment, mutual relationship of
organism and, 160
Epidemics: control of, 55; during
New Economic Policy, 61; during
War Communism, 59; during
World War I and postwar period,
164; elimination of, 167; mandate
of the Commissariat of Health
Protection (1917), 55; measures
against, 21, 22; research institutes
for struggle against, 178; threat
of (1918), 51–53, 162; threat of
in World War II, 69–70, 77
"Ethical universalism," 56

February Revolution, concern with
medical profession, 27–28
Feldsher aid-station, 138, 139
Feldshers: in industry, 196; role in
rural health services, 21, 116, 126–
27; salary of, 130; statistics about,
155; training of, 128
Femister, 185
Financing, of health services, 188–
97
Five-Year Plans: period of, 59; role
in medical research, 183
Fordham University: *see* Institute
of Contemporary Russian Studies

Foreign scientific research, 177
Formalism: interference in health
services, 100; of Health Ministry
USSR, 82
Fox, T. E.: on prevention in USSR,
169; on Soviet medical research,
186
Free University of Berlin, Medical
Section of the Osteuropa Institut,
xi
Freudian psychology, 185

Gantt, W. Horsley, ix
General medical network, 88
"General practitioner," 122
German invasion, 69
Gonorrhea, 154
Gynecology, outpatient clinics for
services, 148

Harmsen, Hans, xi
"Head institutes," in medical research, 182–83
Health: definition of, 4; as strategic
resource of society, 198
Health, publication, 172
Health Commissariat RSFSR: Central Committee's criticism of
health organs, 65; Department of
Health Education, 171–72; establishment of, 50–54; organization
of medical services for Red Army,
60; role of Russian republics, 63;
tendency to neglect clinical medicine, 159–60; and threat of epidemics (1918), 162
Health Commissariat USSR: antiepidemic measures at outbreak of
World War II, 70,71; direction of
treatment for wounded soldiers,
71; establishment of, 67; relationship to the All-Union Public
Health Inspectorate, 163; renam-
ing of, 72
Health Commissar RSFSR: Semashko, 46; Semashko replaced by